BIG WORLD

Claire Brownsworth

BIG WORLD
A GIRL'S OWN ADVENTURE

A SUE HINES BOOK
ALLEN & UNWIN

First published in 2005

A Sue Hines Book
Allen & Unwin
83 Alexander Street
Crows Nest NSW 2065
Australia
Phone: (61 2) 8425 0100
Fax: (61 2) 9906 2218
Email: info@allenandunwin.com
Web: www.allenandunwin.com

National Library of Australia
Cataloguing-in-Publication entry:
    Brownsworth, Claire.
    Big world: a girl's own adventure.
    ISBN 1 74114 308 X.
    1. Brownsworth, Claire. 2. Women travelers – Biography.
    3. Adventure and adventurers – Biography. 4. Voyages and travels.
    I. Title.
910.4

Edited by Karen Ward
Text design by Nada Backovic
Typeset by Pauline Haas, bluerinse setting
Printed in Australia by McPherson's Printing Group

10 9 8 7 6 5 4 3 2 1

*To Mum – for being my ongoing support, my Voice of Wisdom
and my wonderful friend through every challenge in life –
especially the challenge of finishing a book.*

*To Adam – for dragging me out climbing when I was going bleary eyed in
front of the computer, for laughing and not crying every time I said,
'You know how I thought I had finished? Well . . .', and for thinking
that Amazonian-sized women are the best.*

To Dad and James – for making sure I never take myself seriously.

*To my aunt Chris Wallace – for giving me the crazy idea to write a book in the
first place, and for infecting me with the confidence to go through with it.*

*To Allen & Unwin – for taking on a first-time author and giving more help and
support than I ever expected. Especially Richard Walsh and Clare Emery.*

To all my other family and friends – for making life so fun.

And to all the people in the world who are out there trying to save wilderness areas.

That just about covers it, I think.

CONTENTS

PROLOGUE

Above us the remnants of the old volcano rose majestically. Close to the top of Mt Beerwah the high cliff stood proud and, from a distance, the two huge rock overhangs just below its summit looked shallow and insignificant. This was it. The day of our long-planned expedition had come at last.

We did a final gear check, slathered on the sunscreen and decanted a bottle of red wine into an unbreakable container. I shrugged my thirty-kilo pack onto my back and we headed away from the comfort and security of the car and up the steep scramble towards the base of the cliff.

There is an age-old climbing equation that explains what I began to experience next: a climber's bravado is proportional to the distance of the climber from the climb.

The Beerwah Bolt Route is an intimidating rock climb in the Glass House Mountains north of Brisbane. The tallest of this group of mountains, Mt Beerwah, is a volcanic plug with a striking overhanging cliff near its summit. Looking up at the cliff is like looking up at a giant inverted staircase, but a staircase with only two very high and out-of-proportion steps. Together, these steps form about ten metres of horizontal overhang, and the Bolt Route ascends this 130-metre wall of rock and tops out at the summit.

Although I had been climbing for about eight years, the Bolt Route was unlike any other climb I had ever attempted in two very significant ways. Firstly, I had never managed to get my extremely lengthy body up and around anything that jutted that far out over my head. Secondly, unlike all the climbs that I had done previously, you can't hold onto the textures and features in this rock, because there aren't any. The rock is almost completely smooth.

So, if you can't hold onto the rock and the wall hangs ten metres over your head, then how can you hope to climb to the top?

The legend goes that this problem was solved when rock climber Trevor Gynther broke his leg. Unable to do any 'really hard stuff' due to the hindrance of an awkward plaster cast, he undertook the superhuman challenge of hand-drilling a hundred or so bolts into the 130-metre wall of volcanic basalt, turning it into what is known as a 'bolt aid climb'. The only way to get to the top is by ascending the line of pre-placed bolts using specialised equipment and techniques, all of which were new to me.

Apparently, it was just a matter of clipping ladders onto the bolts and climbing the ladders. It sounded easy enough.

I didn't know until much later that the saying also goes amongst climbers that aid climbing is so physically strenuous, and the fear so great that, if it were a job, no-one could pay you enough to do it. Instead, all over the world climbers do it for free. And I was about to join them.

What I did know was that I was about to work my way up an overhanging rock face, completely dependent on about forty kilos of tangled gear and a series of old bolts. And somewhere up there I was going to be spending the night on a portaledge – a flat piece of canvas stretched on a metal frame, suspended from the vertical rock face a hundred metres from the ground. Up until this point, I had never slept on a piece of sagging material any higher than a hammock. Was I kidding myself thinking this was going to be fun?

But my 'Voice of Wisdom' (aka my mother) always told me that the worst thing you can do in life is not give things a go. So, taking a deep breath and with the comfort of knowing that I was merely following motherly advice, I tightened the padded hip belt of my overloaded pack and headed up towards a 24-hour adventure into the vertical unknown ...

WHY WILD PIGS (*SUS SCROFA*) DO NOT MAKE GOOD CAMPING COMPANIONS

- They can grow to 150 kg or more.

- They can be extremely aggressive when they are breeding or when they are threatened or surprised.

- The boars have large tusks, which they can use to rip open prey or foes – or perhaps tents.

- They bulldoze the earth digging for food, and eat eggs, small amphibians and any other small animals.

- They are fast runners and strong swimmers, and despite their size they can move through the bush as quietly as a cat – when they want to that is.

- And apart from anything else they have the very antisocial habit of eating, very noisily, at night.

ONE

Growing Up ... and Up ... and Up!

I wonder at what age people start to show signs of their adult personalities. I know my brother James showed a desire to impress the crowds from as early as I can remember, and I would follow him into danger if it looked like it might be fun. And even as a little girl, when I should have been playing with dolls and make-up and wearing pretty dresses, I was outside barefoot, dirty, climbing and exploring, and just waiting for any opportunity to have an adventure, more often than not limping home with jumper-ant bites and bleeding body parts. I used to complain that even my scabs had scabs.

Growing up on a five-acre Australian bush block meant there were plenty of opportunities to have fun and get hurt, and having an older brother meant that danger was never far away. I mean, I had to follow his lead, otherwise I might miss out on something good. Like the time when he tried to pull off The Tricycle Stunt ...

My brother, the born showman, decided to attempt the long-dreamed-of tricycle stunt just when we were about to leave for a sleepover at the Conways'. Their car pulled up in front of our house and the entire Conway clan, aged three to nine, piled out; as usual our parents started to chat. James – nine years old, blond, freckly and a wild boy – disappeared. Even though I was only seven I sensed an ill wind; he was up to something.

It didn't take long for him to reappear. I should have known – he had been building up to this trick for a while.

Our house was built on the side of a very steep hill. The flat land in front of our doorstep had been carved out of the hillside, creating an area just big enough for cars to turn around. But even this small cutting had left a wall of dirt on the high side, virtually a cliff from our young perspective. Traversing from left to right along the top edge of this cliff, before turning down towards the house, was a footpath. Because half of this path had eroded away leaving just enough width for two wheels, and because it had two hair-raising bends over a three-and-a-half-metre drop, this path was the perfect tricycle stunt run.

James was poised on the pathway high up the hill, five metres above the cliff edge, right foot on the pedal, ready for his debut descent. I knew the rules – both feet on the pedals the whole way. This was going to be great!

'Hey everyone, watch this!'

Mum's eyes flicked from her conversation up towards the sound of his voice, then they widened.

'JAMES! GET OFF THAT TRICYCLE NOW! YOU HEAR ME! JAAMES! ...'

He was off! Now with both feet on the pedals he started his descent. He sure was picking up some speed. He was nearly at the edge when his eyes grew wide and his feet left the pedals to grope madly for the ground. But it was too late to stop. I watched in horror as I realised this was all going horribly wrong. One wheel left the ground as he leaned into an uncontrolled left-hand turn in a cloud of dust.

Oh golly, he'd made it. Hooray! My brother, the stuntman! Now he was careering at full pelt along the top of the cliff. Mum, Dad, the whole Conway clan and I stood, jaws gaping and eyes fixed, powerless to do anything other than watch the cloud of dust as it sped across above us, along the narrowest eroded section towards the corner of the cutting where he could turn back down the hill towards the house to be home free. He was going to make it.

Then a terrible error of judgement. His outside wheel was off the edge; the tricycle started to tip. This wasn't going to be pretty. James, the trike and part of the path were rolling off the edge and, as if in slow motion, were circling towards the ground. I watched in stunned silence as my parents ran towards his spiralling form. Then came the resounding THUMP and the rattle and crash as the trike hit his motionless body on the shoulder. The silence was broken only by bellbirds and then by Mum and Dad's frantic shouts. The rest of the audience stood transfixed as my parents crouched around the crumpled form.

Soon a new sound rose over and above all else as James's piercing wail rang through the trees. My bleeding brother came limping back towards the house, shirt torn, blond hair full of dust, and tears streaming down through the dirt on his grief-stricken, freckly face.

The wails faded behind me as I headed over to where the tricycle lay in the dirt and gravel. Amazingly, it hadn't sustained any real injury. I looked up at the looming drop down which James had been spiralling moments before. Wow! That must have really hurt!

I looked back down at the rusty old tricycle on its side on the driveway. My heart started racing ... He had been so close to success ... I wonder ... It must be possible ... I mean, he had got through the hardest bit ... And it looked like fun ...

My poor mother and father turned from my sobbing brother just in time to see their seven-year-old daughter plummeting down the hill on the tricycle, feet not leaving the pedals for an instant, even as she flew straight over the edge of the cliff and down the three-and-a-half-metre drop to the gravel driveway below.

The Conway clan tactfully left and James and I spent the night at home, picking gravel out of our shredded skin, amazingly without a bone broken between us.

Of course, we did eventually master The Path. But Mum and Dad can't really complain about our reckless natures because, after all, their own sense of adventure was the reason for our very existence, and the reason we grew up as barefooted bush kids.

Although my parents had lived some of their early years within thirty minutes' drive of each other on the Bellarine Peninsula in Victoria, they didn't actually meet until they were in a far more exciting location. Mum had completed her Arts degree and barely survived a mind-numbing year of work in market research, before signing up for two years with Australian Volunteers Abroad. She was posted to teach on Yule Island in Papua New Guinea. Around the same time Dad completed his pilot training and needed to find a job to gain flying experience, so he too headed for Papua New Guinea. Luckily for me, he was hired by the Yule Island Catholic Mission.

His job description? Flying light aircraft full of supplies for delivery to the tiny mission stations perched on the jungle-covered mountaintops of the Papua New Guinea highlands – locations so remote that they could only be reached by light aircraft or weeks of hard walking. Landing on bumpy, home-built airstrips cut into the treacherous mountain tops involved a delicate balance of local knowledge, skill, precise reading of the wind direction and weather conditions, a large amount of luck, and an even larger amount of insanity. The twinkle in my Dad's eye very nearly didn't become James and me many times. But dad was in his element, and even more so when he met a lovely, fresh-faced young teacher at home base on Yule Island.

And so it was that in this remote and tropical setting, Mum, who was petrified of heights, hated flying, and prone to severe motion sickness, was swept off her feet by a shy, handsome and completely broke young pilot.

They married in a whirlwind ceremony in Australia in 1973. This involved flying into Melbourne, meeting their respective in-laws the day before the wedding, tying the knot, and then heading straight back to New Guinea to start work two days later.

A year or so later, with a thousand hours of treacherous and exciting flying and a bout of malaria behind Dad, and a wealth of teaching experience and extended periods of air sickness and trepidation behind Mum, they headed back to Australia to start a new adventure together. Dad had been accepted as a pilot by TAA (Trans-Australia Airlines).

As it turned out, my mother's queasiness hadn't only been air-sickness. To my parents' shock and dismay, Mum soon discovered she was pregnant. Nine months later my brother James was born and two years later I arrived – three and a half weeks late and a strapping ten pounds, already the biggest babe on the block.

So, at the ages of twenty-seven and twenty-nine, my parents, whose romance had been born in a wild and exciting tropical paradise, found themselves with two mischievous children, living in a forest of brick veneers in suburban Victoria.

I have very few memories of this period of my life, but I'm told that from the time I could move independently I was on a single-minded mission to climb absolutely everything and get into sticky situations. In fact, much to my disappointment, I can't even remember my first serious climbing accident, as it happened when I was only two. Mum still cringes when she recalls the sound of my head hitting the brick paving after I attempted to do a solo ascent of the garden table, followed by a BASE-jump with no parachute.

Fortunately, after a moment of stunned silence from my parents as my eyes rolled back in my head, I regained consciousness and appeared unharmed. I suspect that this fall may have knocked some sense out of me.

Anyway, at this time my parents had more to worry about than free-falling babies. They were struggling with the reality that they had somehow thrown a spanner into their dreams of adventure by becoming a 1970s suburban nuclear family. So it wasn't a great surprise to anyone when they began to search for a bush retreat, where the job of raising a family could be mingled with the outdoors and wilderness.

They found a block of five acres of bushland on a little mountain in Queensland, complete with its own rainwater tanks, a little creek in a strip of rainforest and a dense covering of scratchy lantana. They called the property Rivendel, and in 1980 they packed us all up and we headed bush.

At Rivendel I discovered my undying love of all things natural. My days were filled with fascination for the rustling bush, and for the endless cycle of birds, insects, pademelons, butterflies and scrub turkeys. Below the treetop verandah of our house the creek gurgled through elephant's ear palms and tall tree ferns. This winding tributary was the location of some of my earliest adventures into the great outdoors.

But only a very small part of this creek ran through Rivendel. As I became braver I ventured further away from our patch: over the wire fence, along the creek, creeping through the tangled lawyer vine and palms to where I discovered a deep old disused well near a little island surrounded by tributaries of flowing water. In one of these snaking tributaries the creek widened slightly to form a deep swimming hole.

This was the spot that became my secret world, where I dragged even my most reluctant friends to play. As I got older and other kids became interested in clothes, pop music and film stars, I was still trying to persuade them to come and explore the creek with me. I was never one of the cool kids.

By the age of ten I was getting pretty cocky about my survival skills in the bush. I was confident that I knew how things ticked and I sure knew how to survive out there. On weekends and school holidays I would leave first thing in the morning and get back late in the evenings, just in time for dinner. I would have to tear myself away from my cubbyhouse-building and explorations just when the excitement of darkness was coming. My expeditions lasted later and later into the evenings, and eventually I decided that real explorers didn't come home for dinner. What I needed was a tent, and a willing accomplice.

It took a bit to persuade my friend Anna that I knew what I was doing, but eventually I convinced her it would be great fun to stay in the bush overnight. As the sun dipped below the horizon, we sat around our campfire, exhausted from our gruelling day of playing. As I pulled out the sandwiches that Mum had packed in our bags, I felt a pang of regret. Right now Mum would be in our nice safe kitchen, cooking up a hot meal. Maybe I should have asked her to come too ...

We retreated hurriedly into our tent, and then the bush came alive around us with the rustling and whispering of the ghosts from our stories. I lay staring at the canvas roof, cursing myself for feeling much less like the brave grown-up I had been when I strode out this morning. What was I so worried about? This was perfectly safe.

Eventually I drifted into a fitful sleep, imagining with all my might that I was safely tucked away in my bedroom.

A loud crash brought me abruptly back to the reality of the dark bush. Loud thuds and the sounds of snuffling and digging were surrounding our old sagging tent. Any hopes I had of this being a nightmare were destroyed by the whites of Anna's eyes glaring at me fearfully through the darkness. This was real.

For hours we lay looking helplessly at the flimsy tent walls, too petrified to move or make a sound. There was no hope of escape. The terrifying noises continued long into the night, the grunting and snuffling and digging getting closer and closer.

In the early light of morning we cautiously unzipped the fly of the tent, and giggled nervously as we looked from each other's widening eyes to the chaotic scene that confronted us. The ground had been savagely uprooted, and big hoof marks scarred the freshly turned earth right up to the zippered doorway. I was bush-wise enough to guess what was confirmed later. We had been surrounded in the night by a pack of wild pigs.

This incident put a temporary end to camping expeditions to the creek until the family of pigs moved away. However, as with all terrifying and dangerous endeavours, I bathed in the glow of retrospective pleasure. My life of being a 'brave' explorer, facing the wilds of nature, had begun.

Attending the little primary school minutes down the road from Rivendel was like having an extension of the backyard but with permanent playmates. Located on a huge clearing surrounded by bush, it consisted of forty pupils divided into two classes: the Big Kids and the Little Kids. Our education was cunningly disguised as games and bush camps.

And then in Grade Five, when I thought that beating the boys in a barefoot race down our gravel driveway was as good as it got, I found there was more. A new headmaster strode into my life. Mr C ate Mars Bars in class, started a school vegetable patch and added bush regeneration to the school curriculum. He would stop halfway through maths, when everyone was looking bored and sleepy, and bellow: 'You all look like you need to get outside ... Let's go and plant some trees!' He was just plain wonderful, and I was besotted.

At this time my idols were David Attenborough, David Suzuki and the Bush Tucker Man, and from a young age I had been determined that I was going to follow in their footsteps, crusading for the preservation of the natural world. Mr C provided me with my first opportunity to realise this dream when he suggested our school should try to win the Tidy Schools competition by creating some gardens around the grounds. I knew that my time had come.

Some of the other kids decided to build gardens as well, but I made damn sure that I secured the plot at the front gate of the school. I couldn't have those other kids making a mess of this prime land. I would build the best garden in the school and my dedication to the task was absolute.

It was a mammoth effort. This was going to be no simple little flower patch. We made a pond for frogs, a border with old tree stumps, and planted a huge variety of flowering plants and palms that I dug up from Rivendel and other people's gardens around the mountain. I insisted that my best friends and some of the more timid Little Kids stay late after school whenever we didn't reach our goals during the lunchbreak.

Of course our school won the Tidy Schools competition hands down, and continued to win each year following. But for me the best was yet to come. At the end of my final year of primary school Mr C created a new award, which was presented to me at the graduation ceremony. I won the school's first ever 'Environmentalist Award' for my dedication to all things natural. My devotion was complete, and my path in life was confirmed.

But sadly with this award my days of bush regeneration classes had come to an end, and it was time to move on. I would be attending Brisbane Girls Grammar School for my high-school education. My parents had two rather big concerns as I started Year Eight. The first was that Dad was unemployed, having lost his job with Australian Airlines in the 1989 pilots' dispute, and not knowing if he would be getting it back left our family resources rather stretched to be sending a child to this very expensive school. Their other concern was whether mixing with such an affluent group of girls was going to turn me into a materialistic snob. Dad set about making sure the latter wasn't going to happen.

My father had, with the pilots' dispute, been transported from a life of being in charge of jet aeroplanes to a routine of washing up, laundry, housekeeping and picking up the little tackers from school. Showing his true sporting nature he found a way to make even this latter and gruelling task (we lived an hour's drive from school) entertaining.

I would stand and wait at the pick-up bay and watch as all the other girls' parents came to collect them. It was like a line-up for *Wheels* magazine. Porsches, Mercedes and Maseratis would pull in and my peers would climb into plush leather interiors. I would stand and watch the clock ticking, hoping beyond hope that Dad would be late and arrive after all the other girls had gone. But he never was – that would have ruined his fun.

My heart would sink as he rattled into the bay and parked behind the latest-model BMW. He would shudder to a stop in his favourite vehicle, the rusty old Toyota tray-back, and then jump out to help me with my schoolbag. His clothes would be full of holes from working on the property and he would have on what we mockingly called his 'farmer Joe hat'. I would pull my school hat low and jump into the cabin, praying that I hadn't been spotted.

Even though deep inside I knew that the joke was on me, I felt terrible when eventually I couldn't stand the other girls' scathing stares anymore and I asked him to pick me up from the other side of the road. He kindly obliged and from then on proudly honked his horn, waving furiously to catch my attention from across the street.

But it wasn't like I needed a daggy father with an overdeveloped sense of humour to set me apart from all the other girls at high school, because with teenagerdom a tragic thing started to happen. I started to grow or, more accurately, I just didn't stop. I had always been at the upper end of the height scale, but as all of my peers started to plateau out I just kept on going up, and up and up.

By the time I reached Year Eleven I started turning heads in the street. I was, much to my distress, six feet tall. I'd cringe when I'd hear the whispers behind me – 'Look, Mummy – look at that tall girl!' or 'Hey, guys, check out the height of that chick!' Didn't they realise I had ears?

I was devastated. Why did I have to be the one who was different? And it sure was the kind of difference that was hard to hide. I spent many evenings crying on Mum's shoulder. It just wasn't fair that I was the tallest girl in the whole school, probably the whole world!

But still I didn't stop. By the time I reached Year Twelve, at the tender and sensitive age of sixteen, I was nearly six foot two.

'Hey, what's the weather like up there? Ha, ha, ha!' Like they'd just invented the joke. *Really funny*. On Mum's suggestion, I sat down and wrote a list of cutting responses to my most hated of all questions, 'How tall are you?' They ranged from the quite polite 'Eight foot ten', to the somewhat less subtle 'Why? How long's your – ?' (I never did have the guts to fill in the blank.)

But being over six feet tall, it was pointless (and very uncomfortable) to try to hide my height. So I gave up trying and stood tall, though my teenage heart was breaking. Underneath my brave face I couldn't see why I had been burdened with such a terrible trait.

Even when it came to 'tall people's' sports, my height was more of a hindrance than a help. I was recruited without trial into the A1 basketball team, a decision the coach soon came to regret. There just seemed to be too much of me to know how to coordinate all the parts in quick motion at the same time. I was planted inside the defence circle, but here I was hopeless because I didn't want to hurt any of those fragile 'little' girls. I had rings run around me and quickly gave up on myself as a star basketball player.

But feeling like a giant and being at an all-girls' school was a good thing for my academic education. Due to the fact that I didn't have much going on in the romance department (other than a couple of interested men in their late twenties, who freaked out when they found out how young I was) I set my sights on getting top marks.

My strategy was simple. For most of the term I would spend my time away from school exploring the bush and working on my favourite subject, art. Then about five weeks before exam time I would put my paints down and live, breathe and eat study. My end goal? To get into the Physiotherapy course at university, because this required an OP1 (Overall Position), the highest possible university entry grading in Queensland. There had to be something that set me apart from all the other girls, other than my height. And, from what I could work out, physiotherapy would be a flexible career that'd let me work part-time and spend the rest of my time on more creative and adventurous pursuits.

At the end of Year Twelve, 1994, I hit a dramatic six foot two, sold a painting, shocked myself, my teachers and my friends by achieving my OP1, and was accepted into Physiotherapy. And surely at university there had to be a tall man who would like me, and my age wouldn't be an issue any more. I reckoned I had it all figured out.

MY TOP FIVE HOME-BREWING TIPS TO ENSURE A MORE THAN JUST-DRINKABLE BREW

1. As for all cooking, quality ingredients are everything.
   - If possible use spring or tank water.
   - Try less-refined sweeteners like brown sugar, bush honey or malt.

2. Cleanliness is crucial, even in a university share house – otherwise the brew might have a few extra flavours in it from colonies of unwanted critters.

3. While the evil concoction is brewing, insulate the kit with a down jacket or similar item to maintain a steady temperature. Store it in a place where it will not get too hot or too cold.

4. Let it sit for at least a month – resist temptation or suffer the ill effects of a young brew. If you run out of the matured lager then overcome your penny-pinching nature and go and buy a carton!

5. Always save a few bottles from a good batch to sip while making your new brews. It adds to the general atmosphere and does wonders for motivation.

TWO

Discovering the High Life

I knew from the first week of my physiotherapy course that I wanted out. Out of university, out of timetables, out of being told what to do, out of Brisbane and, most of all, out of my Bachelor of Physiotherapy degree. I didn't want to be a physiotherapist and I just didn't seem to fit into the crowd of other students.

As a result, I had an embarrassingly poor attendance record. When I turned up to one lecture, after a particularly slack period, I was greeted with looks of surprise – I had been away from university for so long, my course mates had assumed I'd quit! They were almost right. Thank goodness I had a reliable notes source named Neil, who liked beer enough to trade six-packs for quality lecture notes. My days of academic excellence were well and truly over.

But I came to realise that university wasn't only about lectures; in fact lectures proved to be the only downside as life outside of my degree started to head in an exciting direction. In my first year

I met Kath, a five foot two blonde bombshell arts/science student who was a deep-thinking, brilliant nature-lover and could skol beer better than the average male jock. Despite my spending a lot of time looking at the top of her head, an enduring friendship was born and in my second year of university I organised to do a community physiotherapy placement in Sydney, where Kath had moved to complete her studies. At our first opportunity she took me along to her regular escape zone, the Blue Mountains National Park.

Friday night we hauled our packs into the Youth Hostel in Katoomba, then walked straight out to the famous Three Sisters, a trio of dramatic rock pillars standing proud. From our high vantage point we watched the evening clouds rolling in across the endless expanse of tree-covered mountains and tumbling over the sporadic sheer cliffs that looked like giant bites taken from the mountainsides. We breathed a sigh of relief as we heard ... well, not much at all: no traffic, no people, no car horns, just the gentle breeze rustling through the tall gums. This was where our hearts were, out in the pristine expanse of nature.

Early the next morning we set off in the heavy, damp mist to explore. My head was still cloudy from our night of drinking and socialising with the cute German backpackers at the Katoomba Hotel, and from occasional pounding memories of Kath winning the Limbo Championship and multiple skolling contests. We headed back to the Three Sisters and descended the cliff next to them, down the steep 860 steps of the Giant Stairway and into the forest below. We followed our map along bush tracks, giggling and chatting as we twisted and turned through the trees. Kath's natural energy and exuberance were in full play as she bounced along the bush track beside me, stopping at regular intervals to marvel at this wonderful old tree or that small colourful leaf on the path, or a delicate fern in the bush.

We rounded a corner in the path and our voices faded to silence. The moment of revelation! We had emerged from the bush to find rising before us one of the sheer limestone cliffs that carve through the park. Right there in front of me was a group of young men on the rock face, climbing to the top. They were not just looking, but *experiencing* the scale and grandeur of this stunning place.

The more we watched and listened to their chatter and laughter, the more fascinated I became. They progressed from the ground to the top of the cliff without leaving any trace of their ascent. It was awesome. It was amazing. I couldn't believe that this was something that people could do. They just looked like normal people and yet here they were moving vertically up the secluded cliff face.

The first thing I did when I returned to Brisbane was to join the University of Queensland Climbing Club. I went to my first club meeting at Kangaroo Point (KP), a twenty-metre high cliff in the middle of Brisbane City, abutting the Brisbane River. KP is actually an old quarry that has been transformed into a round-the-clock riverside picnic and climbing area, with big spotlights trained on the cliff all night long.

I wandered along the base of the rock face, heart beating with excited anticipation, looking up at all the climbers and unable to believe that shortly it would be me on the rock, climbing to the top. As I watched people struggling and grunting, I had the warm inner conviction that I would not have the same troubles. This was meant for me, I knew it already, and with my childhood of clambering and tree-climbing behind me I was going to climb the rock like a monkey. University club, here I come.

I saw a group of twentysomethings crowded around a few dangling ropes. One of them had dreadlocks, a few wore bandannas, most looked pretty cool and confident, and some looked fresh-faced and nervous. This had to be the university club. Wow, they were really hard-core! A few people were halfway up already, a whole ten metres off the ground.

Twenty minutes later I was putting on the club harness and sweaty climbing shoes, tying into the rope and looking up at the beginners climb that reared above me. This was it. My time had come. Everybody watch and learn. I looked around. No-one was paying me any attention, other than the tall redhead named Liam who was holding my rope. I was sure they soon would be.

I placed my hand on a big lump and one foot on the rock and pulled my weight upwards. My foot slipped off, and I cracked my knee hard against the rock. Ouch!

Oh well, a bad start.

After half an hour I was a few metres off the ground. My legs and arms were shaking with fatigue and I was hunting desperately for a hold that was bigger than the tiny ledges around me. Oh no ... I was coming off again ... Aaargh!

It rapidly became apparent that I had little natural talent for this sport. But as I heaved and bruised my way higher and higher, looking intently at the beautiful features and textures in the rock while trying to find a way to use them, I knew that I would never look back. I had spent my whole life so far loving and exploring nature, and now I could experience it all in a completely new dimension.

After my first night at KP I felt like I had climbed to the top of the world. I hadn't only discovered climbing, I had discovered an outdoor adventure lifestyle. I had found the niche in life that I fitted into. My life would never be without rock climbing again.

Halfway through second year at university, I moved out of home and into the city with my brother, James. I wanted to be closer to KP and closer to the action. Despite my initial concern, it seemed that James had actually pulled through his horrible teenage days and become rather a nice person. He still had his blond hair and freckles, but instead of being a skinny young boy he was now a strapping six foot four bloke, with proportions that sent the opposition on the rugby field running for shelter. Thankfully, he had grown out of giving me dead-arms or I could have sustained some serious injuries.

Sharing a house in the Brisbane suburb of Toowong with James started an essential new aspect of my education. It was time to make the transition from being a child at home to being an independent adult out in the real world. There sure was a lot to learn, but we tackled the new challenges with gusto.

We found strategies to minimise the impact of domestic chores – we washed the dishes only when we ran out and, because our clothesline was out of sight of the house, we set new records for how many times a single piece of clothing can be rained on and dried out in succession. Eventually we discovered that, if left long enough, clothing actually removed itself from the clothesline spontaneously when the material under the peg disintegrated.

Under the guidance of our student neighbours, we also mastered the art of concocting foul-tasting home-brew. We found out that, after a few gulps, even the worst brew tasted okay; and we discovered the advantages of brown, beer-coloured carpet. Oh, and we even learned that swinging on a termite-infested fence after a pint of home-brew can result in three subsequent weeks of fence-building and painting. Some of these 'lessons of life' sure were tough.

But overshadowing all else was my passage into the world of climbing.

My first adrenalin-charged night of climbing at KP had been doing what is called 'top-roping'. What I hadn't known at the time was that hard-core types consider this the soft option. Top-roping is when you set up an anchor at the top of the cliff and feed the doubled-over rope through karabiners so that it is dangling from the top, with the two ends touching the ground at the bottom. At the base of the cliff the climber ties one end of the doubled-over rope to their harness, while their partner feeds the other end through their belay device (a braking device). As the climber ascends, the belayer takes in the slack rope. If the climber comes off the rock the belayer locks off the rope and stops their fall. It's the soft option because you don't need to be committed to the climb since, when you fall off, you don't fall far. And obviously it is not a very practical technique when out in the real world, because you can't set up your ropes at the top of a cliff when trying to climb a mountain from the bottom up.

The real challenge and adventure in climbing comes with lead climbing, when you start at the bottom of the cliff with your ropes, gear and climbing partner, and you work your way to the top. As you ascend you place pieces of 'natural protection' (equipment specially designed for this purpose) into cracks in the rock, that you then clip your rope through. At the top you anchor yourself to whatever you can find (setting up a 'belay') so that you can then take in the rope as your climbing partner follows you up. If the climb is longer than a single rope length (a single 'pitch') then you repeat the same process until you get to the top, with one climber 'leading' and the other 'seconding'. Getting down from the top can be just as exciting as it often involves abseiling and/or adventurous scrambling and bushwalking (actually, it is often during descents that climbers get injured).

My true climbing apprenticeship started when I left the safe world of top-roping at KP.

I found myself out in the mountains, learning to place gear, to tie the range of essential knots, and to set up a safe belay at the top of the climb. If I fell off, I would fall to below the last piece of gear I had placed. If that piece of gear didn't hold, then I would fall to the next piece down and, if that didn't hold, then there could be serious trouble. This was true climbing – embarking on journeys into the vertical unknown, having to trust yourself, your technique and your partner with your life, and having to be a competent and safe climber that another person could entrust their life to.

I was becoming a real climber. Six months after my first night at KP, I headed back to the Blue Mountains National Park. This time I was up for two weeks of vertical adventure with the climbing club.

And then, at the end of my second year of university, just when I thought I was too tall for any man to fall for me, Anthony rowed his way into my life. He was a tall and handsome elite-level rower with a passion and obsession for the sport that I will never hope to understand.

It was pretty clear from the start that there was really no hope for us in the long term. He hated the very thought of getting dirty and camping, and his interest in climbing died an early death when I proved to be better at it than he was. His idea of a holiday was a five-star hotel, and my idea of a holiday was a bush bash with climbing gear and a tent. He was the most disciplined and focused person I had ever met. At that stage I was attending about fifty per cent of my lectures in a good week.

Nevertheless, we got on like a house on fire. We started out as mates, then embarked on a relationship which was primarily an amazing friendship, and as such was virtually impossible to break up from. How can you break up with a best friend who lives three streets away, and has also become best buddies with your brother and housemate?

In my third year of university Anthony successfully landed a place in the postgraduate medical degree at the University of Queensland and our fate was sealed. We wouldn't be able to break up until one of us left, and I was going to be finishing my degree first. Thank goodness for that because, without his ever-present sense of fun and humour, I'm not sure I would have made it through university.

Even though I knew in my heart that life in the city was definitely not for me, I figured that, when in the city, I should do as the city people do – or at least make the most of the available resources.

It was Carl, a very gorgeous climbing friend and veterinary student, who came up with the smart idea of climbing a 200-metre freestanding radio transmitter situated about twenty kilometres north of Brisbane. He recruited a group of young and foolhardy blokes, and me, and we set about planning our daring ascent.

I thought it might be a good idea during our preparations to assess if there was any danger (other than the obvious) involved. It is actually more difficult than you would think to find out how dangerous these radio transmitters are. The people who own them don't want to tell you about the level of radiation, short of saying that as long as you are outside the fenced perimeter you are fine, and I couldn't exactly ask them if they thought climbing it would be safe. My 'university assignment' story didn't elicit much more information than that 'radiation levels are minor'. I'm sure if I had tried harder I could have found out more, but who has time for research when there's fun to be had?

So our plans went ahead. Dressed in black, the five of us piled into Carl's car, our climbing gear in the boot. Under the cover of night we headed north to our target.

Now, when a radio tower is surrounded by an outer barbwire fence, a kilometre-square paddock with a swamp and bulls in it, then two inner fences – one of razor wire and the other an electric fence on which are signs reading 'High Voltage. No Climbing' –

these are probably indications that climbing the tower is not a good idea. But we were university students and hence lacked any sense or reason and failed to take these signs seriously. Obviously 'the Establishment' was just trying to stop us from having fun.

We scaled the outer barbwire fence without too much trouble, then crept through 500 metres of swamp, skirting around the ominous shadows of the bulls in the darkness. Once we were at the inner fences, our true commitment shone through. We used blankets and bravado to scale first the razor wire, and then the electric fence.

Inside these barricades was an empty watchhouse, next to which the 200-metre tower disappeared high into the night sky. But here our plans began to reveal their first significant crack. The superstructure of the tower started about two metres off the ground. It was secured by a thick metal centre rod that plunged into a huge cement base, rather like a Christmas tree in a pot. During our preparations we had considered that there would probably be some static electricity build-up in the transmitter due to its height, and there might also be some kind of current running through it, to do with transmitting the signal. We knew that if we grounded such a charge we could be cactus. But, with the genius of a bunch of academics, we had reasoned that if we jumped from the ground straight onto the metal superstructure then we would avoid the potentially life-threatening effects of grounding the current.

Unfortunately this bloody big cement platform was creating problems. There was no way we could jump two metres from the ground onto the metal structure without a risk of touching the base at the same time. We needed a new plan. We had come this far, so there had to be a way. The gap between the tower and the fence was too great to bridge, and besides, that would form a link between the tower and the ground.

The watchhouse. Of course! We could climb onto the roof of the watchhouse and then jump across the two-metre gap onto the transmitter. There was no-one inside – we had peeked in through the windows already. It was perfect ... well, according to the blokes anyway.

At this point my enthusiasm was starting to wane. I was beginning to doubt the sense of our venture and was suspecting that under these lunatics' directions I was going to get seriously hurt. In fact my concern overwhelmed even my desire not to be deemed a gutless 'girl'.

'Guys ... um ... maybe we should just leave it, hey.'

'No way, man – this could work. Don't worry, we'll test the current first.'

I felt a wave of relief. Clearly I had underestimated these guys. I hadn't realised they had come prepared with special equipment to check our safety. They weren't as silly as I thought.

Carl pulled out an old piece of bent wire from his backpack. 'Everyone stand back. I'm just going to throw this baby onto the metal.'

I tensed up again. Oh, sure. What was a flimsy piece of wire going to tell us?

We all watched with interest. Carl gently swung his arm through and let go of the piece of metal. We could only see a vague shadow in the darkness as it slowly arced towards the transmitter.

CRACK!

I briefly saw a flash of light and sparks cascading from above me as I hurled myself to the ground. Then silence.

After a few seconds I sheepishly lifted my face up from the grass and looked around. My four brave accomplices were flat out on the ground around me.

'Holy shit!'

'Where'd it go?!'

We all scrambled hurriedly to our feet, and the search for the wire began. We started in circles from next to the platform, and finally found it hidden in the grass next to the fence. It was completely blackened. Well, at least that would be enough to talk these guys out of this crazy idea. I looked hopefully at Carl.

'Right then – there's no way we can climb onto this thing from the ground. We'll definitely have to jump from the top of the watchhouse.'

'No way … I mean … you guys are bloody mad. There's no way. NO WAY!' They were approaching the watchhouse, ignoring my protests. 'I'll just be down here ready to call the ambulance when you're all toasted.'

I watched with a feeling of impending doom as they headed over to scale the outside of the watchhouse. I had Carl's mobile phone ready in my hand.

It wasn't until they were faced with climbing a loose downpipe that sense finally prevailed. A sorry and despondent bunch, we packed up our ropes, climbed back out through the electric fence and past the 'High Voltage. No Climbing' sign, through the razor wire, past the bemused bulls, over the last fence and back to the car. It was a sombre trip back into town. I listened in silent relief to the disappointed mutterings.

'We could have done it, you know.'

'Yeah, it wasn't that far to jump.'

'Maybe we can head back some time and try again.'

'Yeah.'

'Yeah.'

'Cool.'

But, as far as I was concerned, I had seen the last of the inside of that enclosure.

I heard from Carl a few weeks later. He had been chatting to a friend of his who was an electrician. If we had so much as touched the tower without protective clothing, earthed or not, we would have been cooked. That was one tower I wouldn't be getting to the top of. I was going to stick to rock.

Meanwhile, there was more study to endure. My final year of university was my worst. It involved a year of working in hospitals, supervised by tutors, and putting into practice all the knowledge we had supposedly learned over the previous three years. It was a nightmare. Now I was spending five days a week surrounded by sick people and white walls, with a tutor looking over my shoulder. Each patient had to be prepared for and reviewed after treatment, meaning studying after hours, and there were still exams and assignments to be completed.

As the year progressed I became more and more convinced that I never, ever wanted to be a physiotherapist as long as I lived. I hated hospitals with a passion. To rub salt into my wounds there was a minimum attendance requirement which, if not fulfilled, resulted in an automatic fail. The buggers had me snookered, and my lack of enthusiasm was reflected in my marks.

Nevertheless, despite my general lack of commitment to my course – and, I'm sure, to all my classmates' surprise – I didn't fail. In 1998 I graduated and received my Bachelor of Physiotherapy certificate, and attended the graduation dinner in an antique silver dress that I had bought from St Vinnies' charity shop and hand-altered into a slinky midriff-revealing two-piece.

Once again, I felt a little different from my peers. But by this stage I was learning to revel in being the oddball of the group and I received my Worst Attender award with pride. I had made it. I had my bit of paper. My photo was taken in a stupid hat, and at last I could put physiotherapy and everything associated with it behind me, and get back to my life's ambitions – having adventures and saving the environment.

But how? My mother, aka my Voice of Wisdom, tentatively suggested that it would probably be a good idea to consolidate my skills, just in case I ever needed to use them. In fact, as I lay enjoying the summer sun on the beach, contemplating the prospect of turning to bar or restaurant work, a little voice in my head kept suggesting that, as I had spent four years being tortured, I might as well earn some cash for my pains.

However, there was one thing that I was adamant about – the two-year postgraduate rotations in the big teaching hospitals, which were 'essential for career development', could go jump. I didn't want to develop a career and there was no way I was ever going to set foot in a hospital as a physio again. I decided that the best way to utilise my fancy bit of paper was as a ticket to go to weird and wonderful places.

So, while most other graduates were working hard, writing applications to secure the best positions in the best hospitals, I started taking maps to the beach to find interesting places where I could go and use my degree. Soon the parched Australian centre was calling me, and on a whim I phoned a private physiotherapy clinic in Mt Isa, a big mining town in outback Queensland. Sure enough, they were desperate enough to employ a new graduate. I had a job.

Somehow Anthony had put up with my moaning through the whole of my final year of university and had stayed by my side, making me laugh and giving me the strength to finish. He was still one of my best mates but – as I packed my bags, my bike and my climbing gear and said a sorrowful goodbye – we both knew that it was over.

It was tough to be losing a best friend who had been such an integral part of my life for over two years, but it had to be done. My time had come. With iron resolve and new-found purpose I set off on my life of travel and adventures.

And left my wallet with all my cards and money in it on the back seat of my brother James's car. Oops!

AUSSIE ROAD TRAINS

These monsters of the Australian outback, which regularly scare unwitting tourists, are trucks that tow two or more huge trailers. They are used to transport large quantities of goods over long distances to areas where there are no railway lines.

The standard three-trailer road trains weigh in at a whopping 115 tonnes without a load, are 53.5 metres (making them the longest trucks in the world), can carry over 100 tonnes of load, and hurtle along at the legal maximum of 100 km/h (but have a habit of going faster).

Understandably, they are not very manoeuvrable and they have poor acceleration and braking speed.

In summary, they are best treated with great care and respect by us little people.

THREE

The Great Escape

January, 1999: I looked down on the wasteland below me through the small window of the twelve-seater, twin-engined aircraft that roared between Townsville and Mt Isa. Some of the passengers had pulled earplugs from their bags and shoved them into their ears before the engines had screamed into life. But not me. As the little plane rose into the sky, I felt a stab of panic that this might be the noise level for the whole trip. The plane levelled out and my fears were confirmed.

What on earth was I doing? I knew nothing about Mt Isa but I had accepted my first physiotherapy job there. I had left my home and my friends and now I was about to arrive in a huge mining town in the middle of the desert. I hadn't even seen so much as a photograph of the place, or talked to anyone who had lived there.

All I knew was that there was a bloody big mine somewhere near the town and that a guy who rowed with Anthony had a friend, Vanessa, who had red curly hair and would pick me up from the airport. She would be dropping me off at my new home – a spare room that had been offered by some friends of the physio-therapist's receptionist – and then I would be starting my first-ever job as a health professional tomorrow morning. And it was in a private practice, so I would be on my own without the support network of a hospital job.

But a new feeling inside me was coming alive. A deep tingling that rose from my chest up to my throat and out to my fingertips, making me slightly breathless. The piercing scream of the engines lost some intensity as realisation dawned: I was on my way to freedom. I had done my time and now the world was mine to experience, and this plane was taking me there! If I didn't like Isa, who cared; I would be on the next plane out – with earplugs – and off to somewhere new.

Before I knew it, we had touched down and the squealing engines gave way to the silence of the Australian outback. As we walked across the blistering tarmac I was ready to take on the big wide world.

Forty-five minutes later I stood beside my bags and my boxed-up mountain bike in the burning midday haze, alone. The airport had emptied. In the distance I could see a tall chimney with a white pall of smoke billowing from its peak. That must be Mt Isa. My plane had been five minutes late. Maybe Vanessa had come early and thought she had missed me. Surely not ... she would have checked. Maybe she had just forgotten altogether. I sat down despondently on my bags – hot, lonely, and with no purse.

So much for the big wide world.

A dusty white ute screamed into the drive and out of it jumped a woman – a flaming redhead with flashing white teeth. 'So sorry I'm late ... work ... press conference ... delayed ... sorry ... anyway, let's go!'

Within ten minutes of leaving the airport I had my first significant outback cultural experience. I had thrown my bags in the back of Vanessa's car and then, dripping from the forty-degree heat of summer in Central Queensland, we had headed straight for the Irish Pub to cool off with a nice cold beer – the first of many in the following months.

The Mt Isa Irish Pub is not only the biggest watering hole in an extremely thirsty town of 25000 or so people, but is actually the biggest Irish Pub in the whole of the Southern Hemisphere. And I'm tellin' you, it's huge. I doubt that in my whole time in Mt Isa I actually saw every section of it. And we spent a lot of time trying.

An hour or so – and several pints – later, the ute pulled up outside my new home. Vanessa, rushing through some apologies, quickly helped me unload my bags and then screeched off towards her hectic afternoon. I stood shell-shocked on the verge, wilting from the intense heat and giddy from the beer. The low-set brick veneer home matched all the other houses in the street, with some children's toys strewn in the front yard and a Hills Hoist clothes-line dominating the small area of lawn.

With my remaining courage wafting rapidly away on my beer breath I approached the front gate. Around the corner of the house came a yapping dog followed by a slight yet tough-looking lady in her forties with thin, severe lips, short hair and a tattoo on her ankle. Barbara sucked hard on her cigarette as she led me around to the back door, past a much younger and tattooed man lounging in the outdoor set. Even through my beer fog I could see clearly that these two (who I was to find out later were newlyweds) had not been awaiting my arrival with eager anticipation. I was, it seemed, a trial run for a 'bit extra in the kitty'.

The torn back-door flyscreen clattered noisily shut behind us as she led me into the hallway. I dragged my bags over the tile-finish lino, past the Coca-Cola shrine (a lifetime collection of anything to do with Coke), past the purple hand-stencilled dresser, through the kitchen where the new pie maker stood proudly, and into my little room. There had been some obvious effort put into making it homey for me. The lacy curtains lay motionless in the hot breezeless day, trinkets stood on any flat space above floor level and, propped up against my pillows, was a monstrously large and incredibly ugly soft toy. I lounged onto the bed exhausted, and almost hit the floor as the springs sagged below me.

All this was strange, daunting and new but, as I lay awake that night, with my mattress relocated to the floor and the scary-looking toy relocated to the cupboard, my surroundings were the last thing on my mind. Genuine fear had started to grip me, and not just from my memory of the *Dr Who* episode where a hideous-looking toy comes alive in the heat, and attacks and strangles people in their sleep.

At 8.30 tomorrow morning I would be starting my first job as a physiotherapist. I was going to have to take some poor victim from the waiting room into a cubicle, talk to them, work out what was wrong with them, and then treat them. They were going to expect me to know something. I desperately dug around in my memory, searching for something I had retained from my four years of study. But there was nothing there. I'd forgotten everything! My mind was blank with apprehension.

It was dawning on me that now had come the time to pay. If only I had attended more lectures, paid more attention to my tutors and studied harder, but now it was too late. I was doomed. I tossed and turned all night, hoping that the morning wouldn't come.

The dawn light filtered through the lacy curtains and I watched the ceiling grow steadily brighter. My chest was tightening. The alarm jolted me out of bed as it broke through the foreboding silence. There was no turning back now. My patients were probably getting out of bed too, preparing themselves to come to see me, expecting me to make them better. I pulled on my navy-blue trousers and white linen shirt. At least I looked the part.

Breakfast. Food. The one thing in life I could rely on to provide me solace in all situations. I headed for the kitchen, where

Barbara stood blearily watching the kettle. I took a tentative bite from an apple, but my stomach clenched in protest.

Eight am. Right. Time to go. I could do this.

But ... what was happening? The floor beneath my feet started to shake and a low rumble vibrated the air.

Fantastic! It was an earthquake! No-one would have to work if there was an earthquake. I waited for the walls to start crumbling and the windows to shatter but, after a few moments, the stillness returned.

Barbara hadn't batted an eyelid as she topped up her tea with some milk.

'Ah ... Barbara ... um ... what was that?'

'What was what?'

'That noise'

'Oh, you mean the mine blast.'

Every morning and evening, at precisely eight o'clock, Mt Isa residents are reminded that they are living next to a rabbit warren of mine shafts. The kilometre-deep mine fires up its explosives deep underground to open up new shafts in the search of zinc, lead, gold and silver, to extract approximately 35 000 tonnes of ore each day. The scale of these little 'earthquakes' varies, depending on the proximity of the blasting to the town, but every now and then there will be an absolute corker that shatters glass. The life of an aquarium fish in Mt Isa is a tense existence.

The clinic was only just down the road from my new home so I grabbed my mud map and set off past the Coke Shrine and clattered out the back door ... and into a furnace. The sun was only just up, but already the day was roasting. I had barely reached the garden fence before the first beads of sweat tickled my brow. Five minutes later I was dripping and my shirt was sticking to my back. So much for looking the part!

As I slowed my pace in a futile attempt to reduce the sweat, I noticed a strange odour. The faint smell of sulphur hung in the air and burnt at the back of my nose. Later I was to learn that sulphuric acid is used in the processing plant to extract the minerals from the rock and that the 300-metre smokestack that I could see towering over the town had been built in order to lift away poisonous emissions. But on particularly still days like this day, when there is no wind to carry the plume away, the fumes descend in a cloud on Isa and are reputedly sometimes severe enough to give people nosebleeds.

Eight twenty-five. I stood around the corner from Cherie Thumpkin's physiotherapy clinic, drenched. I couldn't go in there looking like this. My head was spinning from a toxic combination of heat, excitement, sulphur, embarrassment and dread. Damn my parents for giving me excessive-sweating genes.

Eight twenty-nine. I gave up hope of drying out and, straightening my shoulders, I headed for the clinic doors. I stepped inside the glass-fronted clinic and my head cleared instantly as I was hit by an arctic blast of air-conditioned air.

The immaculately groomed receptionist gazed with curiosity and concern at the dripping and panicky-looking creature who fitted the description of the new physiotherapist. She directed me to a seat beside an elderly patient and, suppressing a grin, headed out the back to find Cherie, my new boss.

By the time the receptionist returned from the back rooms I was starting to shiver and regretting not bringing a pullover to work. I was introduced to Cherie, a small feisty mother of three who glowed with warm motherly vibes and looked me up and down with maternal sympathy, right before she broke the bad news that took my situation from awful to completely dire.

With only a brief flash of doubt crossing her face, she told me of her plans. She was heading home for the day and I would be taking over from eight-thirty to five, and would be looking after the patients on my own. She had booked all the patients in for double sessions, forty minutes each, which should be 'plenty of time'.

At university we had had one hour per patient. I attempted to appear confident and professional as I resisted the urge to turn tail and run.

Past the reception desk there was a narrow corridor that led into the treatment area. I followed Cherie across scuffed grey lino to where pastel grey-and-pink curtains separated the narrow cubicles, five of which were squeezed into the small treatment space. A few ancient machines crowded into the far corner, and I could hear the hum of others from the two closed cubicles. Tea in hand and friendly smile in place, Cherie gave me the crash tour ... sports tape, ultrasound gel, massage oil, goniometers, interferential, tape measures, reflex hammer, assessment forms, paper, pens, kettle, tea bags, coffee ... everything I would need for the day ahead.

'Oh, and if you have any problems, just call. Look I've really gotta dash ... got to go to the kids' dance rehearsal ... already late ... Good luck ... Oh, and the lady in the waiting room is your first patient. She's a multi-joint rheumatoid arthritis sufferer. Seeya.'

I was trapped. My first patient was between me and the exit. She had the most severe rheumatoid arthritis I had ever seen. It looked as though no part of her body had been spared, and I wondered if she could hear my heart pounding as we walked together into the treatment room. As she hobbled into a cubicle and I pulled the curtains closed around us, I desperately tried to remember exactly what rheumatoid arthritis was, and what on earth to do about it. I looked at her body chart. The whole thing was marked as painful. Where on earth to start?

She sat there with an expectant smile, waiting for me to come to some decision about where this treatment was heading. Did she know I was a new graduate? Cripes. I had to do or say something as this was becoming awkward. Well, what *shouldn't* you do to a RA patient in an acute flare-up? I searched my memory ... no heat, no heavy mobilising, no – this was no good.

She started fidgeting uncomfortably, eyes flicking around the cubicle. Ah, hang on, I had a better idea.

'You've been coming here for a while, right?'

'Yes, dear.'

'So ... ah ... well ... what have you found to be the most effective treatment?'

'Generally heat and mobilising gives me relief.'

Riiiiight then. Let's go.

After I had massaged and mobilised her hands and given her a hot wax treatment, she left happy. One down. A whole day to go.

On to the next patient. A stern-looking man sat waiting impatiently in the waiting room. I looked at the clock. I was already running ten minutes late. He bundled up his paper and stiffly unfolded himself from the chair. This was a new patient so there would be no clues from previous treatments. Start confident.

'Come on through, Mr Brentlin. I'm Claire and it's nice to meet you.'

A few questions, an assessment, a rough diagnosis and some tentative treatment, then Mr Brentlin left with his lower back feeling a little better. Well, he wasn't worse, anyway.

I blundered on through the morning, becoming further and further behind the clock. A football player with a lateral knee injury, an office worker with a stiff neck, a cattle station worker with a huge haematoma where a bull had charged him – these were all at least vaguely familiar scenarios. I started to relax as I realised that although I was far from knowing everything, at least I knew more than my patients did. And it seemed that I knew enough to construct a treatment plan. I was getting away with it – this physiotherapy thing wasn't so hard after all.

And then all my karma from the past four years of slackness came to bite me on the bum, and I realised with a thud that being a medical professional was not going to be something to take so lightly. I went out to find my next patient sitting nervously in the waiting room, cradling his right arm against his body. I stopped in my tracks.

Craig, a super-fit and handsome 21-year-old, had come out to work in the mine and save some money before university. He had been working on some scaffolding inside the mine when the ground below the scaffolding had collapsed down a mineshaft. Luckily, one arm had wedged between the shaft wall and a chunk of scaffolding, halting his fall and saving his life, but leaving him pinned on the side of the chasm with his arm wrenched above his head for six hours until rescuers freed him. He had severe facial and body bruising and continuous pain through his upper back, neck, left arm and right knee. But these were all of little significance compared to his most serious injury. He had no movement or sensation in his right arm.

As we sat in the small cubicle, his deep brown eyes brimmed as he asked me what the prognosis for recovery was, and whether I could help. I shifted awkwardly in my seat and tried to prevent my own eyes from welling up, as I knew too well the possibility of serious and permanent injury to his nervous system. Here was a young man of my own age with his whole life ahead of him and he was depending on my knowledge and skill. I wasn't worthy of this responsibility.

I carried out a gentle and tentative assessment and told him that only time would tell, and that we would do everything we could do to get things working.

In my lunchbreak I sat down nervously with a pile of textbooks from Cherie's collection. There it was: 'Nervous System, Traction Injuries, Brachial Plexus'. It was no longer a matter of knowing just enough to pass an exam. Now I needed to know everything, and fast. During the following weeks of challenging treatment, Craig's injury was to achieve what four years of physiotherapy study had failed to do. It was to turn me into a real physiotherapist.

Compared to the pressure I had experienced in my final year of university, my hectic schedule at the clinic was a breeze. So, with time on my hands and the novelty of money in my pocket, I was ripe for adventure in this new and strange place.

Mt Isa supports a diverse and unusual combination of people so, no matter who you are, it seems you are guaranteed to find a niche that suits you. First there is the huge population of miners of all ages, with or without families, often to be found having their 6 am knock-off drinks in the round-the-clock pub. Then there are the young professionals who have come out west to kick-start their careers and the cowboys from the surrounding cattle stations in town for supplies or a good time. Finally there are the long-term locals who keep the town ticking over. According to Mt Isa Mines data, people from more than sixty different ethnic backgrounds live in the town.

Then there are the local Indigenous people who, to all intents and purposes, seem to be segregated almost completely from everybody else. Considering that the populated area of Mt Isa barely covers an area of several square kilometres, and only has a population of about 25 000, it is really quite amazing how well the two groups have managed to live in complete disharmony for so long. There are 'black' schools and 'white' schools, 'black' pubs and 'white' pubs, 'black' areas to hang out, and 'white' areas to hang out, and then there is the riverbed, where a large Indigenous group lives and which nearly everybody else avoids.

My only experience of Indigenous Australians prior to arriving in Mt Isa was having chatted to a young suburban-born Aboriginal violinist while on a Queensland Youth Orchestra camp, and seeing a few alcoholics around Brisbane city. Nevertheless, with my top-quality education I considered myself to be extremely knowledgeable and open-minded about our 'hunter and gatherer' natives. I had learnt all about their nomadic lifestyles and basket-weaving at high school, hadn't I? I couldn't wait to get out to the real bush

Aborigines to extend my knowing hand of friendship and wait for the grateful tears to start flowing.

But it doesn't take long in Mt Isa to realise that history has left deep scars, and patronising white hands are likely to get slapped. After having my friendly smiles ignored, and my 'noble savage' assumptions challenged by drunken strangers, I started assuming that every Aboriginal in Mt Isa was an alcoholic and began to avert my eyes when I walked past groups of them. I joined the more politically correct of the population by expressing pity rather than hatred. I set about finding my own safe little niche within the colourful mix of cultures, away from the riverbed and any potent issues.

Before I knew it, I was drawn into the party life of the Mt Isa hospital staff, and began my explorations of the Mt Isa Irish Pub in earnest. And one thing is for sure – when a young and single woman is looking for a confidence boost in relation to men, the Mt Isa Irish Pub is the place to go. Given the two primary industries of the area, cattle farming and mining, women are overwhelmingly outnumbered by young men; as a result, you only have to be a fair approximation of the female gender to be considered sizzling hot property. In this environment of appreciation there started growing in me a new and empowering feeling. I was an object of desire, even though I towered over most of the men in town.

Still, despite an increasingly brave exterior, on the inside I was still as shy and unsure in the area of romance as I had ever been. Even if I knew that men were checking me out, what the hell was I meant to do about it? When it came to relationships, all the good-looking and nice men would be going for the pretty little women, not a six foot two Amazon who could comfortably rest her elbow on their shoulder.

On a fateful night in the Irish Pub my bravado was put to the test. I saw Dave across the crowds and I thought he must be all of my dreams answered. He was six foot four of tanned muscle, capped with bleached blond hair ... achieved by working out in the gym, hard work as a builder and a bit too much peroxide. His pearly-white smile melted my youthful heart and I was desperate to talk to him.

To my distress he seemed to be completely unaware of my existence and, after several evenings of unsuccessfully beaming ravishing smiles in his direction and wearing increasingly skimpy outfits, I finally plucked up the courage to make the move. I walked across the crowded bar towards his strong back and broad shoulders. He was deep in a rowdy conversation with his mates: '... and then the bloody wanker went and torched it. Bloody smoke everywhere. You should've seen the bastard run ...'

I tapped gingerly on his high shoulder. 'Um ... hi there.'

His friends were looking curiously at me as he looked over his shoulder. There was a blank moment and then some faint recognition in his eyes. 'Hey ... I've seen you in the gym,' he said.

He glanced back at his friends and then turned back to me with a smirk in his eyes. Wow, those eyes!

'Yeah. I'm Claire. I was just ... well ...' Oh God, this was too embarrassing. 'Look, I've gotta go.'

I turned to leave, but felt a strong hand on my shoulder. 'No, don't go, mate. I'm Dave. I've been wantin' to talk to you for ages.'

'Really?'

'Yeah, man, you're fucking hot.'

We organised to go mountain-bike riding together. Before I knew it, our brief conversation was over and he turned back to his friends. I don't like to regret anything in life but with a little more wisdom, or the gift of foresight at this point, I would have turned tail and run. Instead I tucked his phone number carefully in my bag, and went home with a triumphant glow.

Meanwhile my hospital friends and I planned a three-day weekend that would involve a mere 945 km of driving; 690 km on sealed roads and 255 km on dirt roads. To put this into perspective, having grown up in a family with my father a pilot (he got his job back when I was in Year Nine), I considered 300 km to be a huge drive. If you went any further than that, you caught a plane.

I waited with excited and nervous anticipation as the date of the planned trip drew near. Jules, a doctor from the hospital, and hence someone whose judgement and good sense should be able to be trusted, organised the itinerary for our expedition. In a convoy of three 4WDs full of people we would head to the Gregory River, Boodjamulla (Lawn Hill) National Park and Riversleigh fossil field, and would be back on the evening of day three, ready to start work the next morning.

We were too young and foolish to question his plans and I convinced a doubtful Cherie that it was fine to book up a full day of patients for my return, starting bright and early to make up for my days off. On the map it didn't really look like we were going that far.

Day one started promisingly with a blue sky and an endless horizon. We crowded four people into Jules's 4WD with enough gear and beer to last a month, and food for a day or two, and set off west along the Barkly Highway. The other two 4WDs trailed behind us.

Our first stop would be the town of Camooweal, a two-hour drive away. Geez, it was dry out there. The rocky landscape was parched and dusty with the intense heat. Hardy spinifex grasses and odd spindly excuses for shrubs were the only vegetation to survive in the harsh, undulating landscape. From the road you could walk a long way before finding shade enough to cover yourself. According to Jules, a person would perish in a single day out there without water or shade. The exceptions were the local Aboriginal people who lived in the riverbed, some of whom would head out for weeks at a time and survive off the land.

Camooweal is 188 km from Isa, but it is still under the jurisdiction of the Mt Isa City Council, making Mt Isa the largest city (in area) in the world, and making the Barkly Highway the world's longest main street. The 'town' consists of a dusty petrol station, a convenience store, a pub and a few other buildings and houses near the verge. Beyond this the road stretches out into nothingness again. We topped up the tanks and a cheerily large lady in a floral dress slapped four sausage rolls onto the counter. 'You fellas off for an 'oliday then? You mind them storms comin' over. The weather's gunna turn, you mark my words.'

We looked doubtfully at the arching roof of clear blue sky. Not likely!

Ten minutes later, and almost three hours after leaving the heart of the city, the convoy of three 4WDs turned off Mt Isa's main street to head north, with our vehicle in front. Two and a half hours later it dawned on us – it had been a long while since we last caught sight of the other cars in our rear-view mirror. We had been driving over a sometimes tarmacked, sometimes gravelled, but always potholed and dusty road. There was mounting concern in our car as Jules recalled in graphic detail the accident he had been involved in with Stacey, one of the other drivers, who had managed to roll a car on a similar road and almost kill them both. We pulled over. Ten minutes later there was still no sign. There was nothing for it but to go back.

Twenty minutes later we found them grim-faced by the side of the road. Stacey's old 4WD was tilted up on a jack and its spare tyre, almost worn to the thread, was being slotted onto the wheel hub to replace the very flat bald tyre, that lay in the dust. With the mechanical prowess of a bunch of medical professionals, we put on the spare wheel; an hour and a half later, Stacey's passengers climbed in nervously.

We headed painfully slowly towards Gregory Downs township to get the tyre repaired. Thirty kilometres out, Stacey blew his spare. We limped onwards. But any hopes of salvation soon disappeared as we pulled into the empty car park of the Gregory Downs Hotel. This, it seemed, was all there was! As far as the eye could see, the flat dusty horizon extended, empty of civilisation – broken only by a dense line of vegetation, the Gregory River and a few rusty old deserted sheds scattered nearby.

We headed for the public bar. The clackety-clack of the loose flyscreen echoed through the empty room and the heavy odour of beer seeped from the XXXX towels lying neatly on the empty bar top, and seemed to ooze from the wooden veins of the building. This sure looked like a lonely existence and our chances of rescue were not looking good. When the busty red-faced publican emerged from the depths of the building, Jules half-heartedly asked her if she knew someone nearby who could fix a wheel and a tyre, today. Yeah, right!

Her face beamed with compassion. 'Yeah, mate, no worries. Old Harry out the back there should be able ta help y'out.'

We stood dumbstruck. At that moment I was filled with a profound confidence that, if we had urgently wanted to have a wedding cake decorated, or a suit tailored, she would have known someone out the back who could do the job perfectly. Stacey headed off in the direction of her pointing finger, to one of the rusty corrugated iron sheds that sat shimmering in the haze.

A breeze took the edge off the blistering heat as we sat on the empty verandah, dew dripping down our icy glasses, waiting. Then, as the sun crept lower towards the horizon, a mysterious thing started to happen. Out of the nothingness appeared trails of dust that grew in volume to become vehicles of all sizes and descriptions, which lurched and skidded into the car park. By late afternoon the public bar was filled with dusty, sweaty bodies, sun-hardened faces and the low hum of comfortable conversation. Everyone seemed to know everyone here, except us.

The hours ticked on, the crowd became larger and livelier, and we were absorbed into the sweaty throng until eventually – almost to our regret – a browner version of Stacey, his leg hairs dangling in dags, staggered into the bar. 'It's done. Fixed the spare and everything. Let's go for a swim!'

One thing we had learnt while talking to the locals was that the waterhole we planned to visit got cut off when it rained. The road would flood and could stay flooded for days at a time. Oh, and there was a storm on its way tonight. We were pretty confident it wasn't going to be a problem. Anyway, we had come this far and had been delayed for long enough and, dammit, we needed a swim!

The Gregory River is an oasis. Its deep waters flow north-east through the harsh interior, supporting a lush winding strip of vegetation and animal life. Its banks are supported with thick grass and reeds. Ancient eucalypts reach heavy branches over its depths. It snakes through the dust for about 300 km before joining with Lawn Hill Creek to become the Nicholson River and soon after this union it empties into the ocean at the base of the Gulf of Carpentaria. When you come across this powerful river after hours of dusty desolate driving, well, it's kind of like the crowd in the pub – you just can't imagine where all the water and trees have come from. It is a miracle of nature for the hot and thirsty soul.

At last we arrived and, parking our cars up on the gravel riverbank, we ran fully clothed into the shallow waters of the outer river. Then we gratefully reclined in a wide circle with beers and laughter floating around us, our eskies parked on the water's edge.

Sitting in our river lounge, with the water slowly brushing past my warm body, I watched as the sky darkened and the Milky Way stretched overhead. I was deeply aware that only a few hundred metres away the earth was dry and parched. The electrical storm clashed in the distance and I almost hoped for rain as we pondered how long we would be staying in this paradise.

To my surprise, day two of our expedition had a dry if rather late start. Gradually the field of mattresses stirred as various expeditioners woke with pounding heads and bursting bladders. We had a measly eighty kilometres of driving ahead on dirt roads to get to the place called Lawn Hill Gorge. I had no idea what we were heading towards and the barren landscape gave away no clues until we came to our first water crossing. Lawn Hill Creek is smaller than the Gregory River, but for some reason it is even more of a tropical paradise.

About ten metres from the creek the road entered lush vegetation; at the water's edge it was like being in a jungle, with palms and moss and ferns adorning the meandering banks. We were in no rush. The first crossing was shallow enough to sit in, so we let the cool water wash the heat away from our sweaty and dusty bodies. From then on we couldn't resist the temptation to do the same at each refreshing crossing, and it was late evening by the time we reached Lawn Hill Gorge.

There is something really wonderful about arriving at a place in the dark. Your impressions of your surroundings are based only on a narrow beam of torchlight and the sounds and smells around you. Is that water over there? I wonder if it's a big river or a little stream. Is that the smell of a flowering tree, or a shrub? And gum leaves — maybe there are eucalypts around here. And under my feet, does that feel like grass? Surely not, out here in the desert.

The next morning, when the sun comes up, all these mysteries are solved. And sometimes things are not quite as you expect. On the third and last day of our expedition I woke with the sun and crawled out of my tent into a manicured campground with lawn. Bizarre.

Everyone rose early that day. We all knew we were running out of time. We had to be home that night to start work the next day. We would quickly go up and have a look at the gorge, then pack up and start the long trip back to Isa via the Riversleigh fossil field. I couldn't wait to see the fossils.

The six of us followed the signs towards the gorge, away from the grassy riverside camping ground and up a rocky slope, until only an occasional wildflower brightened the increasingly drab surroundings. Cringeing, I remembered last night's skinny-dipping escapades and my crocodile impersonations. Had I really thought I was funny?

We chatted excitedly about heading to Riversleigh. As we approached the top of the rise, none of us were expecting much. This was just outback Australia – interesting, but hardly the Grand Canyon and certainly not a tourist drawcard. After all, there had only been one other group in the camping ground.

We rounded the top of the hill and our chatter was replaced by a stunned silence, split only by an awed whisper from Jules. 'Oh ... My ... God!'

I sat down and took it all in as the others walked further along the track. I tried to grasp the scale and contrasts of this place. A spindly little shrub grew from the dry rocky soil beside my knee, eking an existence from infertile ground, displaying a tiny miracle of delicate pink blossoms which stirred in the slightest breeze at the end of its fragile branches. But just in front of its narrow stem, the ground stopped. The earth's dry and rocky crust cracked open to leave a great yawning chasm, in the depths of which a wide calm river flowed through dense, lush vegetation and down sparkling cascades. It was simply more beautiful and surprising than anything I could have imagined.

My musings were interrupted. From downstream came two bright red blobs slowly creeping up the calm river towards the cascades.

'GUYS!' I called the others' attention to the two colourful kayaks gliding along the brown water far below us.

Forgetting about our tight schedule we ran back down to the camping ground. Sure enough hidden by the bush but not far from our tents was this same huge river. Next to an old wooden boat ramp was a big rusty boat rack stacked with red plastic kayaks and dented tin canoes. A canoe and a kayak later and we too were paddling our way upstream to the gorge.

As the ravine deepened, the vegetation thickened along its walls, and we paddled against the strong flow of calm deep water. Then we saw ahead of us the first of the cascades, where the river stepped down to our level. It spanned the gorge above us like a wide step, reaching from wall to wall, broken across its width by islands of dense vegetation. The water spewed forth in a frenzy as it surged through openings in the growth, and fell to mingle with the calmer water in front of us. From a distance it looked impassable. We paddled forward in wonder.

To our delight, carefully concealed by the islands of river grasses and palms were wooden boat ramps, allowing passage for boaters like us. The wooden planks were warm and smooth under my feet as I ducked palm fronds to haul our kayak upwards. All around us was the gurgle and flow of the river as it was pushed over the steps. Next to my feet a little whirlpool formed where the water spun off the reeds and tree roots.

As the midday sun grew hotter, we flung out hot bodies from the sides of our boats, naively hoping that crocodiles didn't make it this far upstream. Time was lost and the day stretched on.

Well into the afternoon we regretfully hauled our boats back up to the boat rack, tired and hot. Reality hit us. It was seriously time to make tracks.

Well, Riversleigh was on the way home, wasn't it? We couldn't miss this, the most exciting part of the trip. A field full of fossils like those huge dinosaur skeletons in the museum, only right where they had fallen dead millions of years ago instead of in a glass case.

An hour or so later we stopped at the sign that read 'Riversleigh Fossil Field'. Behind it was a hill. On the hill we saw a path. Beside the path every now and then, if you looked really hard, you could find what might have been a tiny fossil of some sea creature. Where were all the big ones? Hours of searching later we wandered back to the car mystified, disappointed and even more concerned about the time. It was now approaching dusk.

Anyone who has ever driven on outback dirt roads in Australia will know the hazards of road trains. These giant trucks heave two or three carriages behind them as they forge through the Australian centre carrying livestock and supplies, and kicking up an enormous dust storm in their wake. For someone who likes to drive fast on dirt roads, like Jules, and who is in a hurry, as Jules was on this trip, they are a major problem as they tend to trundle along on unsealed roads at about sixty kilometres an hour. As far as I am concerned, overtaking a road train on a dirt road is up there with bungee jumping on the fear scale – only it seems far more likely to result in carnage.

The procedure requires sheer commitment and gutsiness. Initially you stay far enough back from the road train to be out of its dust cloud, watching the outline of its end-carriage flapping through the dust from side to side while keeping a close eye on the road in front of it. Once you see a long straight run clear of other vehicles, you plant your foot to the floor. You penetrate the dust cloud and enter a world of hazy brown shapes, pulling as far to the right as possible to avoid the flapping end-carriage. Then it is all out of your hands. The accelerator pedal is almost driven through the floor as you hold your breath and pray, until you emerge from the cloud near the front of the truck, half-expecting to see the fender of an oncoming road train metres from your face.

Now, if I'd been in the driver's seat, we would have been cruising along at sixty behind a road train the whole way home. But not Jules. I had never been so scared in all my life as I watched my life flash before my eyes again and again. Surely we had to get to a sealed road soon.

But the fear had only begun. I was about to discover another quirky hazard of Australian outback driving. We hit the bulldust.

Bulldust is fine black dust that is extremely slippery in the dry, and treacherously slippery in the wet. We looked at the angry storm clouds breaking the darkening horizon with walls of water and felt traction disappear from beneath us. We had escaped the storm trap in Gregory, but not here. The rain had been and gone, and the road was as slippery as driving on black ice. The only things keeping us on the road were the shallow ruts from previous vehicles. The steering wheel was as good as useless.

Suddenly we were out of control again, spinning off the road into the muddy grass. The second car in our convoy powered past into the lead. Shortly afterwards we came across them in the mud beside the road – their tracks revealing a full 360-degree skid and the passengers wide-eyed but unharmed.

We pressed on past them, but slower now – sometimes too slowly, causing the wheels to lose all traction and spin under our stationary car. Day turned to night. Was this trip ever going to end?

At 8.30, when we hit the sealed road, even the passengers were done in. I had never been so happy to leave nature behind and get some good solid man-made bitumen underneath me. We drove the 130 km to Camooweal in a daze. The town felt like a glorious city.

We slouched over our grainy instant coffee at the road stop, with mud splattered on our faces and clothes, filthy from pushing cars out of black dust bogs. Jules piped up with a beaming smile. 'So, who's been to the Northern Territory?'

'Nope.'

'Nah, not me.'

'No, never.'

'Well, let's go. It's only thirteen kilometres from here.'

'Yeah.'

'Cool.'

'Great idea.'

As we sat in the dark at the border between Queensland and the Northern Territory with the Milky Way bright overhead, I calculated the huge number of hours we had spent driving in the last three days, and the measly amount of ground we had covered compared to the size of Australia. Incredibly, it was still about 2000 km as the crow flies from here to the westernmost edge of the continent.

Despite my exhaustion, I almost wished we could keep driving deep into the heart of our country. But it was already ten o'clock and I had to work the next day. That adventure would have to wait.

We headed back east, away from the deep centre, and at midnight we caught our first glimpse of the familiar billowing smokestack lit up by the lights of the mine. Beneath that huge sulphurous cloud was home. I crawled into my bed exhausted at half past midnight.

The next morning my first patient was Craig. I hauled my aching body out of bed and met him with a strong coffee in my hand. Since his first appointment, I had had my head in books and had been in contact with my university tutors, in particular the neurology tutors and specialist hand therapists, to ensure I was doing everything I could for him. I had carefully mapped sensation down his arm and re-mapped this every three days, desperately hoping for a change. I had recorded the power of all his muscle groups on a long chart, starting from the shoulder and out to his fingertips. We had worked to clear any swelling, made sure that he maintained a range of movement in all his joints and muscles, and kept his nervous system stimulated.

Now at last nature was starting to do the job that I couldn't do. His nerves were starting to repair and some power was returning to his muscles.

This was good news, not only for Craig. Working so closely with him to maximise his recovery had meant sharing his intense ups and downs and with this had come the surprising realisation that my time spent at university hadn't been for nothing. I had gained far more than a way to earn money. Those years of torture had provided me with the knowledge to improve this young man's, and other people's, lives. I had a qualification that meant I could get paid to help people.

Maybe this job wasn't so bad after all.

Several days later it was the morning of my first rendezvous with Dave. I woke up before the alarm at 4.55 am and was waiting eagerly on the kerb twenty minutes later when his huge ute pulled up. Wow, what a man. We threw my bike in the back and drove out to Lake Moondarah.

Then I realised I hadn't thought this through very carefully. Our first 'date' and I would be sweating and going red as a beet-root, as I have a tendency to do with any exercise.

Well, it was too late now. I would just have to impress him with how fast I could go.

We threw our bikes off the back of the ute and hooned around the lake on dusty tracks in the increasing heat. I gave it all I had, feeling my face throbbing and sweat soaking my clothes. But with relief I saw he was struggling to keep up. I pushed myself harder and harder until it was time to head back to town.

I was pretty sure he was impressed. When he dropped me at my door we organised to meet up again in a few days.

Our lakeside biking rendezvous became frequent events but, despite his lingering gazes and sultry smiles, I had started to wonder how things were ever going to progress past a mutual appreciation of our matching mountain-bike frames.

In fact, if I was honest with myself, I had to confess that we really didn't have too much in common. The few times he had invited me around to his place, he and his mates had been sitting in front of video war games with beer and pizza and the limited conversation had been interrupted by frequent gunfire, swearing and cheering.

But he was just so tall and gorgeous, and he was into mountain-bike riding and it seemed as though he liked me. I was sure that, if I looked hard enough, there had to be more common ground somewhere.

It was another morning and I stood outside the fence watching the sky lighten. Here he was at last. I was sure he was keen on me now. The signs were all just too strong. He had repeatedly thanked me for approaching him at the Irish Pub as he had apparently been too shy to do likewise. As I climbed into the high passenger seat of his ute, he reached over and touched my arm in greeting. As we trundled out to the dam he threw cheeky grins in my direction. I sat cursing myself at my inability to be sultry and seductive.

But something about his attitude was a bit different this day. Halfway through our ride he broke the news to me: 'Oh yeah, mate, I'm leaving Mt Isa. Headin' back to Brissie for a bit. But I really wanna stay in touch.'

Bugger. Another one bites the dust.

I didn't see Dave again until four weeks later, when I ran into one of my regular patients, Katie, outside Woolies. She was happy to be able to introduce me to the lovely and handsome guy she had been dating for six months.

Dave looked extremely awkward – he had come pretty close to getting away with it completely.

In retrospect, it is easy to conclude that Dave was a person best to be avoided and definitely not trusted from that point on. Unfortunately, six foot four of tanned muscle and a handsome face can twist a girl's logic. I decided that I had just imagined his flirtations, and he had just thought it irrelevant to mention that he was dating Katie. I had no brutally honest friends around to tell me that behind a handsome face could lurk a lying toad.

Dave left Mt Isa and with him went my hopes of romance, and any of my new found self-confidence with men. I was just an Amazonian fool – what an idiot I had been to even think that he would fancy me.

A month after Dave's departure I had had enough of Isa. After four months – during which I had lived in three different abodes, undertaken countless road trips and enjoyed way too much beer – I decided it was time to leave. Sure, life was great and the parties were endless, but whatever it was I was looking for in life just wasn't there. I hadn't gone climbing for an age and David Attenborough's documentaries were still on my mind.

It was time to get my own wheels so I could drive whichever way I wanted, whenever I wanted.

Somehow I managed to hustle a locum in a Sunshine Coast practice, on the condition that I would do two weeks of 'work experience' before the permanent physio there left for his holiday. If I was too crap, he reserved the right to give me the boot and employ someone with more experience than I had.

So, with this job possibility lined up, I packed my bike into its box and, without a pang of regret and with earplugs in my handbag, I left the smokestack and headed home.

THE ESSENTIAL KOMBI CHECK LIST

What to check prior to leaving (known in campervan lingo as 'tatting down') to prevent serious Kombi mishaps. The kind of advice that my very practical father has always been very good at imparting, but that for some reason never seems to penetrate into my brain.

- All cupboards locked (especially cutlery drawer)
- Pop-top down AND clips fastened
- Gas off at all outlets
- Levelling ramps stowed
- Fuel in tank

Remember: anything that can fall off will fall off.

FOUR

Trusting a Used-Car Salesman

Home again!

It was wonderful to return to my comfort zone. But, despite the glorious sunny beaches, the morning walks with Mum and Dad capped off with cappuccinos, and the joy of being able to be myself around friends who knew me to the core, I knew that I wouldn't be there for long. I had places to go and I hoped there would be a wild adventure waiting for me.

My plans fell into place during a phone call with my university friend Kath. Since our last meeting in Sydney she had quit the hectic stress of the city, the university and her all-girl household for a far more organic and spiritual mountain existence living in the Blue Mountains. Not being one to twiddle her thumbs, she had enrolled in both a bush regeneration course and a three-year massage course.

While at TAFE one day she had encountered a group of Aboriginal dancers. One dancer in particular stole her attention with his bronzed body, deep brown eyes and magical moves. Much to her surprise, she ran into this gorgeous and talented man at a party soon after and things progressed from there. A man who is able to catch goannas with his bare hands and who swerves to hit kangaroos on the road for dinner was someone Kath wanted to know more about. His artwork and dancing skills were renowned, and there was a long list of famous people in Australia and abroad who had his art hanging on their walls.

Through hearing about Kath's new boyfriend, I learnt for the first time about Arnhem Land, a large Aboriginal land reserve in the Northern Territory. He was from an Aboriginal community up there, but he had moved down to Sydney to attend TAFE so as to acquire knowledge he might use to improve his community's quality of life. Not long after meeting Kath he decided to take her up north to meet his family.

This was perfect – Kath had a passport into Indigenous Australia and was heading up there in the next few months. All I had to do was get up there to share at least a part of her adventure.

Without any clear idea of dates or times we made a tentative plan to meet up in Katherine after Kath had emerged from the depths of Arnhem Land. I was going to head into the Northern Territory for real this time, under my own steam. I would drive up the east coast to Townsville, then head west via Mt Isa, until I hit the road that runs up the centre of Australia. Then I would head north to Katherine and, if luck was on our side, Kath's and my paths would cross there.

It was a perfect plan, or so it seemed. But first I needed wheels to get there and I was sure that the only vehicle worthy of such a task was a Kombi van.

Fortunately the Sunshine Coast clinic had decided that I wasn't a liability and so I scored the job and madly saved my dollars, thanks to free board and lodgings at the Parental Villa. I found the Kombi of my dreams at a used car lot. She had pride of position beside the road and her beautiful burnt orange coat with brown side strip and broad shoulders called out to me as I drove past.

The short man with the oily receding hairline and crumpled suit almost wept as he agreed to give it to me for 'practically what I paid for it'. I drove off, surprised and impressed by my advanced haggling skills. Imagine getting such a bargain.

I squeaked the horn proudly as I rumbled into the driveway and Dad tried his best to appear impressed when I gloated at the measly four thousand I had spent on this 1969 machine. But, as with so many impulsive relationships, what began as a beautiful connection between the Kombi and me revealed its first cracks at a very early stage.

When I bought the Kombi I had been swept away by her beauty and stature and had failed to notice that the front seat was just a little bit too high and that at six foot two my head hit the roof if I stretched up straight. I dug into my nearly empty pockets and paid to get a new and lower seat put in. Unfortunately the seat fitter failed to notice the uneven level of the base of the new seat, and hence the right side of the driver's seat sat two centimetres lower than the left.

So it was with a towel under my right buttock that I decided to take off to Brisbane to visit some friends. I slid my U2 tape into the deck, wound down my window, and felt a warm maternal pride at the sweet growl of the engine as I accelerated up the highway. Geez, I had found a beauty. Me and my girl were going places and we were going there in style.

My inner glow was shattered just as I hit a hundred; no more than ten minutes into my journey. There came a loud ripping and snapping sound followed by a very airy and light feeling in the cabin. What the hell had happened?

Eyes wide and with a nervous smile I pulled over to the side of the freeway and looked back over my shoulder. As Bono sang 'Lemon' in the background, I glanced above my head and tried to understand the torn canvas flapping in the breeze, the bent metal jutting skywards, and the grey sky looking down at me through where my pop-top lid had once been.

Worse still, dramatically silhouetted against my new skylight feature were the clips that Dad had suggested I check every time I got in to drive. Dammit! I must have left them undone.

This was worse than terrible. I was never going to live this one down. A manic giggle started to rumble in my chest as I realised what had happened. This was a shocker – even by my standards.

But then my laughter stopped and my eyes widened even further as I bit my bottom lip. If the lid wasn't on the top of my van anymore then … where was it? Cripes! I was on the highway. I looked back along the four lanes of tarmac where cars were whizzing past. There, on the central strip that bisected the freeway, my Kombi lid lay on its back like a flipped cockroach with spindly metal legs flapping in the breeze. As I breathed a sigh of relief, the first drips of rain started to fall. Bugger!

I made a suicidal dash through a gap in the traffic to rescue my lid. Standing on the central strip with the Kombi top on my head, I imagined the other drivers sniggering at me. A few mocking horn blasts later and I was back across the road.

But there was a new snag. The lid was not going to slip back into its old place to hide my mistake, and there was no way it was going to fit inside the van. I was going to have to leave it on the side of the road. As the drizzle turned to rain, I trundled home. I dreaded the ribbing I was about to get, as water poured in through my new skylight feature onto my fold-up bed, and into the sink and stove.

Well, at least I was keeping my family entertained. We had to call on Dad's friend Bjorn to come to my rescue with his Kombi.

We tied my lid onto his to bring it home, but the damage was done – my pop-top mechanism was no longer popping up, and I had to permanently attach the lid to my roof.

At this stage I sensed an ill wind, but ignored it. The show had to go on. I had a road trip to the Northern Territory planned and there was no way a silly accident was going to put me off.

As the city lights of Townsville faded in my rear-view mirror, the sun dipped below the distant horizon and stained the sky pink and orange as it melted away. Ahead of me the road stretched long and straight as it left the east coast behind and plunged west towards the centre of Australia.

I had made my way lazily up the east coast over the previous weeks, pulling over to camp when and where it pleased me, staying for a time in spots that took my fancy, dropping in on friends, and generally revelling in the freedom of the open road and my self-sufficiency. I had only run out of petrol once, which hadn't been a problem as it was broad daylight and I had walked to a nearby petrol station to fill the jerry can. But back in my now familiar position behind the wheel with a towel under my right buttock, I felt a pang of concern as the horizon darkened.

I had put the warnings about the dangers of this section of road to the back of my mind as I had whiled away the afternoon, drinking tea in Townsville with my friend Jason. The rapes, the murders, the robberies; all had seemed like a distant myth. But as the darkness stole away the sides of the road and my headlights became my world, these stories began to play back in my mind.

'Whatever you do, don't pull over because there are creepy men scouting these roads for parked cars.'

'Did you hear about the family who had everything stolen at knife-point?'

'Young lady, you be sure to only ever drive on that section of road in the daylight.'

Anyway, none of this was going to be a problem. I would just drive the three hours into Charters Towers and then find a nice friendly street to park in and have a safe night's sleep and continue westward in the morning. There was nowhere to stop between here and there anyway.

I popped in my Beatles tape, which always lightened things up, and let it rip. It always felt great to be playing tunes from the Sixties while motoring in my Kombi. I would just have to drown out those voices of dread. As I trundled along singing 'Hey Jude', the uneasiness slipped away and the familiar feeling of excited anticipation of new adventures ahead crept into me. I could almost smell the Northern Territory air.

There is something captivating about driving alone along the endless roads that cross Australia. The vastness and power of the landscape stretching out to the horizon makes you acutely aware of your own insignificance on the planet: just a tiny speck on a long straight road. This was my first solo journey on one of these roads and, even though I soon couldn't see more than the tarmac in front of me, I knew what was in the darkness around me, and it was intoxicating.

So it was with a happy heart that I was on my second round of the Beatles, and building up to a crescendo with 'It's been a hard day's night', when I heard the awful screech and crunch of metal twisting and snapping. I just managed to veer off to the side of the road as my beloved Kombi and I lurched to a stop. I looked up – my lid was still on – but ... My eyes widened as I watched smoke billowing from our rear end in the soft glow of the brake lights.

Trying not to panic I sat frozen in the driving position, eyes fixed on the dark road ahead, my heart thumping in my ears. The silence was broken only by a sizzling sound coming from behind me. I couldn't get out of the car. What if one of those dangerous men came along and plucked me from the side of the road? But I couldn't stay there, I was a sitting duck. I looked at the clock. I had been driving for an hour and a half. I was in the middle of bloody nowhere.

My mobile phone. I unfroze and desperately fumbled to find it in the glove box. No signal! Silence and darkness overwhelmed me.

My throat was dry and tight as high-pitched sobs squeezed out. Okay, this was not going to get me anywhere. I sucked in deep calming breaths and took hold of myself. I was just going to have to get out and survey the damage. With hands shaking, I fumbled with the lock and the door handle and, with all the lights off, I crept around to the back of the van.

Any hopes of being able to continue my journey disappeared. Smoke still billowed from the Kombi's rear-mounted engine and there was the heavy smell of oil in the air. There was no way I could deny it – I had killed my Kombi! I was stuck on the open road in the pitch black with no phone and no transport.

Off in the distance a pair of headlights lit the horizon. I scuttled around the back of the van and crouched there trembling. As the vehicle drew closer, its engine slowed. Please don't stop! Please don't stop!

The car crawled past and I imagined a surly man with a mullet and goatee and evil eyes drooling out the window with his rifle on the seat next to him. But then the engine picked up speed and roared off into the distance. I breathed again and peeked out from my hiding spot. There was only darkness.

After another survey of the situation, I came to a simple conclusion. My mobile phone was my only hope. I had to find some reception.

Finding the number for the Royal Automobile Club of Queensland – the good old RACQ – snugly stowed in the glove box (and fleetingly thanking Mum and Dad most sincerely) I inched my way up and down the highway, never straying too far from the car. Several other vehicles passed, but luckily their headlights betrayed them in time for me to run behind my van and hide. Each one slowed down, causing my heart to skip beats, but then sped off, obviously curious about an empty smoking Kombi on the side of the road but too wary to get out and check it out. They had probably heard the stories about this road too.

Eventually, choking with sobs and almost out of hope, as I watched the battery indicator on my phone flash on its lowest rung, I climbed up onto the roof of the van. I was completely alone, looking into the blank sheet of night. The reception band at the bottom of my handset flicked on, and then off again. I moved slightly. It flicked on again. Yes!

Shaking, I dialled the RACQ.

'Hello. You've reached RACQ. All our operators are currently busy but we appreciate your patience and will be with you as soon as poss –' BEEP. The reception band flicked off.

'Ohhhhh, nooooo.' (Plus some other words to that effect.)

I tried again. 'Hello. You've reached RACQ breakdown service centre. This is Katie. How can I hel –'

She didn't get a chance to finish. God knows how I must have sounded from their end. Through the broken static my hysterical voice screamed that I was almost out of credit and batteries and about to get raped and murdered.

Three cut-offs later I was put through to Charters Towers, the nearest RACQ depot. Two panicked attempts later, with the battery warning beeping and knowing I was almost out of credit, I managed to communicate my location. I didn't need to spell out how desperate I was for them to get to me.

Forty trembling minutes later a truck pulled up behind the van. I peeked in the rear-view mirror from my hiding place to see the glorious sight of the black and gold RACQ logo. I have never been so happy to see a redneck in a big truck in all my life.

Butch was a big man of about fifty. I had an overwhelming urge to wrap my arms around his stubbly neck and plant a huge kiss on his cheek when I saw his fatherly proportions emerge from his tow truck. But that feeling disappeared an hour later, when he towed the Kombi into what resembled a scrapyard.

I filled out some papers and then climbed back into my dead van. I pulled the curtains tight and locked all the windows and doors, before curling up in my jeans and sweater to try to get some sleep amid the night sounds of dogs yelping and metal clanging.

The next morning Butch and Jack, a younger man of half his size, delivered their unequivocal verdict to me: 'Your engine is completely stuffed.'

I wasn't that surprised, but it was still a shock to have my fears confirmed. Half an hour of slow and painful questions later, I began to understand that driving the pistons through the engine casing is not a good thing for an engine. And that destroying both the top and bottom half of an engine, as a result of this, means a mechanical medical emergency – i.e. a complete heart transplant, and big bucks.

But Butch, with eyes full of sympathy and the confident air of someone who retrieves a lot of desperate people off the highway, assured me that fixing a Kombi was a piece of cake. They didn't do it very often but Jack knew a bit about Kombi engines, and they were basically the same as any other car. A new engine was not available in Charters, but that wouldn't be a problem. All I had to do was get one freighted in from somewhere. They could put it in for me, no worries.

Sometimes I can't believe what a sucker I am. In retrospect, if at this point I had just let the Kombi roll off a cliff, cut my losses and headed off with my backpack and bike, I would have saved myself a lot of money and heartache. But, alas, I have never been one to give up easily, or to be suspicious of people.

Butch reached across from the other side of his jumbled desk and with a stubby oily finger pressed the Line One button. I dialled Cherie Thumpkin's number in Mt Isa. I was going to have to earn some dollars to get my baby fixed. Cherie sure did have work for me and I could start the next day if I wanted to. I packed my back-pack and jumped on the first bus to Mt Isa.

Once back in Isa I surprised even myself by working six- and seven-day weeks, desperately hoping to get the finances together to get back on the road again. The Northern Territory was waiting for me and Kath's Arnhem Land adventure was almost in sight. But things weren't going well with my poor stranded Kombi.

Butch had left the job of finding the replacement engine in my hands, which of course meant Dad's hands. The subsequent and tragic drama unfolded slowly over the phone in the Mt Isa physio-therapy clinic and, as time went on, three things became clear – the Charters Towers team had no idea about Kombis; the whole episode was going to cost me a lot of money; and, if I wanted to get to the Northern Territory in time to meet Kath, I was going to have to find another means of transport.

When I first thought of the idea of hitching a ride with a road train I felt the excitement that only a slightly dangerous and crazy escapade can bring. It was perfect. Road trains trundle all over Australia carrying with them their precious cargoes. If there is a main road going somewhere through Australia's centre, there are certain to be regular road trains on it hauling their two or more carriages. It is even more certain that there will be a truck stop where the truckies take their rare breaks to eat and drink and flirt with the service girls. I found out that there was such a truck stop on the western side of Isa, and this was where I was certain I would find a truck that was heading where I wanted to go.

I was more than a little nervous as Deb (Cherie's receptionist) and I pulled into the big dusty car park. We were dwarfed beneath the road trains, which seemed to be sprawled carelessly around. As a safety measure I had asked her to drop me off and take down the numberplate of whichever truck I got into. In a kind of nonsensical way this somehow made me feel like I was being sensible and grown-up, but deep down I knew that it would make Buckley's difference to my safety. I would just have to trust in my instincts to choose a good truck.

Reluctantly I got out of the comfort of her car and adjusted my jeans and very loose-fitting shirt. Right. I was going to do this. I twisted my face into what I hoped looked like a confident smile, pulled myself up to my full six foot two stature and, as I stepped into the dusty truck-stop shop, I managed to get tangled up in the plastic strips that hung in the doorway, knocking my sunglasses onto the concrete floor. Great start.

The conversations around me stopped as I walked to the counter where a rough lady with peroxide hair stood behind an array of frankfurts, hot baked beans, chips and other greasy food.

'Hi ... ah ... I'm actually looking for a ride up to Katherine. You wouldn't happen to know if there is anyone heading that way?'

'Wouldn't 'ave a clue, luv. You'll 'ave to go ask.'

I turned to the cluster of plastic tables and eyes that were drifting from my butt back to their plates. There were a few lingerers. Maybe this was a bad idea. Deb sat outside safely in her car.

Ah, what the hell – you only live once. I headed over to the tables. All eyes turned back my way.

'Hi. Is anyone heading up to Katherine? I'm looking for a lift.'

There was a clatter of fists on tables and disappointed curses. Then two hands shot up in the air.

'Yep, we are. We're leavin' in ten.'

A chorus of 'you bastards' went around the room and once again I questioned whether this was such a good idea.

'Right. Um ... well I guess I'll just wait outside then.'

Ten minutes later, with a quick flick that belied his sinewy frame, Jacko loaded my heavy pack into the side box of his truck and slammed the lid down. I rushed over to check that Deb had taken down the number. She looked more than a little worried, but I resisted the urge to jump back in her car and get her to drive me to the bus station. I was on my way up north now and a few nerves were not going to stop me.

I reassured her: 'Don't worry, babe, I'll be fine.' But I wasn't so sure.

'Hey, girlie, we're outa here. Ya comin' or not?' Jacko shouted impatiently across from where he was dwarfed by the giant truck. I gave Deb a final nervous hug and tried to avoid Jacko's 'helping' hands as I climbed up the steep ladder and into the cabin.

Only a truck this big could have a cabin this big. Up the front were two enormous leather seats for the driver and co-driver; behind them was a bed that was easily big enough for two people. In fact the size of it concerned me somewhat as I sat cross-legged behind Jacko and Kevin.

Jacko fidgeted in the co-driver's seat. His oily singlet covered little of his scrawny chest and arms as he sprawled with his knees wide apart. Despite his crude attempts at being charming, there was a manic glint in his small eyes, which were flicking excitedly between Kevin and me. I could imagine the serving girls doing up their top two shirt buttons when he arrived in the truck stops.

Kevin, on the other hand, had a gentleness to him that was evident in all of his mannerisms. He was well-padded and thirty-ish and was behind the wheel for the first leg from Isa. If it wasn't for Kevin, I would have climbed straight back out of that cabin.

The passenger door slammed shut, the engine grumbled and the wheels crunched over the ground far below us. I'm not sure what I had expected, or whether I had really thought it through, but certainly being trapped in a small cabin with these two blokes and about to head into nothingness didn't feel like the most sensible thing I had ever done.

The conversation started a little awkwardly.

'So, do y'ave a fella?' Jacko's beady eyes flicked from me back to the road.

I have always been a terrible liar. My face gives me away every time. It's a bugger as I never win at poker, and have come to accept that I am completely incapable of carrying off a practical joke. But there are times in life when the ability to tell a convincing story is a must. So I have a strategy – in order to carry off a lie, I first have to convince myself that there is some truth in what I am saying. If I can manage to convince myself of this, then I can convince bloody anyone.

Although I hadn't expected it to be the conversation opener, I had spent the last few days preparing myself for the boyfriend question. I had figured that since Anthony (my boyfriend from university) and I still had some unresolved issues (i.e he still had a CD of mine, and we hadn't caught up for a cappuccino in ages) we were technically not completely broken up.

'Oh yeah. He lives in Brissie.'

'Ooooh riiight.' Was that disappointment in those crazy eyes? Yuck. I hoped not.

As we trundled away from Mt Isa and into the emptiness of the Australian centre it occurred to me that in some other respects, besides the financial ones, this was even better than catching a bus. I not only had stacks of leg room, stretching my lengthy legs out on the huge bed, but even better, this massive truck was a relentless, round-the-clock moving machine. It didn't have to make rest stops every four hours, or to pick up passengers at bus stations.

Kevin and Jacko were its non-stop navigators, operating in shifts. One of them drove for ten hours while the other rested, then they swapped, then they swapped again, and again, and again, and again. These two guys had been thrown together by their work and now spent nearly all their time together in this cabin trundling in an endless cycle of movement across Australia – sleeping, talking and driving. Having a third person to add to the conversation was a huge bonus for them. This gave me a new perspective on the groans of disappointment back at the truck stop. Taking on board random travellers, male or female, meant a whole new life story to while away the hours.

And I found out that it was not uncommon for penny-pinching travellers such as myself to utilise this speedy and economical form of transport. But I had been lucky – the drivers were discriminating. Some were reluctant to pick up women for litigation reasons, and most were reluctant to pick up men. I thought this was more than a little dodgy and unfair, until I learnt why.

We had not been on the road for long before Jacko started rustling away under his seat. I tensed. Was he going to pull out a knife? Or maybe a gun? Shit!

From the depths he pulled out an opaque plastic supermarket bag. He reached into it and pulled out two smaller transparent bags, each about the size and shape of a one-kilo pack of flour. The contents of one were green and the other white. With deft efficiency he removed the elastic band sealing the bag that contained the white powdery substance and sat it opened on his knees.

I watched on in amazement as he delved into the bag and constructed a long white line of powder on the dash. I had figured that he wasn't about to talcum powder his armpits but, as I watched him inhale the white powder through half a pink straw, I realised with a shock that I was looking at enough drugs to get several people put away. With bloodshot eyes he turned my way.

'Mate, you should try some of this gear. It's fucking great.'

He was fondling the bag now. This was just fantastic. I was stuck in a cabin with two strange guys, heading into the middle of nowhere, with enough drugs to send fifty people off the planet. And one of them wanted to get me wasted. Kevin was staying very quiet.

'Aw, come on. It'll be fun. You should just have a little bit.' His face had taken on a look of childish excitement.

Now I reckon there is an obvious logic that says not to take strange substances offered to you by a shifty-looking truckie when trapped in a cabin with him, his mate and a bed. And anyway, I have never had the urge to indulge in social drugs other than alcohol, even around my closest friends. However, I felt more than a little concerned at what Jacko was going to do if I refused his offer. His red eyes were wide with anticipation.

'Look ... um ... I'd really love to ... But I have a terrible allergic reaction to amphetamines. I go into anaphylactic shock.' Thank God for my medical training, which helped me to confuse him with long words. Jacko's wiry frame seemed to droop a little, and he turned back to his bag, from which he carefully laid out a second, even longer, line for himself. I'd done it – I'd lied, and he'd believed me.

'It's the job that turns me t'this stuff, ya know. It's for safety. Ya gotta stay awake somehow!'

I didn't think it was the right time or the place to debate the issue, or to point out that he wasn't on driving duty for another nine hours or so. But the issue wasn't over yet.

When he finally decided he wanted to get some sleep he unravelled the second bag to reveal an even larger clump of marijuana. I'd used up my best excuse – I wondered if he would believe I was allergic to two completely unrelated drugs. I didn't think so.

'Look, sorry, but I really just don't like smoking.'

'Aw, come on. Just a little bit won't hurt.'

'No ... ah ... really ... um ... No thanks.'

He reluctantly accepted that he was going to smoke alone. We swapped positions, him in the bed and me in the co-driver's seat.

The sound of his bubbling bong and raspy inhalations were occasionally replaced by his reedy voice and warm breath next to my ear: 'Look, mate. Are ya sure?' (Cough, splutter.) 'It's great stuff. You'll love it.'

Eventually from the bed came the deep rhythmic breaths of slumber. I heaved a sigh of relief. Now it was just me and Kevin, and I was much happier with the situation. Kevin seemed relieved as well. According to him, I had just been a perfect case study for why they (or he and many other drivers, possibly excluding Jacko) preferred female hitchhikers. Most male hitchhikers, lacking concern for personal safety and with nothing better to do during the long trip, diminish the ample drug supply considerably, making them costly passengers. It's only an occasional female who will partake. I couldn't imagine any woman being so stupid.

Kev and Jacko had only been caught out on their female-only policy once. They had pulled over to pick up a female hitchhiker from the side of the highway and couldn't believe their luck as, even from a distance, they could see that her enormous bosom was practically bursting out of her skimpy top and her lengthy legs were clad only in a tiny miniskirt. It wasn't until she climbed on board that they noticed her five o'clock shadow and her deep guttural voice.

With Jacko safely asleep, and me in the co-driver's seat, I started to regain my confidence. And it is hard not to feel pretty confident sitting at the helm of a road train. In fact you feel damn well all-powerful. You are the king of the road, looking down on all the little cars that seem like ants. Thankfully Kevin, unlike Jacko, didn't feel the need to talk continuously and, between intermittent conversations about his girlfriend and the job, we sat in relaxed silence. He took occasional sips at a can of Coke that he had laced with amphetamines to keep him awake.

From the bird's-eye view of the co-driver's seat I saw a new perspective on the mini-drama of cars overtaking road trains.

Watching the last of our three carriages flapping from side to side in the rear-view mirror, we could see a 4WD coming right up to our rear.

Kevin was muttering to himself: 'They couldn't be stupid enough to go now. Yep, they *are* stupid enough to go now. We are just about to hit a bump and the end carriage is going to go crazy. Those bloody idiots.'

Meanwhile the little 4WD pulled out to the right side of the road and started roaring up the side of the train. I imagined all the passengers with their eyes wide with fright, the driver pushing the accelerator down as hard as it would go, and everyone's fingers crossed. As we hit the corrugation in the road, the end carriage flicked out and the 4WD veered hard to the right, its wheels skidding in the dust there. From the safety and comfort of our cabin I imagined the passengers having heart attacks as the driver rammed his foot through the floor. After what felt like half an hour, they pulled in front of us and roared off into the distance.

Kevin chuckled. 'So, anyway, what the hell is a young girl like you doing hitchhiking with road trains? You must be crazy.'

After telling me about some particularly unfortunate incidents involving girls and not-so-nice road-train drivers, he made me promise that, if I ever planned to hitchhike anywhere again, I would call his mobile and he would make sure I got a lift with decent chaps. If not, I was to catch a bus.

He was bloody right. What the hell was I doing?

After seven hours on the road, I was certain I couldn't keep my leaden eyelids open any longer. The need for sleep overcame all logic and I crawled onto the spare half of the bed hoping not to disturb the inert form. Soon I was woken by the shuffling sound of a scrawny body inching towards me in the darkness. Logic returned with a jolt and I jumped back into the co-driver's seat. There was going to be no sleep for me tonight.

Ten hours after leaving Isa, we arrived at a truck stop. Thank goodness. We could get out for a while, stretch our legs and relax with some food.

But, after a whirlwind five minutes of freedom, we were back in the truck with some takeaway and with Jacko in the driver's seat. He took a few lines of speed and then pulled back onto the road again. I wasn't at all happy when Kevin had a smoke and collapsed into bed.

The road stretched empty ahead of us, lit up far into the distance by our vehicle's powerful headlights. Jacko hummed to himself between bursts of reflection about life, love and everything. I couldn't always keep track of exactly what the conversation was about, but he had obviously spent many of his lonesome hours in profound musings and he wasn't going to waste this opportunity to share them.

Mid-reflection, a tall majestic shape hopped into our path and stopped. As we rapidly drew closer our headlights lit up the strong male kangaroo. His face was turned to us with eyes fixated on the two big round lights bearing down on him. This was a scenario that instinct had not equipped him for. Out in the bush you only have to make a rustle near a group of kangaroos and they stand erect, ears twitching to locate the sound, on full alert for danger and ready to bounce off to safety. This proud male was on full alert all right, chest pushed out towards the roar of the engine bearing down on him, but he stood mesmerised by the light, helpless to do anything.

There was a thump from somewhere down below my seat and then the road was empty again. I sat cemented to my seat as we trundled forward. Jacko had not even paused in his musings. Kangaroos are a major hazard when driving through Australia in a car, especially at night when they are dazzled by headlights. Hitting a big roo can mean a serious smash, and even death, to the occupants of a car.

Not so in a road train. All you know of hitting a roo is the muffled *thump*. The momentum of the truck is so great that you can't even feel the bump. Even if the driver wanted to, they couldn't slow down in time to avoid the collision and Skippy definitely comes off second best. Indeed, most of the dead roos that lie scattered along Australia's roads have met their fate in this manner. We had just added another big male roo to the national roadkill.

Hours later, the sky started to brighten and the scale of where we were hit me. Early in the night we had entered the Northern Territory and now from the elevation of the cabin the horizon seemed endless. All around us, as far as the eye could see, the flat land was etched with hardy grasses and spindly shrubs softened by the rosy light of dawn. I watched as the sun poked its head over the pink horizon and the soft glow smoothed out Jacko's lined face. He smiled as he shared this moment with another person, or maybe he just smiled every day at sunrise.

'Isn't it a beauty? I love this time of day. It's like the world is clean and fresh and bright and ready for life. And mate, its fuckin' good being the only person to see the world wake up from where I sit … Not that I mind ya bein' here right now! It's pretty nice actually. But sometimes, when it's just me, I feel pretty damn lucky. We'll pull over soon. One of the choicest spots on the road is coming up. Ya gunna luv it.'

I was wondering what could be so different about their special spot in this seemingly uniform scenery. As our momentum slowed and Jacko pulled the three huge carriages off into the dust it all looked the same to me. I wrenched the heavy door open and climbed down the ladder to the bare rocky earth below, happy to stretch out my lengthy frame. By my feet lay a few old wrappers and cans. I still couldn't pick how this was any different to what lay behind and ahead of us.

Kevin climbed sleepily down after me. 'Mornin' mate. Not bad, eh? This 'ere is the highest spot on the road. Great, isn't it.'

And then, as I looked around, I could see that ever so slightly the ground dropped away from where we stood. We were at the summit of this seemingly flat world, watching as it came alive. The pink horizon faded into blue as the sun rose over the earth's edge.

Jacko emerged from the other side of the truck carrying three large rockmelons: 'One of the farmers filled up our luggage box with the best of 'em. They're fuckin' beauties.'

Sitting next to the road train in the middle of nowhere at the high point of the road, Jacko, Kevin and I watched the sun rise as we ate the most delicious rockmelons I have ever tasted. For a moment I understood how someone could love this life.

We finally arrived in Katherine and, armed with Kevin and Jacko's mobile phone numbers scribbled on a piece of paper and under strict instructions to organise lifts through them in the future, I was left on the side of the road with my pack on my back. That scrap of paper I had in my hands was the gold card for road trains to anywhere I wanted to go in Australia. Cool.

Sitting with Kath at a table in the Katherine pub, it felt like we had years to catch up on. We had both done so much since we had last seen each other less than a year before, but nothing I'd experienced compared to Kath's stories of Arnhem Land, still so fresh in her memory.

I sat mesmerised as she recounted meeting her boyfriend's family, sitting around campfires as the only white person and trying to communicate with people who spoke broken if any English.

She had been taken out hunting in a beat-up old 4WD and they had headed straight out into the bush, where there were no roads. They had driven through dry creek beds, bouncing up their steep walls, traversed up and down sandy slopes and found their way to deep waterholes in the seemingly dry land. They had shot kangaroos and caught fish to cook up on the fire at night. They had sat around the campfire with their beers and grub and talked and sung long into the night.

But Kath had left Arnhem Land on her own and come into town to meet me there. It had not all been fun and laughter. There had been a lot of alcohol and almost complete unemployment and this was having serious consequences in the community. Her boyfriend was showing the strain of the tension between his life in Sydney and his responsibilities back home. So, although Kath was bubbling from the experience, she was clearly overjoyed to be sitting in a pub and drinking beer away from it all. I couldn't understand why she didn't want to take every day she could to be out in such an excitingly different place, but I would come to learn exactly why.

I was desperate to find a way to get into Arnhem Land. But without a vehicle we couldn't get a permit, and without a permit we couldn't get in. There was no way we were going to sneak in by hitchhiking because the shame for Kath if she got caught would be too much, and it seemed disrespectful for her to ask the community she had just left for a pass to take her friend sightseeing. So I had to find another way.

Then another moment of revelation. I was a physio, wasn't I? Surely they were desperate for health professionals out there. So Kath and I hitchhiked the short distance to Darwin to see if I could wangle a job in Arnhem Land.

No jobs going. I offered my services for free. But they couldn't accept volunteers because their insurance didn't cover them and the risk was too high due to 'violence in the communities'. I begged and I pleaded, but to no avail. Arnhem Land seemed out of my reach. I had hit a frustratingly solid wall.

Almost completely broke, Kath headed back to Sydney for uni and I phoned for a road train to take me back to Mt Isa, where Cherie was offering me work until the Kombi was ready.

After several weeks of work in Mt Isa I got the call: my fickle vehicle was ready and waiting. So yet again I left Isa and Cherie behind me, and headed to Charters Towers. But my reunion with the Kombi was not to be a fond one. As we putted out of Charters Towers on the road towards Cairns, where I was starting work the next day, I had a dreadful feeling of impending doom. Was I just imagining it, or had a new stuttering noise joined the myriad of Kombi sounds? I buzzed and spluttered along at sixty km/h.

When I finally arrived in Townsville she was sounding like a chronic asthmatic. A fully qualified Kombi mechanic delivered the diagnosis. Butch and Jack hadn't installed the new engine correctly. They had forgotten a crucial piece, and I had stuffed the top half of the engine by driving it. The cylinder heads were done in and they were going to need replacing ... again. If I drove it any further I could completely wreck the engine. He could fix it for me in a few weeks if I wanted. It would cost $1500.

Enough was enough! I drove out of his garage and straight to a car freighting company. The Kombi was heading home without me and I was heading to Cairns to start a job servicing three separate physiotherapy clinics. I was going back to the simple life, with just a backpack and a bike. The last I saw of my former pride and joy was when I kicked it as I ran for the taxi that would take me to my bus.

I realised the serious flaws in my new plans while gazing out of the bus window. I was completely broke again and I had nowhere to stay. I had just sent my accommodation back to the Sunshine Coast, and I had no vehicle to drive between the three clinics for the job I was supposedly starting the next day.

Later I sat bemused on the Cairns Esplanade, with my bike in its box leaning against a tree, looking out at the ocean while munching on the hot chips I had just paid for out of my last ten dollars. Out there was a limitless horizon and under that blue water was hiding one of the Seven Natural Wonders of the World, the Great Barrier Reef. *And* the Kombi was out of my life. Things were pretty good, really.

I used fifty cents to call the Gordonvale Hospital, one of my three work locations. They could give me a bed for a bit. I used the last of my money to get a taxi that would carry my bike with me out to the hospital. The hospital administration lent me some money to survive until my first pay came along. Life works out.

While in Cairns I had an all-time classic work encounter. Part of my job was to work in a small, one-therapist clinic, which only opened two afternoons a week. I was a one-man band there and, after Reginald turned up, I nearly closed up shop. He was a Veterans Affairs patient and I had been warned about him by one of the therapists in the town clinic.

'Good old Reg has been coming to us for ages,' Jenny said. 'He had a tough time in the war and he has pain absolutely everywhere. Now I know that strictly this isn't the done thing, but we let him tell us what he wants treated and just do what he asks. This seems to keep him happy. He's a good regular client so I hope that's going to be okay.'

I wasn't so sure, but there didn't seem to be an option number two.

When Reginald hobbled confidently into the cubicle, I wondered which part of his tall, thickly padded and hunched-over frame I was going to be addressing today. I hadn't even finished introducing myself before he had unbuttoned his almost transparent old shirt, whipped it off and settled himself on his back on the plinth.

The skin of his face was battle-scarred, red and bumpy. His thick lumpy torso was criss-crossed with jagged scars, and in the supine position his face was taking on an unhealthy purple hue. It occurred to me to call for a doctor, but he got in before I had the chance.

Looking at me over the top of his set of thick-rimmed, almost opaque reading glasses, he started: 'Now, my dear, the problem is my chest ... here, see? This bit near the chest bone. Now there is only one way that helps it and I will give you the instructions. What it needs is pressure downwards on my ribs see here ... and here ... and here.' He gestured.

'Oh sure, that's easy.' I moved into position by the plinth and placed my hands on his costo-sternal joints ready to do the appropriate mobilising technique.

'Oh, no. You can't do it that way. It doesn't work.'

'Really?' That was odd. I waited for further instructions.

'No, dear. What you have to do is put one knee here [gesturing to the left side of his head] and one knee here [gesturing to the right side of his head] and then you can lean forwards over me and put downwards pressure on my chest.'

For a brief confused moment I processed his instructions, trying to figure out if I had heard him right. My musings were interrupted.

'Don't worry, dear. I'll take my glasses off.' He carefully took the cloudy glasses from his nose, then lay expectantly looking towards the ceiling.

'Um. Look, that really isn't going to be necessary. I can do a technique perfectly well from the side. See, if I just ...' I attempted to place my hands back on his sternum but he brushed them aside. Impatiently, he repeated his explanation.

'One knee here and one knee here and lean forward. I promise I won't look. The other girls all do it that way.'

Not bloody likely.

After five minutes of fierce debate I'd had enough. 'Look, I'm really sorry. But either I treat that area the way I would normally treat it, or we can address another issue today.'

A very disgruntled Reginald left after a brief and half-hearted calf massage. I booked him back in for three weeks' time when the other therapist would be back from her holiday. Not sure whether to be shocked or amused, I returned to the main clinic in town, and debriefed to Jenny, who was writing up her daily notes.

'You wouldn't believe what that guy Reg asked me to do today. He wanted me to get up on the plinth and ...'

She looked up at me with an eager glint in her eyes. 'Oh, yeah. He's tried that one on all of us. So ... did you do it?'

I couldn't believe it. She hadn't warned me. '*No!*'

A hint of disappointment flashed in her eyes. I was struck by a sudden thought: 'Why, has anyone ever done it?'

A red flush crept up her neck and overwhelmed her face. 'Oh ... ah, yeah.'

'Really! Who?'

She looked back down at her notes. She was trapped.

'I did.'

The great part about working in Cairns was access to the Reef. I had seen many pictures of this magical place, but I wasn't prepared for the wonder of scuba diving amongst schools of colourful fish and fabulous corals, and the emerald green clarity of the water. It sure was great to be back in the ocean again.

The downside to working in Cairns was that in my heart I still yearned to be in Arnhem Land. I couldn't explain exactly why. It was just a deep force within me. So, between boat trips out to the reef and riding my bike and catching buses between three clinics, I set my mind to getting myself there.

I discovered that there was a full-time physiotherapist position in East Arnhem Land, in a town called Gove. Unfortunately, this position was filled by a permanent staff member and she had been there for over ten years. I figured she must really love her job.

Maybe she wanted a holiday?

I found the phone number for the Gove District Hospital and was put through to Physiotherapy.

'Physiotherapy Department. This is Ruth speaking.'

'Hi. My name's Claire and I'm a physiotherapist and ... well ... I was just wondering if you wanted a holiday. I can come out and fill in for you if you do.'

'Can you be here in three weeks?'

'Sure.'

'Great. I'll sort it out.'

I gave her my mobile phone number and put the phone down in stunned silence. After all my deliberating and scheming, could it really be that easy?

Two days and a few telephone conversations with Gove District Hospital administration later, I had my flight organised and paid for by Northern Territory Health. I was booked on the Cairns to Gove flight in three weeks' time and I would do a three-week locum job to fill in, while Ruth was away.

It wouldn't be for long, but the job was perfect. It was to be based at the hospital in Gove, which was a town right at the tip of Arnhem Land. I would be treating patients in Gove and also flying out to all the remote Aboriginal communities. I was on my way into the heart of Aboriginal land, and the Northern Territory Government was going to pay me to go there!

But I have to be honest. Although my adventures were taking me to places I wanted to go, my mind was in overdrive trying to figure life out, and find my place and path in it. I knew I didn't want to head back home to safety and security, but it sure was an unsettled and confusing time being twenty-one and out in the big wide world on my own.

And thrown into the equation was the fact that I still felt like a giant living in the land of the little women. The lack of real bosom buddies around me made my insecurities all the more over-whelming. What hope was there for me with all those gorgeous petite females fluttering their eyelashes and looking helpless? I was far from being overweight, but just felt enormous.

Reducing my weight was the only way to make myself any smaller. Unfortunately (or fortunately for my long-term health) my regular resolves to diet were constantly undermined by my love of eating. Good sense always prevailed with the first grumble of my stomach.

Before I knew it, I was on the plane heading for Gove. I was still six foot two and a trifle confused about the world, but I was on my way to a new adventure. Maybe I would figure out about my life and love there. One thing was for sure – fun and challenging times lay ahead.

THE STARFISH

One day a man was walking along the ocean shore. As he looked down the beach, he saw a human figure moving like a dancer. He smiled to himself to think of someone who would dance to the day. So he began to walk faster to catch up. As he got closer, he saw the young man was reaching down picking up something and throwing it very gently into the ocean. As he got closer he called out, 'Hello, what are you doing?'

The young man paused, looked up and replied, 'Throwing starfish back into the ocean!'

'Why are you throwing starfish into the ocean?'

'The sun is up and the tide is out. If I don't throw them back they will die.'

'But, young man, don't you realise that there are miles of beach and starfish all along it? You can't possibly make a difference!'

The young man listened politely and bent down, picked up a starfish and threw it into the sea, past a breaking wave. 'It made a difference to that one.'

Unknown author
Found on a cereal packet

FIVE

Aboriginal Land

Gove airport was a tiny one-building affair, surrounded by sparse bush, where red dust coloured everything from the ground up. There was no sign of civilisation anywhere in sight – nor, for that matter, was there any sign of my luggage. With nothing more than my little hippy handbag and the sweaty clothes on my back, I jumped into the dusty white minibus that was waiting patiently for me. After all, this was what adventures were all about – meeting challenges head-on and dealing with them, even if it meant being smelly.

As I climbed onto the bus, any concern I had for my worldly possessions was overwhelmed by a tingling anticipation in my veins. I was on Aboriginal land now. I was in a place where there would be racial harmony and mutual respect and I could learn about our traditional land-owners. I could feel it in my blood that this, my first taste of raw bush physiotherapy, was going to be a mind-expanding experience.

The white bus driver smiled cheerfully as I handed over my money.

'To the hospital, thanks.'

'No worries, mate.'

As the bus pulled away, I looked around me. Was I in the right place? I acknowledged the curious smiles of my fellow passengers who were all – well, white!

We trundled along the bitumen through the spindly bush and copper-coloured earth for half an hour. Then, to my surprise, we emerged into grassy suburbia. One by one the passengers were dropped off at affluent-looking homes, with their driveways sporting boats of varying sizes and expensive four-wheel drives. Eventually we arrived outside the hospital and I was directed by a white staff member to the nurses' quarters, which were filled with lots of white health professionals. Where were all the Aboriginal people?

Slightly mystified, I refrained from asking one of the pale faces in the corridor: 'I was just wondering – am I in Arnhem Land? And, if so, which way to the blackfellas?' Instead, I asked how to get to the shops for some food. I left my gapingly empty new box of a room, and headed down the road. Ten minutes later I was in town.

Aha! Bingo. Here they all were. Large groups of dark-skinned people lolled around the shops – some standing, some sitting. And one was approaching me.

'Hey, chicka, ya got a dolla?'

'Yeah … um … sure.'

The battle-scarred man staggered with his bounty back to his mates, who were eyeing me off suspiciously. Around me, distinctly Caucasian people were everywhere – busily going about their lives, walking out of Woolworths with their well-dressed children and bags full of groceries, or sitting outside dusty cafés drinking cappuccinos and chatting. They were for the most part completely ignoring the Aboriginal people who seemed to be sitting uncomfortably at the edge of this activity, looking disorderly.

Hell. Here came the first chap's friend stumbling towards me. He looked drunk. Damn it – this wasn't how I'd wanted things to be. What to do?

I ran for cover in Woolies.

This was my first taste of the sad reality of Gove. I had, it turned out, inadvertently landed myself once again in a mining town where race was a divisive issue. Only, this one was smack bang in the middle of Aboriginal land. I soon came to learn the history behind the clash of cultures.

In 1931 the Australian Government gave back the territory of Arnhem Land to the Aboriginal people. At last the traditional land-owners had a sizeable area of Australia that they could call their own. Sure, missions were established there and westernisation crept in – in the shape of missionaries and bargeloads of supplies once every couple of months – but the Aboriginal people were mostly in charge of their own lives. There was no alcohol, nor any drugs, and the people caught most of their food by traditional methods. The most rich and productive area of this land was the coastal strip, and hence this was where most of the population was located. Photographs from this era show a happy and healthy people living in harmony with their land.

Then in 1955 it was discovered that the north-eastern coast of Arnhem Land was rich with bauxite, the raw material from which aluminium is extracted. The Australian Government hadn't realised *that* when they gave the land away. Suddenly the Aboriginal people had something of material value to other Australians.

So on 13 March 1963, without informing the traditional land-owners, the government reclaimed this prime 300 square kilometres of coast from the Arnhem Land reserve and started mining it for bauxite.

The local people were devastated. The land and sea contained many sacred areas, and they were an important source of food. The Aboriginal elders took the matter first to the House of

Representatives in 1963, and were ignored. They then took the matter to the Supreme Court in 1968. The judge accepted evidence that the Yolngu had been living in the area for tens of thousands of years, and that their law was based on intricate relations to the land. He held, however, that Australian law could not recognise these as property rights. In 1971 their petition was turned down.

It was too late anyway. The Commonwealth of Australia had already granted the mineral leases; building of the mine was under way. In 1972 the first shipment of bauxite was exported. The whopping great multi-million dollar mine took over the pristine coast and now removes two million tonnes of bauxite from the earth, including from sacred areas, each year.

The mine owners offered royalties to the one family who claimed to be the traditional owners of that site. (There is some dispute as to whether they actually are.) Clearly there was no point in not taking the money as the damage was already done. Consequently, there are now a few *very* rich Aboriginal people in Arnhem Land who own helicopters and huge houses. Others have suffered as a result of this disastrous series of events.

The elders went into crisis mode; damage control seemed the only option they had left. They put forward a proposal to the Australian Government to ban all alcohol in the whole of Arnhem Land. At least, if there was going to be a mine and a town in the middle of their land, they could try to keep out the toxic drug that was ruining the lives of so many in the cities. Needless to say, their plea was ignored. How were they going to get mine workers to move to Gove if there wasn't any beer? The elders attempted to sue the Liquor Licensing Commission, but the case was overturned.

So the miners got their drinking clubs and the rest is history. Alcohol was banned in Arnhem Land everywhere except for Gove, which is smack bang in the middle.

On my first day of work, still wearing my sweaty travelling clothes, I was dealt a crushing blow. I wouldn't be flying out to any of the communities that were scattered through Arnhem Land. Instead I was going to be the Gove District Hospital in-house physiotherapist for three weeks until Ruth returned and took over again. I had battled my way into getting all the way out here, and for what? To treat white mine workers with sore necks and backs! I might as well have been back in Isa.

But there were things going for this little seaside town that I couldn't have anticipated, particularly in the shape of my enduring friendship with the wonderful Alison Dunn. The story of how Alison came to live in Gove made me more determined than ever to see for myself the traditional lands and mysterious people beyond the borders of Gove.

Ally, a gorgeous busty blonde from Adelaide, with an Arts degree majoring in Anthropology, and a Science degree majoring in Psychology, had been taken out to Arnhem Land for an arranged marriage. Not that she had realised it at the time.

Israel (the lucky man) had moved to an out-station in Arnhem Land about five years earlier to live in harmony with nature and the Aboriginal people. He had learned to speak fluent Yolngu Maata, and had become a part of their family. The older women at the out-station had eventually decided that it was about bloody time that Israel had a wife, and that he clearly wasn't going to do anything about it for himself, so on a trip to Darwin visiting family they had commenced their search. They found Alison, who was protesting in Jabiluka with hundreds of people opposed to uranium mining in Kakadu National Park. They picked her out as his 'soul mate', and invited her to their out-station in Arnhem Land 'for a ceremony'.

Now Alison, through her studies, thought she knew a little about Aboriginal people, and one thing she 'knew' for sure was that it was very impolite to ask questions. Being an anthropologist and sensitive to their culture, she accepted their offer without knowing where she was going, where she would be living, what she would be living on, how long she would be there for, or what exactly she was going for. They just handed her a one-way plane ticket and, with a small bag of belongings and no money to her name, she was on her way to – well, somewhere exciting.

Unbelievably, after some extraordinary misadventures, Alison and Israel did ultimately hit it off, which didn't surprise the women who had been responsible for their meeting. Of course it had worked out – did anyone imagine that they would bring back the wrong woman for him?

By the end of my three weeks at Gove, I had decided that I wasn't ready to leave Arnhem Land. I had been enchanted by Alison and Israel's stories of the 'real' Arnhem Land; I no longer had to hand-wash my clothes every night as my luggage had finally arrived, and I had settled into my room. But Ruth was coming back, my return flight was booked, and then the doors to this wealth of experience were going to be closed.

Ruth returned from her holiday and, without giving it too much thought, I took a long shot: I offered to permanently take over the job that she had been doing for the last ten years. Well what was the harm in asking? The next day, to my great surprise and shock, she accepted. She packed her bags just like that, and she was gone.

'But hang on, what exactly do I have to do?' Half the town, her patients and the hospital staff didn't even know she was leaving until she had left. The hospital had little choice but to take me on, as there wasn't exactly a queue lining up to apply for her position.

And suddenly I was it – less than a year after graduating, I was in charge of my own hospital department (including the budget) and was the only physiotherapist for the whole of East Arnhem Land.

I should probably have taken Ruth's rapid departure as a clue to what awaited me. She left so quickly because she didn't want to miss her chance. It might be ten more years before there was another person foolish enough to take over. I excitedly and naively signed my contract.

That night I went out with Alison and another of my new girl-friends, Debby, to celebrate at the Arnhem Club and saw before me an apparition of golden ringlets, tanned skin and big brown eyes. I looked at him, he looked back at me and there was no denying it, he was gorgeous. His name was Kel. The heavens sure were shining on me today. Or so I thought.

What was it with me and men who were obsessed with hob-bies? At least with Anthony (my boyfriend at university) I had some previous experience and interest in rowing, so I could partly understand his passion. I could see the health benefits and under-stand the thrill of winning races. But *fishing*? Puhlease!

Enter Kel. Kel's lifetime ambition, his holy grail, his dream, was to catch a marlin! (For those non-fishers out there like me, a marlin is like the Rolls Royce of fish – big, powerful, and extremely hard to acquire.)

I knew that people liked fishing, but I didn't know that there were people whose photo albums were filled entirely with pictures of fish, fishing rods, fishing boats, and people holding fish. I didn't know there were people who sat for blissful hours polishing lures, looking through fishing magazines, watching fishing videos of 'great catches', or just fishing.

We were doomed from the start. Other than a mutual love of his Staffordshire bull terrier (Jack) and grilled crayfish with cheese on top, we had absolutely nothing in common. I wanted to find vertical rocks big enough to climb on. Kel liked rocks that were low and flat, preferably positioned near river mouths, and just big enough to stand on with a bucket and an esky alongside. I dreamed of finding more than just a ripple in the flat blue ocean, to ride a board on; Kel awaited the calm flat days with excited anticipation. My mouth watered at the thought of nutritious fruit and yoghurt smoothies; Kel's nectar of the gods, his constant and reliable companion, was icy cold XXXX. Sadly for me, our location gave Kel the upper hand – all the cliffs in Arnhem Land are sacred sites, there was never much more than a tiny ocean swell (thanks to the proximity of Indonesia), and beer was much easier to fit into an esky. However, despite the odds, soon after my arrival in Gove we embarked on a tumultuous relationship.

Why couldn't I just fall in love with someone? Where the hell was my Mr Right? What was True Love anyway? Maybe this was it. Maybe falling in love was about making compromises and accepting another person for who they were, even if it wasn't quite right. Maybe I just had to change a little and then he would fall in love with me.

After all, what were the chances of meeting someone who was totally compatible, whom I found attractive, who was honest and grounded and good, and whom I fell in love with and who would also fall in love with me? Maybe it wasn't even in my nature to be capable of such complete devotion, and unquestioned commitment, to one person.

I persevered with Kel. And Kel persevered with trying to catch a marlin.

I hardly needed this added complication in my life as my new job was more than enough to keep me occupied. I realised pretty early on that I had actually been employed to do two completely separate jobs, each of which had the potential to keep at least two therapists very busy. A cunning cost-minimisation strategy by Northern Territory Health.

My first job was to be the one and only Gove District Hospital physiotherapist. Without even the luxury of a receptionist, I had to provide a physiotherapy service to all the sick people in the hospital, all the workers compensation patients from the mine – who couldn't go to a private physiotherapist, because there wasn't one – and all the injured people in the general population of 3000-ish people in Gove. Some minor responsibilities to fill in all my free time included screening of young athletes for the NT Academy of Sport (without which the kids couldn't be selected), in-services for nursing staff in the hospital, and attending a weekly playgroup for children with developmental delay.

My second job was with the Aged and Disability Team, and I suspect this was some kind of sick joke that someone high up in Northern Territory Health was chuckling about. The team consisted of one occupational therapist, one speech therapist, one care coordinator and me (or 'half' of me anyway). Our job? On our tiny budget we were supposed to provide *all* of the aged and disabled people within the 13000-odd population (most of whom lived in remote settings) with a reasonable level of services and care. Yeah, right!

In our attempt to achieve the impossible, the four of us divided up the nine biggest remote communities and I was the primary provider for Ramingining and Milingimbi. Somehow, alongside my overloaded job as the hospital physiotherapist, I had to fit in one visit of two to three days to each of these two communities every month, and then try to get out to each of the other communities at least once every six months to see people with specialised physiotherapy needs.

On the morning of my first community trip I woke well before my alarm. I had nothing to distract me from my eager anticipation as my bags were already packed and ready by the door. Miriam, the occupational therapist, was going to come with me for this trip to show me the ropes. I would spend a total of five days going first to the small island of Milingimbi, then to Ramingining, and then back home. Ramingining had a reputation for being particularly rough and dangerous.

Clad in appropriately long skirts and modest shirts we boarded the single-engine aircraft that transported people around Arnhem Land and twice a week did the round trip via all the communities west of Gove. Looking at its old exterior I tried not to think about when it had last been serviced. The inside of the aircraft was crammed with hot and sweaty black and white bodies hard up against each other. There is no such thing as air-con in the Arnhem Land branch of the Missionary Aviation Fellowship airline.

After three hours, with two bumpy stop-offs to load and unload people and boxes in Gapuwiyak and Ramingining, we arrived at the island of Milingimbi. I was drenched and exhausted from the travel. My long green skirt hung wet around my legs, and my forehead streamed. The dust from the unsealed airstrip clung to my sticky skin and crept into my nose. The heavy, hot air buzzed with incomprehensible chatter and laughter from the crowds of dark-skinned people who were organising their friends, the mail and the supplies from the plane into old 4WDs.

Through my hot sweaty daze I realised this was it. I was out here at last! A Land Cruiser pulled up in the red dust and Miriam waved in greeting to a large, energetic looking lady with long blonde hair down to her waist, a long floral skirt, old white T-shirt and a wide, friendly – if slightly stressed – smile, as she jumped out to help us with our bags. Regina had been working as a nurse in Milingimbi for almost three years.

We dumped our bags at the staff accommodation and then reluctantly left the air-conditioning behind to head through the township on foot to the medical clinic. It was already nearing midday and the flies pestered my sweaty body and tickled my nose and eyes. Clusters of dark people turned to us as we walked. A group of young boys rattled and laughed along the bumpy dirt street on old bicycles. The houses were open, some of them completely lacking doors, and all were discoloured with red dust. The ground was covered with rubbish.

We were the outsiders here all right. In fact, I had never felt so conspicuous in all my life. Not only was our colour different, but my height was creating a bit of a local spectacle and small children were pointing and giggling. My oddity was accentuated by the fact that Miriam only just cracks five foot, taking her to somewhere near my shoulder.

As we approached the clinic, I couldn't believe my eyes. It was silhouetted against the blue ocean – a beachfront surgery! On its verandah stood a group of dark women in long flowing floral clothes. Like the rest of the community, their faces turned as we walked towards the building and their jaws dropped somewhat as they looked me up and down, and up and down.

We had only just stepped onto the verandah of the medical centre when one of the women reached out and grabbed me by the hand, drawing me towards her. She was short and round with a face that looked as though it was permanently split by her wide grin, ready to break into laughter at the slightest excuse. She planted a firm kiss on my cheek.

'Hey, you that new physio? You a tall one ay!'

All the other ladies giggled.

'Yeah, hi – I'm Claire.'

'Yo yappa [means literally 'sister', but is a word used in reference to nearly any woman]. My name is Djiliri. You adopted as my daughter. That means you a Wamutjan.'

'What? Really? I mean … thanks.' I looked helplessly at Miriam for some guidance but she was already deep in her own conversation. Had I just been adopted by a complete stranger or was this some little joke on me? I tried a chuckle, making out that I was in on it.

'So, um … What exactly does that mean then?'

'Hey … that means ya gotta get me cups a tea and give me shoulder rubs!' Her hands were holding her belly tight as she shook with throaty chuckles. 'Hey, everyone. I'm ganna be gettin' shoulder rubs from the physio!' All the women were laughing now and watching for my reaction as Djiliri pointed flamboyantly to her shoulders.

'I'll show ya to the tea room ay.' Eventually, after preparing a cup of tea for Djiliri and myself, I had a chance to talk to Miriam and find out what on earth was going on.

It was no joke. I was now Djiliri's daughter and shared her skin name, Wamutjan. Wow!

Adoption of white workers is actually standard practice because in Arnhem Land the whole social system is based on where you fit into the family structure. You have to be a part of it so people can know how to relate to you. Based on my adoption I now had a set relationship with all the people in Arnhem Land, which affected whom I should and shouldn't mix with (especially men), whom I should be subservient to (Djiliri!) and who should be subservient to me, and so on.

One of the traditional benefits of this system is that in a closed group of people it prevents marriages in the same gene pool. It's extremely complicated and I wasn't really expected to abide by the rules. The important thing was that I fitted in. I had a place, and people henceforth could say: 'You know the Wamutjan, Djiliri's daughter, the tall one. She your aunt/sister/mother/grand-mother/cousin' or whatever applied.

Oh, and to Djiliri's continuing amusement, she got to boss me around. She had figured she was on to a good thing, adopting the physio as her daughter!

The clinic itself was a small, simple building with its back wall practically built on the sandy beach. Its white walls and lino floors wore their share of the red community dirt, from the continuous traffic that passed through the clinic's doors every day. It was a simple set-up, but the colourfully dressed staff and the view from the windows out to the children splashing and laughing in the ocean gave it more charm than any other health-care building I had ever seen.

It was staffed by two full-time trained nurses and a team of local health workers who were mostly women. Djiliri – or should I say 'Mum' – was one of the dedicated health workers who earned a meagre wage and were invaluable as translators, as most of the clients spoke little if any English.

In my first two days there, with Miriam and the other health workers I drove and walked around the community and was introduced to as many of the aged or disabled clients as we could find. But, despite Miriam's warnings, nothing could have prepared me for the appalling conditions that many of them lived in.

One of our first visits was to a demented old man who had had a stroke. We were ushered into the house by his wife, who was also his full-time carer. She took us through to his room. As we entered through the narrow door, the acrid stench of his stale incontinence hit me like a tangible wall of fetid soup. He lay looking blankly at the dirt-smeared wall as flies buzzed around his motionless body. I squatted by his side and, as Djiliri explained who I was to the family, I held his hand and his eyes shifted briefly from the wall and fixed on me as he gave me a gentle toothless smile.

Later we met a young paraplegic man who was unable to get into his own home because there was no ramp access; he had to be carried in and out by friends and family – very humiliating for a man in his twenties. Even worse was that he couldn't get on and off his bed – a mattress on the floor – without help.

Then we moved on to a house by the beach. Here was a large young girl of fourteen with severe cerebral palsy, who was in an old wheelchair that should have been condemned years ago and was far too small for her. Her deformed limbs and spasmed legs jutted out from its rusty frame at cruelly comical angles. Her mother was in permanent pain from injuring her back carrying her daughter up and down the stairs, and lifting her to and from the relic of a chair onto her stained old mattress on the floor.

These were just some of the people I met that day, and their lack of enthusiasm for my arrival was understandable. They had been promised a lot in the past and were yet to see even close to an acceptable level of equipment and services.

Miriam was more battle-hardened than I, and the harsh reality was that there just wasn't enough time or funding to supply the services required. It was just a matter of doing the best we could.

Milingimbi gave me an inkling of the tough job I had landed myself in. The trip to Ramingining confirmed it with more of the same, but the latter community's reputation for violence seemed completely unjustified. Its people were wonderful.

The danger in Ramingining came not from man, but from beast. Dogs were in plague proportions. They were starved and aggressive, and instinct told them that people's calf muscles could be their next tasty meal. Many locals wore scars on their legs, bodies and arms from run-ins with the dogs, and the dogs carried scars from their run-ins with the locals and their sticks. Unfortunately the animals had figured out that we white workers were soft touches, and on the way around the community we had to carry big sticks to scare off the snarling packs of these famished creatures.

After my mind-boggling first trip out bush, I returned to Gove thankful to be back in a mining town and to have a wonderful clean room with running water and air-conditioning, and as much fresh (well, relatively fresh) and healthy food as I needed. Some of the wind sure had been taken out of my sails. How was I ever going to do anything to make a difference out there?

They had been waiting for years for the services they needed and Ruth hadn't been able to make it happen. How the hell could I do any better – an inexperienced new graduate who was probably well out of her depth? I had been so focused on getting a job out here for my own benefit that I hadn't stopped to consider whether I was experienced enough to do it. What if I was completely inadequate? Those people deserved better than that.

I returned to my office on the Monday to an answering machine of angry messages. The people of Gove sure didn't like to have to wait for a week when they had a sore neck. This was to become my regular routine. Fit in the community trips to see people calmly putting up with horrific conditions, only to pay the consequences back in town on my return, in the shape of a longer and longer waiting list, and more and more irate patients suffering from sore necks and shoulders.

But despite the community trips being by far the hardest part of the job – or of any job before or after for that matter – they also provided some of the most unique and fulfilling experiences of my physiotherapy career.

One such experience that particularly sticks in my mind was the recovery of 'Jimmy', a young dancer and hunter who had been injured in a car accident. When I met him he had been hobbling around the community on a pair of wooden crutches for over a year. Not having been told anything to the contrary, he had assumed that he would have to use these crutches for the rest of his life, and would never be able to dance or hunt properly again. His foot dangled lifelessly from his lower leg because the nerve to an important muscle had been damaged beyond repair, causing the muscle itself, which should hold his foot up, to become completely useless. His leg was wasted and weak from being broken in the accident, then not being used for a year. But otherwise he was fine.

Enter Claire, the Wonder Therapist. A permanent but simple splint to hold up his foot and do the job of the lifeless muscle, plus an exercise program that he followed like his life depended on it to strengthen all the undamaged but weakened muscles, and within a few months he was good as new. Back to dancing and hunting with the best of them. He used the crutches for firewood. 'Hey yappa, what'll I hit the dogs with now ay?'

There were a few other intensely rewarding cases like this, where I felt that my physiotherapy skills had made a significant difference to someone's life. And then there were opportunities to relieve more commonplace problems, like the people who couldn't get up from bed (by providing them with a proper bed, rather than a mattress on the floor) or off the toilet (giving them a handrail), or the full-time carers who hadn't had a break for years. These people's lives were eased by providing equipment and services that we in the rest of Australia take for granted – handrails in bathrooms, respite for carers, wheelchairs, ramps and beds, When I hear people saying how good those 'dole-bludging Aboriginals' have it, I just wonder if they or anyone they know has ever been stuck on their bed or toilet with no way of getting up.

These were some of the small successes I had, and over my time in Arnhem Land the 'Age and Disability Service' was improved greatly with the dedicated work of a new care coordinator, Rhonda. But I was constantly aware that the little help I was giving was completely unrelated to the deeper problems. Really I knew nothing about these people and their ongoing plight.

On my second visit to Ramingining I met an elder. I admit it – I thought I was an archangel there to help my Indigenous brothers and sisters, and immerse myself in their culture. But he took one look at me and told me to come back and talk to him if I was still there in a year. He suggested that I, like most white workers, probably wouldn't be. My time there would just be a short and interesting experience for me, and then I would leave them and head back to my own world. He was right.

The simple fact was that in the end I got far more from my time in Arnhem Land than I was able to give. While I was out in the communities, I realised the dream I'd had for so long: I at last had the opportunity to meet Aboriginal people on an equal footing and it was a humbling experience. I met some wonderful families living mostly off the land in out-stations, their children happy and healthy and relatively free from racism and oppression. I met strong Aboriginal people in the communities fighting the battle to help and motivate their people. I was taken out bush hunting by the ladies in Ramingining and given a glimpse of their profound understanding of the land and its resources. I was invited to traditional ceremonies, and watched the men and women dancing and singing like their world depended on it. I sat back and laughed till I cried with women who I shared little language with. Funny how humour doesn't need many words.

And I was lucky enough to be in Ramingining when a momentous thing happened in Australia. I had retired to the staff accommodation after a long and hot day and sat eating my dinner and reading a book alongside a few other white workers out from Darwin. From the darkness of the dirty township and into the clean western locked-up world of the staff house, a loud voice boomed in the Yolngu Maata language. It was coming from the community loudspeaker.

There was a feeling in the air that something big was happening. I disturbed the others from their books.

'Does anyone know what's going on?'

'Nope.'

We went back to our books and the TV, but the voice in the background continued and was cutting through my thoughts. Eventually curiosity got the better of me. I unlocked the front door, grabbed the two huge 'dog sticks' I had leant strategically against the front stairs, and headed out of our locked compound and through the darkness towards the commotion.

The community loudspeaker was mounted at the top of a pole next to the council house, and on the dusty grass around it many people of all ages had gathered in the soft glow of a single light. Only the small children chattered and laughed.

Despite not understanding a word of what was going on and feeling very out of place, my curiosity got the better of me and I sat down in the dark periphery to watch.

I was spotted. A woman of about thirty came over and sat next to me. "'Ello yappa. You that physio ay? You're a tall one.' The large lopsided gap in her front teeth was bared in a friendly grin. I couldn't help laughing with her.

'Yeah, hi. I'm Claire. So ... ah, what's going on?'

'Ahh yeah, it's a big day in Sydney!'

It was 28 May 2000 and around me, a little Aboriginal community in the middle of nowhere – one that most people in Australia would never even know exists – sat entranced as the loud crackling voice translated into Yolngu Maata a live radio broadcast of events on the Sydney Harbour Bridge. Over 150 000 Australians (not including Prime Minister John Howard) were marching together over the bridge in support of reconciliation. This event was the culmination of a three-day festival marking the end of the ten-year official reconciliation process. The word 'sorry' was written in jet stream across the sky above the opera house.

As my companion translated some of the proceedings back into English for me, I watched her beautiful happy face as light caught the tears on her chocolate skin. I was moved beyond tears. I only wished those people on the bridge could in some way have shared this moment, and seen the effect that their simple action was having. I had a sudden strong feeling that this was what these people needed more than anything. Pride. Confidence that the rest of Australia wasn't looking down on them as poor dependent cousins and dole-bludging alcoholics, but loving and respecting them as a people. I so wanted to help these quirky laughing characters maintain the culture and insight and humour that is so uniquely theirs. But how? God only knows. What can you do when most Australians will never realise the mystical wisdom that is held within our own country until it is too late?

While I was out in Arnhem Land I would have had to keep both eyes and ears shut to deny that the locals have an uncanny and seemingly supernatural understanding of – well, stuff. One of my experiences in this regard was particularly memorable.

About six months after my arrival in Arnhem Land I was in the health clinic at Milingimbi. I had brought Miriam out to the community to see to a few clients with specialised occupational therapy needs. It was a hot, dry and still afternoon and the health clinic was nearly deserted save for the nursing staff and us. Miriam and I stood discussing our action plan, procrastinating under the cool whisper of the fans.

As we talked, a tall young man of about thirty wandered through the open doors past us and into the back office. His presence barely registered amidst our deliberations until Regina came hurtling out of the office into the treatment room, and then back with a stretcher. As she struggled past us looking flushed and anxious, we asked if we could help.

'No.' And she was gone.

'We'd better clear out, Miriam. I feel like we're in the way.'

We walked unfazed out the front door and into the courtyard and were met by an eerie sight. The people of the community were heading towards the clinic from every direction. And with them came a strong wind blowing past the clinic and out to sea, carrying with it leaves and dust that skipped over the courtyard and around our feet. Miriam and I stood looking around, bewildered.

Things got stranger. The people's facial expressions all lacked their usual cheery grins and the atmosphere was ominous. The first arrival, without pause, asked me who had died. I said that, as far as I knew, no-one had died. As the community gathered around the clinic a low wailing started.

Miriam and I escaped to the tearoom.

'What's going on?'

'I have no idea.'

As I sipped my tea, to the background howl of wailing and wind, I felt a pressure on my shoulder. 'Claire, could you come inside please? We need some help in there.'

I followed Regina inside and into the treatment room. On the stretcher in the middle of the room the young man lay unmoving on his back. Drips had been fed into his arm. His expressionless face was half-covered by a mask, through which a health worker was inflating his lungs with an air bag, and his open eyes gazed unseeing at the roof. One of the nurses was leaning her whole weight on his chest in regular compressions.

'He has had a heart attack. It's a very bad one. We are going to have to continue with CPR. Could you please step in for a while?'

'Sure.'

I laid my sweaty white hands on the smooth dark chest as the nurse moved away. I was close to his face now and could see the rough stubble around the mask and the big brown eyes bordered by thick dark brows. I put my weight behind my hands and pushed down.

His ribs bounced beneath my weight and I felt the resistance against the deep tissues. *One ... Two ... Three ... Four ...*

The health worker squeezed the bag and his lungs filled and then emptied. *One ... Two ... Three ... Four ...*

Come on, friend, wake up from your sleep. You are so young and fresh, and it doesn't make any sense that your body has stopped.

The wailing outside the clinic grew louder as more and more people arrived. How the hell did they know? The only people who should know were with him now in this room, trying to bring life back into this body that I was compressing.

Regina was receiving phone instructions from the doctor, keeping him on the line continuously while carrying out each direction. She was placing little electrodes on his chest to read his heart activity. Nothing.

'Yep, okay. I'll get it ready.' She pulled the defibrillator machine away from the wall and turned it on. The heavy metal pads that she lifted off the machine looked cold and hostile.

'Everybody stand back.'

As his body arched violently with electricity, it seemed that life had returned. But the buzzing line on the ECG was soon replaced by a continuous flat line. His lips and fingers were going cold and purple.

Another violent arch, and then the flat line again.

I continued my compressions. Time blurred and my arms started aching from the effort.

'Sorry, guys, but we have to keep on going until the doctor arrives. It could take quite a long time because he has to fly out from Gove. Claire, are you okay?'

'Sure.'

I didn't understand why we had to keep on going, but I focused completely on keeping an even beat and the right depth of movement. Deep down I knew from my physiology training that after this much time his brain would certainly be dead, but I had to believe there was hope that he could survive. I couldn't do the job in half measure with this young man's body empty and helpless under my hands.

As the hours passed, I developed an oddly intimate relationship with him. I came to know all the details of his body, the way you would know those of someone very close to you. I knew the dark hairs on his chest, the shape that his wide ribs made as they rose and fell with each bag inflation, the outline of his Adam's apple, and the strong curve of his jaw. His full lips filled the mask and his big dark eyes, framed with thick lashes and dark brows, continued their empty stare at the ceiling. I watched as his blood vessels gradually deflated, starting from his hands and working up his arm and his neck, as the pressure left his veins.

Two and half hours after we started CPR, the doctor arrived from Gove, his presence required to take the responsibility of death away from the nurses who lived amongst the community. I registered vaguely as the wailing outside ceased just before he entered the room. Dr Wal was a Papua New Guinean man who worked at the hospital, and lived in Gove with his bubbly wife and three of the cutest children you could hope to see. But now, with his scrubbed cleanliness and this morbid task to perform, he was an unwanted outsider invading a private world. He was going to declare the end of my friend's hope, his life.

The assessment was quick and routine; as he scribbled down the time of death in his notes, he gently asked us to cease. No! I didn't want to. It surely couldn't be that simple.

All over. Final. I am sorry, friend – I couldn't save you. You are gone.

I stopped my now instinctive pressures on his beautiful choco-late-brown chest and mechanically peeled my hands away from the cold skin. Our bond of touch was broken. The mask was taken away from his face and I had a chance to see his strong dark features in full – his lips blue, his eyelids being gently stroked shut. My heart ached painfully for the loss of this person I had never met in life.

When the news was taken outside, the wailing reached a deaf-ening volume. I was ushered out and left my companion with his relatives and the doctor. I found Miriam looking drawn and tense in the tearoom. She came and gave me a hug.

'Are you okay, Claire?'

'Yes. You?'

'Yeah ... How did they know?'

'I've got no idea.'

And to this day I still have no idea. There is no logical explana-tion because the reaction of the community had been instantaneous and from every direction. And, they had known he was dead before we did.

As the months went by, I returned from my bush trips enlightened and inspired, yet frustrated and despondent. The exhilaration of obtaining even a tiny insight into the mystical wealth that is con-tained within the Aboriginal people was juxtaposed with a growing feeling of helplessness to do anything to help these same awesome people in crisis, and a kind of fury that many of them didn't seem to want to do the things that might help them.

It was one of the few problems that I had encountered in my life so far where the harder I thought about it and the more I talked about it, the further from any solution I seemed to get.

I had my moment of truth about Gove, and finally resolved to leave the place while in the local fish and chip shop one day. I had been in the town nearly twelve months. I pushed through the plastic strips into the shop's sweaty interior: standing there on the dirty lino was an Aboriginal lady of about fifty, uncomfortably shifting from foot to foot as if she had been there for a while.

As soon as I entered, a peroxide-blonde teenager emerged past the greasy fryers and, without looking twice, asked me for my order. I looked at my fellow customer who had cast her dark eyes to the floor. The bare toes of one foot now scraped the lino distractedly. She was waiting for me to be served.

'Hey … um, you go first.'

There was no response from her. After an awkward silence I turned back to the service girl, who was tapping her pen impatiently on the counter, a scathing look on her pimply pubescent face.

I placed my order and left with my number to sit and wait in the more muggy, but less greasy, conditions outside. I could still see through the grease-smeared glass into the shop and my feeling of anger grew as the blonde girl went casually out the back and dropped off my order, before returning to finally serve the other lady.

I realised as I sat there that this had become a familiar situation to me, as it obviously was for the Aboriginal lady, and yet I had never seen anyone kick up a stink about it. What was the point? Aboriginal people faced blatant racism every day of their lives, even here in Arnhem Land. This lady could be a medicine woman, a health worker, a political leader, a teacher or anyone, but that wasn't the point. Because she was an Aboriginal Australian she was getting served last.

And then it occurred to me that maybe my very presence in Arnhem Land was a part of the problem. The more we outsiders were around, trying to 'help', the lower we pushed Aboriginal self-esteem, by confirming their dependence and lack of self-reliance, by showing off how much more stuff we owned, and by participating in situations like this one.

Everything came into focus with sudden clarity, telling me it was time to move on. I couldn't find a clear direction forward in my job here, and just pressing on with a feeling of futility has never been in my nature. Something deep inside me was still trying to find my true calling – the job or vocation that would need my particular strengths and skills to create positive change. And this job wasn't it.

Besides, it seemed like forever since I had been climbing; occasional mountain-bike riding in buffalo-ridden bush, surf-skiing in crocodile-infested waters and staring down dogs in remote communities were just not a fitting substitute. I liked being consumed with adrenalin, not consumed.

And the clincher was that, if my past was anything to go by, the only way I was going to finally break up with Kel was if I got the hell out of there. Throughout my life I have learnt that it is dangerous to stand on a soapbox and take the moral or personal high ground, because time and time again I have proved myself a complete hypocrite. In the past I had certainly seen women staying in relationships in which their confidence was crashing around their feet and I had been quite vocal about the fact that I would never be so stupid. But, sure enough, here I was in such a relationship, rapidly losing my self-confidence but seemingly unable to escape.

The few times Kel had come to a meal with my friends had been disastrous. From his perspective I'm sure we seemed a bunch of weird hippies when we sat around on colourful rugs on the floor with the food spread out like a big picnic, talking passionately for hours about the issues facing Aboriginal people and the world. He would fidget uncomfortably and then leave at the first possible opportunity. And no matter how much I tried, I just couldn't find his shiny little fishing lures exciting and I had nothing in common with his friends or their girlfriends. Our relationship was causing my self-esteem to plummet to a new low that I didn't even know I was capable of, but because he lived just around the corner I seemed unable to find the strength to break up.

In all my travels since university I had yet to set foot beyond Australia's shores. Heading to the other side of the world seemed like the most appropriate way of ending things with Kel for good, and what better place to start than England, where I could work as a physio and earn pounds, and have easy access to Europe. Besides, reputedly there was some great climbing in the UK.

In Gove I had met Michelle, a nurse originally from Lismore in New South Wales but who had spent much of her qualified life working in Alice Springs. She had a way of observing from the sidelines, her wicked sense of humour hidden behind huge watchful brown eyes. On the surface we were complete opposites – I was big, she was small; I was loud, she was quiet; I told everyone everything about me within five minutes of meeting them, whereas Michelle took time and quietly worked out where she stood before opening herself up; I was brash, she was measured. We had an instant and profound connection.

Michelle too was ready to leave and had been planning to head abroad for some time, so together we organised our working visas and medical registrations from Gove. I left Arnhem Land a month after Michelle, with a lot of the wind taken out of my sails, but ready to find new horizons.

My passing shadow left little, if any, lasting trace on Aboriginal land. But these Indigenous Australians certainly left a permanent mark on me.

THE TOTALLY DELECTABLE TURKISH BREAKFAST

Serve it on a big platter with small plates for each person so that you can help yourself to as much as you can possibly fit in. A huge advantage of this type of breakfast (apart from being delicious) is that unlike the good old greasy fry-up, you can eat until there is no room left and not feel like you have to have a nap to sleep it off!

- Turkish bread (preferably warm)

- Big chunks of fetta

- Kalamata and green olives

- Fresh tomatoes, sliced

- Fresh cucumber, sliced

- Boiled egg (optional – I have a suspicion that the Turkish hostel owners only add this touch for us Western tourists, having heard of our big greasy fry-ups)

SIX

Journey to the Middle East

I headed home from Arnhem Land to gather my very confused thoughts before leaving for the other side of the world. My return to Brisbane was surreal. This city, which had once seemed so small and friendly, now felt like a concrete jungle, noisy and hectic and confusing.

My friends in Brisbane noticed the change in me immediately and commented on how serious and introverted I had become. I couldn't believe that they could just be content with having fun in light of the problems that were facing Australia and the world. I quickly sought refuge in the tranquillity of my parents' house on the coast.

Four weeks later I arrived in London, the cornerstone of the old British Empire, on a predictably bleak and wet day. But this wasn't proper rain; there were no Northern Territory downpours. It was just an endless grey drizzle that drifted into the dirty cracks in the pavement and washed irreverently past the litter. After the pristine expanse of Arnhem Land I had thought Brisbane was big, but now it paled in comparison. London seemed like the most massive, smelly, dirty and lonely place I could possibly imagine. Everyone ignored one another and me, and the noise and filth were unbelievable.

Even through my jet-lagged daze I could see clearly that I had to get out. And so, from a guide book in my overcrowded hostel, I planned my passage to one of the reputed meccas of climbing in Britain – Llanberis, a little town nestled amongst the mountains of Snowdonia National Park. I left London on the first available train.

And thank goodness for being a climber! Before darkness blanketed the mountains on my second day in Llanberis I had found myself some climbers in the rugged cloudy peaks and planned a climbing adventure with a cockney bloke called Johnny-Boy for the next day. Walking down from the wet, misty mountains we had considered different routes and possibilities, until we finally decided on an action plan. We would head for the tip of North Wales, where I would do my first ever climb on the sea cliffs of Gogarth. Perfect.

How lucky can you get? Not only had I found myself a climbing buddy, but I had found one with a crooked grin and eyes sparkling with dry British wit, ever ready for a laugh.

We arrived at the sea cliffs of North Wales in the late morning. I hadn't been climbing for more than a year now and was feeling far from strong. Looking out at the horizon, doubt was setting in. Maybe he just hadn't noticed that enormous sheet of solid water approaching us ...

'Hey Johnny, do you reckon we have enough time? I mean it's chucking it down over there.'

'Oh, yeah. No worries, mate. It's dry now, isn't it?'

What I was yet to learn is that climbing in the UK requires a different attitude to the prospect of bad weather. Back home in Australia, rain generally means a cancelled trip, but if you had this attitude in the UK you would never go anywhere. A small window in the weather is enough to send Pommie climbers running for the cliffs; waiting just long enough for the rock to dry, they set up and climb in the hope they will get to the top before the next downpour.

Oh well, when in Rome ...

We hurried to the cliff, ignoring the rapidly approaching clouds, and abseiled down to a little ledge near the bottom.

The rough swell threw itself violently against the rock, the spray reaching just below my feet. On a nearby ledge stood a seagull, and this fearsome creature was far from happy at our intrusion. I was feeling even less happy at having upset it because my own narrow ledge was barely three feet across, rendering me effectively trapped. This is not a good situation to be in with a British seagull.

Now, here I have a bone to pick. Poms make such a bloody song and dance about the size of the spiders in Australia, but they have kept awfully quiet about their gulls. Let me tell you that there should be warnings handed out with the entry visas into the UK. They seem to have bred up a super-race of chicken-sized gulls, with tempers to match. At least spiders don't have whopping great beaks and a vendetta against all humans.

I looked from the gaping beak of the angry bird to our only escape route. The first drops of rain splashed against the rock. Great.

After an embarrassing half-hour of untangling the mess I had made of our ropes, Johnny left the ledge. To my profound relief he turned out to be a fantastic and very fast climber and I fed out the rope quickly, nerves jangling from the incessant squawking from my left.

Once he had set up his ropes at the top, with relief I started to work my way carefully up the rock face, leaving my unhappy feathered companion screeching up at my backside. The waves thundered below, wetting me with a thin mist of salt water. The rock was dripping and slippery under my fingers and climbing shoes, but I was determined I was not going to fall off on this, our first climb together. The world around me receded, and all that mattered were the textures and features before me and the position and movement of my body. Peace, beauty, challenge and tranquillity. It was breathtaking.

To my surprise, and to my own and the seagull's immense relief, I pulled myself over the lip of the cliff and onto solid ground, where Johnny-Boy sat with rain pouring off his raincoat, laughing in my direction.

'I guess that rain was a bit closer than I thought!'

I didn't care. The rock, our gear and I were soaked, but my head was spinning from the kind of high that comes from absolute and intense happiness and exhilaration.

We ran for cover through the now steady rain to the nearby climbers café. It was crammed with steaming bodies and the rowdy chatter of the other climbers who had retreated to wait for the next break in the weather. This was my next lesson in climbing in England. Due to the regularity of crappy conditions, near every good climbing site is a fantastic café and/or favourite pub to retreat to. No matter how cold, wet, hurt, frustrated and exhausted you are, you can rely on there being a mug of steaming hot tea with an enormous flapjack waiting nearby.

After we'd bought our food, we pushed through the steaming crowd to join an already overcrowded table, shouting in conversation above the uproar. They crammed in even tighter, and we exchanged stories and contact details over a pint of tea.

The old me was back. My memories of Arnhem Land and Kel were fading into the background of new friends, climbing, buttery oats, fun and adventures. I was ready to start again.

Of course, when a cappuccino ends up costing about six Australian dollars it doesn't take long for the good old Aussie bank balance to take a serious blow. At this time the Australian dollar was worth just over thirty pence so the cost of living was scarily about three times as much as back home. There was nothing else for it but to get myself a job. However, there was a problem, other than not wanting to end my holiday – my registration to work as a physiotherapist in Britain had still not come through.

There was another option for the interim. I could work as a locum physiotherapy assistant for a much better wage than most other work. The only such job going? Six weeks as assistant in the Geriatric Rehab Unit, North Middlesex, in the outskirts of London. Back to the city where I had sworn I would never stay, to take a position in a hospital in an area of physiotherapy I had sworn I would never work in.

But at least by the end of this stint, I had saved up some cash and was ready to catch up with Michelle, my friend from Arnhem Land. Together we were planning to head to the Middle East for three weeks.

From personal experience I have a word of advice for women planning a trip to Turkey. Unless you're after 'that' kind of a good time, whatever you do, don't choose a pretty girl – or any girl, for that matter – as your travelling companion. Take a bloke, and you'll have a ball.

Michelle was probably the worst person to be travelling in Turkey with because every cell of her delicate and wide-eyed self seems to magnetically attract men. It is a completely involuntary effect and happens almost despite her efforts to the contrary, but it brings them swarming to her and they just won't go away. She looks at them quietly and curiously over the rim of her glasses, and they fall at her feet.

This effect was magnified in Turkey to a painful degree and the fact that she is also the kind of person who would be horrified at the thought of hurting someone's feelings made things a whole lot worse.

I had to get out of Istanbul before the trail of Turkish salesmen panting at our heels drove me mad. We left this hectic city to discover the west coast of Turkey's 'Tourist Road'. Quite contrary to my preconception that being in Turkey would stretch my cultural and travelling horizons to their outermost boundaries, our journey down the west coast was kind of like being on a guided tour but without the guide. All the systems, transport, information, and accommodation are designed to steer everyone in the same direction – through all the 'best' spots, and into all the rug shops. Our travels were punctuated with the familiar faces of the hordes of fellow travellers armed with their Lonely Planet travel guides following the same route. It was easier to find a bus to where you wanted to go than it is in Australia.

Unfortunately, Michelle and I as a team just didn't seem to have what it took to escape the stream of tourists and get off the beaten track. We were doomed from the start in any case as it rapidly became apparent that Michelle and I, despite our friendship, had very different agendas. I wanted to get away from the cities and explore the 'real' countryside and mountains, whereas Michelle wanted to explore the historical and spiritual wealth of this vibrant nation.

As a result, we could agree on nothing, and consequently got sucked along with everyone else on a tour of Gallipoli, exploring ancient Roman ruins and roaming through noisy souks in bustling cities.

By the time we reached the seaside town of Oludinez – a very beautiful and sleepy spot nestled beside the Mediterranean – we finally had to admit to each other that if we were going to stay sane we would need some time apart, at least for a day or two. We left the beachfront camping ground on our first morning there and headed in different directions along the dirt road that stretched along the coast. Michelle headed towards town and I headed for the hills.

I breathed a sigh of relief, and imagined Michelle doing the same. Now I could explore. I threw my daypack on my back, craned my neck to look up at the mountaintops and found what looked like a track off the dirt road heading uphill away from the ocean.

Finally, no people, buses, fumes, markets, salesmen or carpets. I was back to the simplicity of working my way, step by step, through trees and grass. In time I lost the path and the close branches scratched at my bare arms and legs. On impulse I started running through the bush, my lungs taking in the clear air and my ears filling with the sound of my own deep breaths and the rustling of the bush. Freedom! I lost all thoughts of where I was going, why I was going there – or whether I was going to get lost. I was alone, where I wanted to be, and my mind was clear at last.

Three hours later commonsense returned with a flood. I looked around at my scrubby world and realised that I was completely disoriented. I tried to recall the tracks I had taken. I had spent the last hours going up and down in the foothills and twisting and turning with each new whim, assuming that I would find my way out eventually.

But now I wasn't so sure. I considered my supplies: no map, no more water, no more food, no watch ... and absolutely no idea of where I was. How could I have been so stupid? Involuntarily, I giggled as I considered what Mum would think if she knew of my predicament – lost in the bush alone with no supplies or warm clothes, near a remote town in the middle of the 'dangerous' Middle East, and it was getting late in the day.

Still, it didn't really matter. This was kind of fun, really. I had wanted an adventure and this was certainly it. I knew that there were only two ways to go, up or down, and if I kept on heading down I would eventually get to the sea.

But it's amazing just how confused you can get when the sun is hidden by trees and the land is hilly. My attempts to maintain a straight direction were futile, and I pushed on with increasing apprehension. Time went by and the sun drifted across the sky. I tried not to panic. I had no idea how long it was going to take to find my way out of here. I prepared myself mentally for a night in the open. In shorts and a shirt it was going to be cold, and I was already getting rather peckish and thirsty. I wondered if there were wild pigs in the Turkish bush.

I had almost given up hope when I stumbled across something worthy of a bad ending in a trashy adventure movie. The bush opened into a clearing and at its centre sat a small ancient ruin – complete with a group of overweight American tourists crowded around it. Obviously I couldn't be far from the road.

Just a ten-minute walk and I was back in Oludinez and heading for the sparkling waters of the Mediterranean. Exhilaration tingled in my fingers and toes as I ran down the beach and jumped into the warm emerald ocean fully clothed. Then, dripping and happy, I stretched out on the beach of smooth pebbles, my face and body bathed in softening sunlight, smiling as I looked deep into the perfect blue sky. Alive. Free. Happy. Exhausted. This was the life.

But what was that racket behind me? I turned to see a jeep being loaded in front of a shop, with 'Paragliding' splashed in bright colours across its sides. I had seen the brightly billowing sails of paragliders around the Sunshine Coast, like parachutes but with a person dangling in a comfy seat as they spiralled up and down in coastal air currents. Now was surely the perfect time to give it a go. Tourists were clambering in and their bags were being thrown on top. I ran across the beach, its pebbles loose under my feet, just as the jeep pulled out and roared off towards the mountains. Damn it. But maybe it was still worth asking.

'Hi there, um – you know that jeep that just left. Is there any chance of me joining it?'

'You serious?!' He was looking me up and down. Not another bloody Turkish man cracking on to m – then I realised he was critically assessing my dripping shorts and shirt and sandals. Not ideal paragliding attire.

'Absolutely!' I grabbed some money from my handbag and placed it on the counter. Nothing talks louder in Turkey than US dollars.

'Okay, lady, but we must hurry. We have one pilot left.'

The pilot, his paraglider, the store owner and I squeezed into a clapped-out old ute and roared off up the road after the jeep. Twenty minutes of stomach-churning driving later and we had caught up, but by the time I transferred across to the jeep I was starting to shiver uncontrollably. My pilot jumped onto the roof with the luggage, and now we started the steep upwards climb.

Apparently it is not uncommon for people who have paid up in full for their paragliding to lose their courage halfway up this treacherous mountain road and elect to get out of the jeep and wait for a lift back down. Luckily I couldn't focus too clearly on the dangers of the road because I was preoccupied with the icy chill that was seeping into my bones. The braver of my fellow passengers clicked away at the view with their cameras as I tried to huddle out of the icy cold breeze coming in the windows. To amuse myself, I once again thought about my mother's likely reaction were she to witness my latest predicament.

The road went on and on, and I felt my lips getting cold and hard. I rubbed my hands together to bring blood and warmth to them, and then held them over my chin and neck. In some places nearly the whole road had broken away and plunged down the steep mountainside; at such points our jeep negotiated its way over the narrow sliver of track that remained.

After ascending 2000 vertical metres we finally pulled up onto the top of Mt Baba Dag (*Father Mountain*). There were paragliders and tourists everywhere. We were in a line-up of about twenty gliders and I was going blue with the cold.

At least I had plenty of time to meet my pilot, who had climbed down from the roof of the jeep. One good look at him and it didn't take a rocket scientist to figure out that I might be doing the drive back down. We were definitely not a well-matched paragliding team.

Randy wasn't Turkish. In fact he was about as far from being Turkish as you can get. Rather than being small and slight with black hair and a moustache, he had sandy hair, was well over six foot, and was built like an American footballer. It was going to take one hell of a strong wind to lift the combined weight of the two of us off the ground. For the first time I started to evaluate the relative risk of what I was about to do, and I didn't much like my computations.

'Um, Randy ... Do you think we are too heavy to fly together?'

'Yeah, maybe. Especially today, because the wind is very light.'

'Oh. So you don't think we'll be flying then?' (Phew.)

'Oh, don't worry about that – we'll take off. We'll just have to wait a while. The wind should pick up a bit later.'

I looked at the sun, which was already nearing the horizon. Pilots were lifting their sails to take off. Some were aborting due to lack of lift, but some were launching themselves off the cliff and disappearing into the valley below. They were all about half the size of Randy and me.

'Look, Claire, I'm sorry if I seem a little distracted. It's just that one of my best mates, a really experienced pilot, took off from here and crashed into the mountainside and died a few weeks back. Just over there [pointing just to the left of the launch site]. I was pretty shaken up and I haven't flown since. This is kind of like getting back on the horse for me.'

'Oh – I'm sorry.' And really I was. My stomach was starting to crawl with millions of little ants. This, combined with the cold, was beginning to make me feel a bit sick.

'Hey, you don't look so good. You must be freezing. Do you want a cup of chai?'

'What, up here?'

'Yeah, sure. There's a hut over there.'

And so there was. Hidden just below the flat mountaintop perched a little tin shed. Inside it the Turkish paragliding pilots were clustered around a big pot of chai tea while their clients shivered outside.

'*Merhaba.*' One of the ten or so short, dark-haired men greeted Randy as we entered.

'*Merhaba* ... No wind, eh!'

The chai did little to warm my frozen bones.

'Hey, Claire. You take my jumper. I'm too hot really.'

'No, I couldn't. I'm all right' (Best to keep the pilot healthy).

'Take it.'

I wrapped his enormous jumper around my shoulders and, combined with the chai, I started to thaw a little. But the cold was the least of my concerns. At least I was alive at this point.

When we finally left our haven, a sharp breeze cut through the loose weave of the jumper and Randy pulled his bare arms across his body. The wind was picking up, and the number of paragliders at the top had thinned in our absence. Still, there wasn't much left of the day.

'I reckon we are going to get off.'

'Really – Great.' (Dammit! Why was I doing this?)

Randy heaved the bulky bag containing his paraglider off the top of the jeep and we plodded closer to the launch site. Then he started the meticulous process of setting up his glider on the ground: first, he laid out the billowing sail of brightly coloured material. Then he sorted and arranged a bewildering array of strings leading from the sail, that attached to a double-seated harness. Even though I didn't know him, I could sense a reservation in his actions. He mumbled under his breath as he worked.

'Geez, I'm really feeling nervous about this jump.'

'Hey, look, we don't have to go. I don't mind. Honestly!'

'No, no – I really need to do it. It was just so horrible to see him spiralling out of control ...'

I hoped to God he was just stirring me, that perhaps he did this to all of his passengers, but there was a sincerity in his eyes that stopped me from questioning him further.

Finally, it was our turn to jump. The breeze still seemed very light to me as I looked nervously towards the edge, where the top of the mountain just ended, abruptly plunging into a deep valley that spanned between us and a high summit in the distance. Then Randy said we were all set up and ready to go.

'Are you sure the wind is strong enough?' Geez, I sounded like such a wuss.

'It should be fine. Now, Claire, what you have to do is run as hard as you can towards the edge of the cliff and just keep on running and running and running, even after you feel your feet lift off the ground. Don't stop running until I say so, then you can slip your feet into this little ladder and sit back in your harness. Okay?'

'Yep.' My voice squeaked from somewhere far away.

No! This was far from okay. I didn't know how the hell I was meant to run with this harness on, which felt like an enormous second butt hanging off my back. I was in front of Randy, who stood with his second butt securely attached, close behind me. Trailing behind us was the tangle of strings and sail that would theoretically stop us from plummeting straight down to join his friend in oblivion and a very messy end. It wasn't okay at all.

'Remember – just keep on running as hard as you can. We are really heavy so we'll have to go extra fast to get our weight off the ground, and I can only go as fast as you do so it's up to you. If you stop too soon then we could just go straight down off the edge. So remember just keep on running. You still okay?'

'Yep.' (Nooooo!)

Randy pulled on some strings and our paraglider's blue sail lifted into the sunset-stained sky.

'Right. GO!'

Eyes fixed on the horizon, I dug my feet into the ground and pushed my body forward. We didn't move – the resistance from the sail was too strong. But I pulled harder and felt Randy straining forward behind me. We started to move in slow motion towards the edge of the cliff. I pushed my feet frantically with all the power I could muster.

The edge got closer and closer but we were going painfully slowly. Then gradually we built up speed, faster and faster. The edge was just there, rapidly approaching under my nose. Now we were going too fast to stop. We were never going to get off the ground!

Then the ground disappeared from beneath my feet. I kept on pumping my legs manically but there was nothing there, nothing to push on to make us go faster. We'd had it! We were going down for sure. HEELLLLP!

'Okay, you can put your feet up now.'

I looked down to see my feet dangling in nothingness. The ground had gone, dropped all the way to that distant valley below, deep green in the evening shadow … and we weren't plummeting towards it. I put my feet in the little ladder and pushed myself back into my seat harness.

And then I had a chance to take it all in. We were floating through the air. Around me and below me little puffy clouds drifted aimlessly, tinted pink with the sunset, and we were flying with them. We swung from side to side as Randy effortlessly tugged on the strings. There was nothing tangible below us, beside us, above us.

'Claire, that was amazing. In all my time doing paragliding doubles, I have never known anyone to run without any hesitation over the edge of a cliff on their first jump. You are one fearless chick. That was really cool.'

Fearless? From behind me he had thought my petrified attempt at gaining speed was bravado. Bonus! Who was I to shatter his delusion? Anyway, I was too overwhelmed with sheer joy to answer. We had done it – we were flying! The horizon opened out as we rounded the side of the mountain to reveal the sun beginning to dip down below the ocean.

'Hey Claire, do you want to go through a cloud?'

'Wow! Yeeeah!'

We floated like a brightly coloured feather towards a little puffy cloud and silently drifted into its cold, misty whiteness. The world was gone. There was nothing, just the whisper of passing through pure, pristine beauty. That a place like this existed in the world – and I was living and breathing it – was beyond belief.

'You know, Claire, you should really learn to fly. It's in you, I can tell.'

'Yeah. I think you might be right.'

Although taking off hadn't proved a problem for two very large people, landing on the beach in a light breeze was a different matter altogether. Thankfully, as the passenger, I was practically sitting in Randy's lap so he caught the brunt of our crash-landing on his tailbone.

Later, when we got back into the town, Randy limped off to the shop with his paraglider while I ran back to our camping ground to meet up with Michelle. I was already two hours late, but I didn't care. My feet still weren't touching the ground. I could fly!

I dragged Michelle into town to meet the paragliding pilots at their local bar. Randy was knocking back stiff scotches to numb his aching back, and shifting uncomfortably in his seat. He moved across to make a wide gap and we joined the table. All eyes, other than Randy's, landed appreciatively on Michelle, who was looking more than a little uncomfortable with the unwanted attention.

Before I had downed even my first beer, Randy was looking deep into my eyes and, with the sincerity of three scotches and a pint of Guinness, he offered to give me free instruction to the point where I could get my paragliding licence, no strings attached (other than perhaps some free physiotherapy treatment). I could stay in Oludinez for two more weeks, and then I would have my licence to fly.

It was like a wonderful crazy dream.

Michelle, it turned out, wasn't that keen to wait in this tiny little town while I learnt to paraglide. She intended to head off regardless.

Which to choose – friendship or fun? I chose leaving for the sake of our friendship, although maybe staying would have done more for the cause. Michelle and I organised to join a tourist boat heading south to the ancient city of Olympus. My paragliding dream was going to have to be put on hold.

'Claire, I'm going to head back to Istanbul early to see the Blue Mosque before I leave. We've been in Turkey almost three weeks, and I still haven't been inside a mosque!' Strain was showing on Michelle's face. By now friendship had been taken to and beyond its tolerance limit with the clashing of our expectations. We had tried to talk things over during the course of many deep and draining conversations, but we just didn't seem able to find a happy place together.

Unlike Michelle, I still hadn't decided what on earth I really wanted to do in the Middle East, but I knew I would feel cheated if I left now. I had seen some amazing things, but I still felt my experience of this place had been limited to just 'seeing the sights'. The paragliding had blown me away, but however hard I tried not to regret my decision to leave, that particular memory was laced with disappointment at the opportunity lost. There must be another, more authentic experience – something that would maybe strike me at my core – waiting for me in this place that was so different from my own country and reality.

When Michelle left, our parting had an awful feeling of finality. As I waved her bus away, the sadness of a changed friendship was laced with the exhilaration of independence. Now I could do whatever I wanted. I didn't need to consult and deliberate about decisions, I could just *do* and *experience* as I wished!

So here I was alone in the amazing centre of Turkey, in a town called Goreme. Surrounding me was a famous landscape, created from volcanic tufa and looking so much like it belonged on another planet that it was used as one of the locations for *Star Wars*. This incredible landscape was formed sixty million years ago by the eruption of nearby volcanoes, which spread a deep layer of ash over the land. This dust hardened into the soft porous stone called tufa. Over time the erosive forces of air and water shaped the most intriguing landscape you can imagine, not dulled by the fact that cut into the sides of the tufa landforms are doors and windows. Many of the local inhabitants still live in caves carved into this compressed dust. In fact I was sitting cross-legged at a low table, in a tufa cave hostel, with a thick cushion between me and the rug-lined floor. The smell of breakfast – fetta, tomatoes, olives, eggs and wood-fired turkish bread – warmed the dining room. From the windows I could see out across the rooftops to the tufa caves beyond. Music wailed in the background as groups from all over the world huddled discussing their plans.

The owner of this dining room, a young Turkish man, had just moved from speaking fluent English to me, to fluent French at the table next to me, to fluent Japanese at the table in the far corner, to fluent German with the two at the counter. One thing was for sure – these Turkish people sure took tourism seriously, and I had to admit, they did it well. He spoke six languages, and most of the hostel owners seemed to speak more than one. I was still struggling with getting the English language right.

I wasn't alone at my table. Jane, a New Zealander, was enthusiastically piling her fetta, tomato and olives onto a slab of spongy warm bread (a breakfast to recommend to anyone!) and next to her was Marty, who turned to face me:

'So where are ya heading now, Claire?'

I had first met Marty in the ancient city of Olympus, while staying there in a very groovy tree-house hostel. I had come to loathe running into the same fellow-travellers wherever we went, because it destroyed any sense of having a personal and exciting adventure. Comparing travel tales just became a familiar and predictable ritual. (*So you've been to … Yes … And you've been to … Yep … Oh and how about … Yeah!*)

But seeing Marty again was different – a real buzz, in fact – because he was a climber and, like myself, he had packed his climbing shoes and chalk bag, just in case. We had scrambled around on some rocks in Olympus and then said goodbye, as Michelle and I had moved on. But now here he was in Goreme, just when I was looking for a new direction.

His mischievous eyes looked expectantly at me, his blond brows creased with the anticipation of a possible adventure, his scruffy travelling beard and long hair symptoms of more than a year on the road. Like me, he assumed that any fellow climber must have something fun planned.

'To be honest, Marty, I have no idea. But I've had it with tourists. I want to do something exciting. Any ideas?' The ball was back in his court.

'How about Syria? I'm thinking of crossing the border. I'm just not sure at this stage whether to go home or go on.'

Bingo.

Jane looked up from her bread. 'Really? That sounds pretty cool.'

And I had to agree with her. 'Syria sounds awesome. I'm in.'

'There are a few other Aussies who are keen to come along. We could probably get a crew together.'

Our plans were made. Jane and I would be catching a bus across the border together, and we would meet up with the others in Aleppo. I emailed Mum and Dad:

Things are great. My plans have changed again. Michelle has headed home, and I am heading to Syria with two Australians and a New Zealander. Apparently there is no email and very poor phone contact from Syria so don't worry if you don't hear from me for a while. I am having a blast.

Love Claire.

My parents were not impressed.

I have a second word of advice for people travelling to the Middle East: whether you have made the mistake of travelling with an attractive female or not, never, I repeat *never* get off a bus without your bags.

Jane and I boarded our bus in Goreme, and then lost it at the Turkey/Syria border. Or more accurately it left without us, with all our bags (and maps) still on board. We looked with not a small degree of confusion around the bleak and desolate surroundings of the border post that was now minus our bus. Cripes.

My apprehension didn't lift when we managed to hitch a ride with a non-English-speaking Arab man into Aleppo, where we hoped like hell we'd find our bus. Being squeezed between Jane and our turbaned driver – with four of his mates in the tray-back, while heading out into the desert – wasn't exactly a relief.

But this seemingly dodgy situation turned into our first eye-opening insight into a culture that is often feared in our own countries. In Syria it seemed that, when asked for help, whoever we asked would drop whatever they were doing, find a family member or friend to take over their job, and then commit themselves entirely to our cause, even if neither party could understand a word of what the other was saying. It was only with the help of our turbaned driver and countless random Syrians that we finally managed to find the bus station and, incredibly enough, rendezvous with all our belongings.

As we wandered bemused from the bus station, for once happy to feel the weight of our packs dragging on our shoulders, we realised that we had landed in a place that was very different to Turkey. Apart from Jane and me, there were no other westerners in sight. The people were dressed in exotic costumes, many of the men turbaned like Yasser Arafat, some of them with long white Arabian dresses, and the women covered head to toe with their gowns. There were no signs in English, no restaurants offering a menu of pizza and hot chips. No-one was beckoning us into their shops. The only people paying attention to us were those staring curiously at us as we struggled along with our backpacks.

The city of Aleppo reverberated with the buzz of life and activity – voices shouting, children screaming, traffic blaring, blasting horns, screeching tyres and noisy throttles. Huge bags of olives sat next to sacks of spices and nuts. Pita bread hung out to dry on the railings between the pedestrians and the motor traffic, or was laid out flat on the dirty pavement, to be picked up later and sold by the store-owners.

As we walked by, a young man spilt a huge bag of olives all over the pavement. He scratched around people's hurrying feet, grabbing handfuls and putting them back into the large sack. Dogs sniffed around, babies screamed, young boys sat on the pavement offering to polish the shoes of passers-by. Groups of men with moustaches and exotic looks crowded around their favourite falafel stall, congesting the narrow walkways while eating the delicious falafel and salad-filled pitas that had probably just been picked up from the pavement.

I was thankful we were on foot rather than driving a car. The roads were a battleground and there were no rules of combat. It was every man for himself. There were no lanes, just cars filling the tarred surface wherever they could squeeze in.

My relief to be a pedestrian was short-lived as we came to a distressed halt. We inspected our map more closely to make sure we were on the right track, but there was no other way – we were going to have to cross a major road to get to the hostel.

We stood hesitantly, heads turning from side to side as the never-ending stampede of cars surged forward. Our jaws dropped as we watched the locals weaving across. They just stepped out into the moving traffic and, with a cacophony of horn blasts, the oncoming cars would somehow manage to stop just before bowling them over. They would run and weave through the traffic, sometimes having to stand stationary amongst the tide of flashing metal until they did their final dash for the other side. There was no system, no order, no right time to go, no right of way. We were never going to get across.

'Hey Claire – there's someone about to go. Let's follow her.'

We loped our way over to a fully gowned woman, her tiny frame poised as she watched the traffic intently. Just as we got to her side, she was off. Sticking behind her like glue, we followed her into the chaos. Bumper bars came within inches of our thighs, horns blasted in our ears, cars swerved in front of and behind us. She was going for it without hesitation. We made it unscathed to halfway across and then there was the turmoil coming from both directions around us – cars, buses, trucks, and motorbikes, all fighting each other and the pedestrians to get to their destination. Then she was off again, scuttling fearlessly through the frenzy with us on her tail.

'Holy cow!' Jane cried as we slumped, sweating, at the other side of the road. 'That was mad!'

The little lady had walked off serenely along the busy sidewalk.

Although her eyelids were hidden from view behind her black veil, I'm sure she didn't so much as bat them. This place was surreal.

What was the deal with these Syrian women? I am reluctant to speculate on what is outside my own cultural experience, but based on my own observations there was something so quirky going on with women in this country that I just have to mention it. On the streets, women – hugely outnumbered by men – were hidden behind the hijab; shrouds of material covering their body and head and often covering the whole face. Mostly these costumes were in colours, some drab and some bright, but many were clad entirely in black. Apart from anything else they had to be roasting – we were sweating in our long skirts and T-shirts. But there was more going on than met the eye.

In the souk, nestled between rugs, clothing, olives, soaps and smoking pipes were displays of flamboyant and raunchy female underwear that made us liberated western women blush like schoolgirls. And they were lit up with bright spotlights for everyone to see. They looked like costume displays, with frills and lace and vivid colours, and excruciatingly narrow G-strings. What *did* those women have on under their gowns? Did their men buy them these items for their own entertainment, or did these women have a concealed world of sensual extroversion, liberation and opulence?

I desperately wanted the chance to communicate with some women, but they were out of reach, hidden away behind veils, closed doors and a foreign language. What was their life like? It didn't look that great from a western point of view, but who was I to say? I hadn't met a single woman since arriving. These questions went unanswered for me.

In the bigger cities it seemed to be a little different. Westernisation appeared to have seeped in and some young women were dressed in western clothes, wearing bright lipstick and heavy eyeliner. I learnt that some of them were attending universities. Change was afoot. But such women seemed by far the minority.

My big chance to see behind the veils and into the world of Syrian women in the flesh came one day with an excursion to a bathhouse. Jane, Sarah, two other girls from our hostel and I were taken by the hostel owner on a zigzagged path through the city, and into a narrow back street. He stopped at a curtained opening in an old brick wall and knocked. The stained yellow drape was pulled aside just enough to allow a scarf-covered head to poke out through the gap. After a hushed conversation our guide disappeared into the streets, and the curtain was now pulled aside sufficiently to allow us through.

We entered into the world of the steam bath. Before us was a room that was dark and dank, with fingers of mould and mildew streaking down from the corners of the walls, smudging the dirty paint. The woman threw off her headscarf and to my surprise I realised she was in a singlet top, with her skirt pulled high and tucked into her elastic waistband, revealing skinny hairless legs that suggested she was an old woman. But how old I couldn't tell. Her hennaed hair shone bright red against the pale, sun-starved skin of her wrinkle-free face. Much better than any results obtained from Oil of Olay, I'm telling you!

She took us to some wooden benches and gestured for us to undress. Yikes. I wasn't getting all my gear off around people I hardly knew, and my western hygiene alert was on full. I looked around at the others.

'Do you think we should keep our pants on?'

They looked around and to my utter relief replied: 'Yeah ... definitely.'

We sat on our towels on the benches, our underpants on and our arms folded shyly around our naked bosoms. Our host returned, casting a slightly disgusted look at our modesty. What was she going to do with us?

We followed her through deeper into the building, our arms still crossed, until we emerged into a world of steam and water. A high shadowy ceiling hung over an area about the size of an average living room that was lined completely with stained white tiles, and darkened with the dank light and years of moisture. Around the edges water ran in deep, green channels.

Filling the room were women of all ages – some with young children – sitting and talking. They were completely naked as they slowly washed and massaged, and hennaed their hair. There was a ring of deep orange ochre staining the wet floor around them. Their skin, having rarely seen the sun, was milky white and flawless; their hair grew nowhere except on their heads.

The floor was discoloured from years of henna and bodies naked against it. We wore the only items of clothing in the room, but there was no way I was taking off this last vestige of modesty. We sat nervously in a circle around our host, wondering what came next. God, I couldn't lie on the floor near-naked with everyone sitting right next to me watching! I hugged my bosom tighter. Please don't pick me first.

Our host grabbed my arm and I was firmly guided onto my stomach. Well, that made that decision easy. But at least I had my undies on. Then I felt the sides of my pants being pulled away from my buttocks and pushed between the cleft. Then a set of strong hands started into this seldom-exposed area of my body. Yikes!

We western women must seem pretty filthy to the average Muslim lady. Sure, we shower, but how can you compete with someone whose skin never sees the outside world? It seemed that this little lady was determined to set me right. Just when I thought her hands had rubbed off any surface grime there could possibly be on me, a new sensation hit my now-tender skin. Cripes, what was this? *The loofah!*

I had never thought of using what is effectively a kitchen scourer on my skin, but she was going to stop at nothing to get me clean. She was going to strip me back to the basal layer if she had to. I couldn't believe there could be so much brawn in a woman of her size and age. She scrubbed and rubbed and pulled and stretched until she had covered every inch of my body, front and back.

Finally allowed to struggle back into an upright position, I wasn't at all sure I could stay there. I felt like a piece of bread dough that has just been kneaded to within an inch of its life by one of those buxom country women in floral dresses and which is consequently a sagging mound, unable to maintain its shape.

One by one the little old lady took my companions and laid them out on the tiles, and her sinewy arms and strong hands set to work on their near-naked bodies. I watched in a daze as my friends endured her onslaught. How she kept on going I don't know.

By the time we left, we had been in the intense humidity for about three hours. We had had any remaining modesty ripped from us; our skin was stripped and puckered from the moisture.

The rest of the residents of the bath we left still sitting and washing – for them, there seemed to be no sense of time. We paid our extraordinary host and in a delirious state wafted calmly through the bedlam outside, over the main road, and all the way back to the hostel. Despite seeing them in the flesh, the world of Syrian women was even more of a mystery than before.

But some things in Syria aren't quite as hidden and mysterious, although they really should be. Take, for example, the toilets. Anyone who has travelled extensively has at least one horrific toilet story to tell and Syria provides plenty of fodder for such heroic accounts.

Up to now I wasn't going too badly in that department. By the time we got to the seaside city of Latakia I was actually getting pretty cocky. All the travel guides had warned against unpackaged local foods, especially fruit without a covering (bananas and oranges are okay), but most of all it was said to be dicing with the devil to drink the water. Bottled water had to be checked to make sure the seal was intact, and watermelons were best avoided as the rumour was that they were sometimes filled with local water by injection to make them feel heavier and juicier. Water was a time bomb in westerners' stomachs.

But I had been eating at street stalls, restaurants, and even occasionally brushing my teeth in tap water. Everyone else had had 'the runs' except for Sarah and me, and life was good. I could usually hold on long enough to find a toilet that was remotely acceptable, sometimes longer than a day or two. Whenever asked, I could proudly say, 'Solid and functioning, thanks!'

I shouldn't have gloated. My undoing came from a plan of my own instigation: a great idea, but predictably lacking research and preparation. I had searched through the town for the tourist information centre, to try to find an exciting and adventurous destination, preferably involving some climbing or mountains off the beaten track. Unfortunately, what I found was not a tourist information centre for foreigners but for travelling Syrians.

No-one spoke English. There was some mild amusement as I tried to communicate with the receptionist with the help of an Arabic language book, embellished with what I thought was perfectly clear sign language, indicating mountains, rocks, and so on. The woman pulled out a map and pointed to a big lake. It looked like there were hills surrounding it. A single dead-end road headed out to the lake and a town was marked at the end of the track. There must be some rocks out there, I thought.

I bought the map and returned to the others. Marty, Jane, Sarah and Chris all thought it was a great plan, and we naively set out to get to the lakeside town by whatever means we could. Under the guidance of yet another typically helpful Syrian we found a minibus that was heading in the right direction. An hour or so later we were unloaded in the middle of empty hilly terrain next to a tiny shop with bananas, biscuits and apples spilling onto the pavement.

We showed our map to the curious crowd of villagers and children and they pointed down a rutted dirt road, looking bewildered and mildly amused. We pulled our backpacks to the side of the road and waited for a ride. Nothing came. Wasn't there a town at the other end of this road? Where were all the cars?

An hour later we were giving up hope. Jane was getting bored and entertaining herself by making monkey faces at the staring children and scratching her armpits and head, and Marty was playing hacky sack. As per usual, the local men were gaping eyes wide at Sarah's blonde ringlets that bounced behind her fashionably placed headscarf, and her busty figure that was barely hidden beneath her singlet and trousers (this outfit had caused a stir pretty much wherever we had gone so far). Eventually even she was enticed into borrowing my long-sleeved red shirt.

We toyed with the idea of buying supplies here but decided against it. That would just be more to carry. We would be able to get food and accommodation in the next town if we ever got a lift. Bad decision. *Very* bad decision!

At last! A tractor dragging a fully laden trailer trundled towards the shop. The first vehicle in two hours, and ideal for a party of five hitchhikers. What a stroke of luck. We put out our thumbs and it stopped.

An hour later, our vision blurry from sitting in the back of a tractor with no suspension on a dirt road, we rounded a corner and before us the lake stretched into the distance. We'd arrived. But where was the town?

A confused sign-language conversation ensued. Apparently there was no town. Only a bloody big lake, with dusty brown hills rising around it, and two tiny dwellings perched high on the hill, which were the houses of our drivers, who were now heading home for the night.

After another confused sign conversation (our drivers had absolutely no idea what on earth we were doing out there) we were dropped by the side of the lake. The earth was hard and dry. We had no food, barely any water, and a single one-man tent between us. It was going to be a cold night.

Things went from bad to a little better, to much *much* worse. Hungry and thirsty we huddled in the darkness around the tiny fire we had managed to build, the cold wind cutting through our clothes. We cheered as we saw the lights of a motorbike heading down the hill. Please let them be bringing us some food.

The three tractor drivers piled off a tiny scooter. And food they did bring. Out of a satchel came a gift from the gods. Hot chicken casserole and a big bowl of watery tabouli were laid out in front of us, along with a bag of oranges and of course some lukewarm chai tea. As I tucked into this wonderful gift of sustenance I was over-whelmed with a feeling of love for this country full of people ready to help us foreigners at every turn. The warmth and spice took away the chill of the night air.

We laughed and signed for hours across the campfire to the three Syrian men, who were still looking at us like we were crea-tures from another planet. When the last embers of our fire died, they piled back onto the tiny motorbike and we all curled up in and around the tent trying to shelter from the icy wind. At least our bellies were full.

I woke early. Something was not right. Deep inside my stomach a strange new sensation was curling its fingers, tighter and tighter. I lay still trying to get some warmth from the bodies that lay close. The tightening increased until it moved – downwards. I stood stiffly and looked around me. Oh no!

Anyone who has ever had diarrhoea will understand the panic I felt as I looked across the flat empty expanse of the lake's shore, and over to a single clump of bushes up the rocky hillside at least a kilometre away.

I seized the roll of toilet paper that every backpacker has at hand in the Middle East and started a slow waddle towards the bushes. I was in a horrible predicament. The faster I went, the more I felt my control of the situation slipping. But if I went too slow – I just had to get there soon or . . .

Time stood still and my world became a screaming war with my internal functioning. Willing myself to hold on, but about to lose control with every step, I felt like a marathon runner with the end in sight but not sure if they are going to be able to reach the finish line.

When I finally made it – thank God I made it! – well, I don't think I should say more. It was the beginning of my end. The end of enjoying my travels in the Middle East.

We packed up camp and, after waiting for two hours by the road, we managed to hitchhike with the same three fellows back to the shop. From here we found our way back to Latakia, by which time I was completely green.

My memory of the rest of the trip is only a painful blur of a fierce battle raging inside me. I remember curling up in pain as our bumpy minibus took us south towards Hama. Please just let me survive this six-hour drive, and then we can find a bed and a toilet. My stomach twisted in further anguish at the thought of a Syrian toilet.

It took us until midnight to get to Hama, by which stage I was in a sorry state. I admit it, I am completely pathetic when it comes to nausea and I was consumed with misery.

As much as I like to think of myself as a 'traveller' who doesn't need to use Lonely Planet guides (they are just for all the tourists), the fact that we ended up staying in one of the few hostels in Syria with clean western toilets was entirely thanks to the author of the Hama section. (Thank you, thank you, thank you!)

I spent the next eight days either in this pristine bathroom or curled up in a ball in bed in a state of complete devastation. I couldn't eat or drink. Surely there had to be nothing left inside me. But still it came. Several times when standing up to get to the toilet I blacked out, landing in a crumpled mess on the floor. Sarah, Jane,

Marty and Chris – although only recent acquaintances and ready to move on with their own travels – loyally stayed with me.

The clean white porcelain and tiles were only a small comfort. This was my first ever taste of being really sick and I didn't like it one bit. I, the independent brave international climbing explorer, just wanted my mum. I called home. As soon as I heard her sleepy voice, I broke down in tears. Between sobs, I managed to squeeze out the information that no parent ever wants to hear over the phone: 'Mum … I'm stuck … in Syria … and I'm … really … really … sick.' Both Mum and Dad still haven't forgiven me for that.

But I *was* stuck. I wasn't getting better. I was in the middle of Syria and everything just seemed to make me sicker. I just had to get back to hygiene. I managed to walk down to the hostel phone a second time to make enquiries about flying to England from Syria, but it was more than I had in the bank. I already had a return ticket to England but it was from Istanbul, all the way back in Turkey. So I booked a sixteen-hour bus ride back to Istanbul. Jane went to a chemist and bought me a cocktail of medications for the trip.

My short moment of euphoria when I lay down on the empty back seat was destroyed as I saw the bus driver approaching down the aisle with two turban-clad men in tow. I was, of course, unceremoniously removed from my prime location, despite pretending not to understand. Bloody men.

I was relocated to the last remaining aisle seat next to a huge lady who, before I managed to sit down, shuffled her rump across to claim half of my seat and stayed there for the sixteen hours it took to get to Istanbul.

Economy airline seats had never felt so spacious. Back in England I headed straight to the next best thing to my Mum and Dad – family friends in Bristol. I just wanted some grown-ups. But, despite their TLC and nursing, I wasn't able to hold in a solid meal until about two weeks after my return. My attempt to go on a twenty-minute walk through some nearby woodland a few days after returning had a messy and somewhat embarrassing end. Within the space of a month I lost over ten kilograms.

But no experiences in life are without positives. I had learned two important lessons.

The first: ten kilograms less makes a hell of a difference when scaling high walls. Despite feeling weakened and shaky, as soon as I was able, I headed to an indoor climbing wall. I had never climbed so well as after this month of being severely ill.

The second: be warned, unwary travellers – never accept tabouli from three Syrian men on a moped.

The world is the perfect size for the traveller's imagination – small enough that you think you can see it all, and big enough that you never will.

SEVEN

On the Move

My British physiotherapy registration had finally come through and so I headed up to Liverpool for a short stint of work to restock my coffers, working in the Orthopaedic Unit in the Royal Liverpool University Hospital. Immediately I experienced the Liverpool Christmas Rush ... but not the one to the shops. It goes something like this.

The wonderful Christmas spirit is everywhere; the streets are filled with happy shoppers and sparkling tinsel. Television sets are endlessly beaming reassuring images of smiling families opening gifts and laughing and drinking merrily around big colourful Christmas trees. Families everywhere have spent months preparing, in eager anticipation of gathering together for this joyous occasion. The shops are full to overflowing with happy faces and hands passing over credit cards.

At last the Big Day comes and all these meticulous plans come to fruition – but not quite as expected. Relatives all around the city remember that they can't stand the sight of each other. When forced by foul winter weather to spend prolonged periods trapped indoors together, otherwise peaceful folk turn to violence. Thus my colleagues experience their 'Christmas Rush', repairing people who have been punched, kicked, pushed off chairs and into walls, and injured in a multitude of fascinating ways by infuriated family members. This is invariably the busiest time of the year for the Royal Liverpool Orthopaedic Unit.

After six weeks of work in this city – building snowmen, gazing dreamily out of hospital windows at drifting snowflakes, going for walks through the lightly frosted mountains of Snowdonia, laughing at the awesome 'Scouser' accent, and being attacked with snowballs by random carloads of people – I knew it was time to go home. It seemed like a lifetime since I had seen my family and friends, and I was sick of having a permanently cold, red nose.

So, at the very end of December 2000, I flew back to Australia.

As soon as I arrived home I had an unexpected but profound impulse to head down to Victoria to see my two grandmas. Despite protests from my mother and father, on the grounds that I should recover from jetlag first, I at once packed my bags and headed south. Maybe some of that Arnhem Land intuition had rubbed off on me.

Mum decided to come with me and we stayed for the first night with her mother in Geelong. Jetlag hit me with a blinding thud as I unpacked my bags from the hire car. All I wanted was sleep, but that feeling wouldn't go away. Between yawns I told Mum.

'I'm just going to call Bea before I crash' (Bea being my father's mother).

'Darling, you should get some sleep and call her tomorrow.'

'No, I'll just call her now. It won't take long.'

I dialled the number and, sure enough, there she was. We had one of those conversations that you have with an older person when they have finally realised that you are an adult too. What had at times in my past been an awkward relationship, with me on the defensive against grandmotherly wisdom, seemed to have found a new comfortable level.

My grandmother Bea had weathered a tragic life. She had been born into an unhappy marriage, and had grown to be a stunning and highly intelligent young woman. At the age of eighteen she married Graham, a tall, handsome soldier who was ten years her senior. They set off on a life of adventure, sailing up and down the Queensland coast, and then exploring the Daintree in a Land Rover, with their steadily growing family. Just after the birth of their third child, tragedy struck. Graham suddenly became ill and had to be hospitalised. The nursing staff sent Bea home to be with her children, assuring her that after a night of care he would be fine. That night Graham died in hospital, without so much as a chance for her to say goodbye.

Bea was a shy, underconfident 27-year-old, with three children, no husband, and no home. She was avoided by her few friends because, as a young and beautiful widow, she was considered a threat. Her cherished, much older brother had been killed in the Second World War, so she was left depending for some financial support on her one remaining relative – Graham's very unsympathetic estranged father.

But Bea never dwelt on her past, although it lived with her in her eyes. Instead she filled her life with art, stylish clothes, Radio National, and the one cigarette she allowed herself to smoke each day. Her home, her food, her life were always impeccably organised and tidy.

Just recently life for Bea had finally taken a turn for the better. She had moved into a retirement village and established a close-knit bunch of friends. She was looking forward to the trip she was planning with my father (her eldest child) to revisit the places she had lived with her husband. Things were on the up.

'Hey, Mum, that was the nicest conversation that I have ever had with Bea. I'm so glad I called. She sounds happier than I have ever heard her, and she is chuffed that I have come down to visit so soon after getting home from the UK. I really think I am going to enjoy seeing her this time.'

I fell asleep happy and excited. I knew she would be proud of all I had done since we had last seen each other.

The next morning Mum popped into town, and when she came back she was white and shaken. 'I just saw the most awful car crash. The traffic is terrible. Those poor people.'

After breakfast we set off to visit Bea as arranged. Strange – she wasn't home. If there is one thing that Bea was, it was punctual and reliable, but there was absolutely no sign of her. After a long fruitless wait, we returned home.

Dad was on duty that day as a pilot and it was as he was taxiing into Brisbane airport that he received a message over the intercom to report immediately to the aerobridge as soon as he had left the plane. He knew from the tone of the message that it was bad news.

My brother James received the news at work. He headed straight for the airport to make sure Dad was okay. He wasn't. They arrived together in Melbourne. Dad hadn't seen his mother for several months.

The car was on the front page of the newspaper the next day. It was crushed beyond recognition: 'Two elderly ladies, 76 and 91, killed instantly in horrific accident on the corner of Noble and LaTrobe streets ... The 76-year-old driver failed to stop at a red light and drove directly into the path of an oncoming truck ... The driver of the truck was unharmed.'

Poor Bea. Just when life was starting to be good to her, it ended in twisted metal.

Following my brother James's lead wherever he went, and showing early climbing ability, pulling off a classic heel-hook and about to do a rock-over move.

Starting my lifetime mission of trying to get to the top of things.

A young love of nature.

A typical climber's rack – the gear used to place into cracks in the rock as protection.

Feeling pretty hard-core while top-roping at Kangaroo Point in Brisbane – before I realised that this was the soft option.

Living it up university climbing club style in a rented house in the Blue Mountains.

Leading up a crack using natural protection. Beautiful rock!

Having a blast seconding on an exhilarating sea cliff. Sometimes you don't have to be leading to get a serious rush.

The morning vista from my Kombi van, looking out over the RACQ depot in Charters Towers – a lovely place for a 21-year-old girl to spend the night on her own.

Luxury transport from the airport to the centre of Ramingining township.

Out collecting bush food with the ladies from Ramingining, about two hours drive away from the community in a 4WD.

Kel, a crayfish and a fish. Need I say more.

The surreal landscape around Goreme in central Turkey.

Inside a tufa cave with one of the locals. She invited us in, fed us Turkish coffee and cake, taught us how to tie head scarfs and showed us her handmade wares. We left her cave the proud owners of our very own socks, gloves, mini rugs, doilies and of course head scarfs. The Turkish have tourists totally figured out.

Sampling the apple-flavoured smoking pipe in Istanbul. Well, even a non-smoker has to give it a go. It apparently has no tobacco in it, and is the ultimate Turkish social experience.
(From left Michelle, another backpacker and me.)

Hitchhiking into the unknown in the back of a tractor in Syria. At this point we were all feeling so chuffed to have scored a lift that could carry all five of us, and our backpacks, that we didn't care too much about where exactly we were heading. That changed pretty soon after this photo was taken.
(From left Marty, me, Sarah and Chris. The Syrian blokes are in the front. Jane is taking the photo.)

Hanging out with Johnny-boy at the top of my first ever sea cliff climb in Gogarth, Wales. Wet, cold and ecstatic. This random and brief acquaintance opened the world of climbing in the UK for me.

Climbing in Cornwall with Roland and Angela (the couple I met on my first climbing trip to Wales). Roland is belaying me up to his perch on a multi-pitch climb in typically lovely English climbing conditions. Cold and wet, on green rock but exciting.

Flower Power and me in the backyard (our shed is just over to the right).

The *Endeavour* – taken from a rubber ducky in the middle of Bass Strait.

Vanessa and me at the wheel of the *Endeavour* on a windy evening in Bass Strait – it is really very hard to keep the ship going in a straight line.

Mum and Dad after spilling the beans about my ticket on the *Endeavour*.

Catching a breath. Note the harness – this was used to clip to the rigging when dangling at the top of the mast working with the sails – a very comforting thing when the boat is rocking from side to side.

Pia the Princess of Power at the top of Downhill Madness with another nervous tourist.

The most dangerous road in the world – this photograph doesn't come close to doing the steepness of the valley walls justice, but it gives an idea of how bloody long the ride was.

Bogged in a twenty-tonne truck in the middle of nowhere in Peru – fun!

Standing in front of the Big Red Truck, with Mt Chimborazo looming in the background. This photograph was sent to me by Pia with the title 'Claire looking grumpy'. Pretty much sums things up I think.

Sandro abseiling back down Mission Lunatica after our first ascent – what a view.

Triumphant at the end of the first-ever free climbing ascent of Mission Lunatica. Me, Mike and Sandro.

The Llaca valley. The refugio was situated just to the right of the lake at the bottom of the glacier. Mission Lunatica ascends the wall on the left side of the valley, but is hidden from view in this shot.

A wonderful little old lady in the marketplace in Huaraz, Peru. Note the angle of the photograph taken from my eye level.

Looking out past Adam's legs from the portaledge on the Bolt Route.

I have discovered a fantastic use for a freshly cooked pancake – the ultimate camping hot pack. When you get peckish simply pull it out of your pants and add your choice of toppings. Hmmm.

Adam in his element, and me in the background, before we hit the hard stuff and I dropped my bundle.

Adam and me looking out over the hills at Lindis Pass, New Zealand.

My flight back to the UK was scratched, and I stayed in Victoria to help sort out the threads of a life ended without warning. After six weeks of picking up the pieces of a devastated family, the strain was showing on all involved and we needed some light relief. Dad made a suggestion: 'Claire, there's a full-size replica of the *Endeavour* sailing ship moored in the Geelong harbour. I want to take you down there for a look.'

Not exactly my idea of an exciting outing, but what the hell. Dad needed to get away from all this and it was the sort of thing he would love.

Mum, Dad and I headed down to the harbour and there, moored with thick heavy ropes to the wooden dock, bobbed a vessel straight out of my history books – a tall ship identical to the one in which Captain Cook journeyed to Australia. Its wide wooden hull contrasted quaintly with the steel giants around it. Its high wooden masts were adorned with thick canvas sails neatly rolled up and tied with ropes to the horizontal struts. Ropes, wood, huge black pulleys ... it was from another time.

Inside was even more fascinating. The ship was an identical replica down to the materials used, the position of the hatches in the wooden deck, the knots used to hang the hammocks, the tables, the captain's cabin, the five-foot ceilings. All just as they had been 200 years before.

I got chatting with the second in command. The *Endeavour* replica – as distinct from the *Young Endeavour* which is a metal ship, not a replica – was on its way around the world, following in Cook's footsteps – and it was taking people on board as paying crew whenever it stopped.

It was a strange kind of revelation when I realised that I could do it. I could join this ship. The familiar anticipation of a new adventure beckoned. Why the hell not?

But not now of course. It was leaving in four days, and I needed to stay here with Dad. James was back at work, Mum had to return to Brisbane, and I couldn't leave him down here alone at this time. Not now, but soon. The *Endeavour* had woven its spell around me. I was bewitched by the groaning of its wooden hull, its tall strong masts, its polished deck and its swinging hammocks. I emerged onto the old wooden deck. Dad was looking distracted.

Something strange was going on here. I had expected Dad to be full of chatter about the intricate details of the ship, but he wasn't asking me any questions. In fact he was practically avoiding me. Maybe it was the strain of Bea's death. But that wasn't it – his thick brows were pushing together to form a deep frowning furrow, but the telltale laughter lines around his eyes were giving away something more.

He turned to leave. 'Right, we should get going then.'

The only person I know with a worse poker face than me is my father, and by now his whole face was creased with the strain of hiding something. Mum was looking on with obvious amusement. I looked from one to the other and stood my ground.

'So what's going on, Dad?' He was giggling helplessly now.

'Oh, okay – I was trying to keep it as a surprise. We've got a little present for you for all your help over the last weeks.' He handed me a receipt, which read: *Claire Brownsworth ... sailing Geelong to Hobart with the* Endeavour *replica*. 'I thought you might like it.'

All traces of the strain of recent events had left my mother's face. She was laughing out loud: 'Claire, it's almost killed him trying to keep the secret from you since yesterday afternoon.'

I couldn't believe it. I was going on my first real journey out into the open ocean – my first sailing adventure – in this beautiful ship that stood before me, the exact replica of the ship that brought Cook to Australia. I was beginning a totally new chapter in my life, in four days. Maybe I was born to be a sailor ...

The *best* thing about being gainfully unemployed and single is being able to change life completely in an instant to go on a new fun-filled adventure. One minute I was planning to head back to England, the next I was planning to stay in Geelong, and the next I was booked to sail with the *Endeavour*. If a better option were to come up then hooray, why not? Though I couldn't imagine that happening now.

I never knew what I was going to be doing until I did it, because I knew better than anyone how easily my plans could change. As one of my friends put it, my plans were not fluid but gaseous. But I loved it.

The *worst* thing about being gainfully unemployed was being broke, because most of the really fun things required at least a little bit of cold, hard cash. Finding the balance was the hard bit. Finding fun, spontaneity and adventure combined with an income was my ultimate dream.

Four days later I stepped on board my home for the next month. First of all, the fifteen new crew were taken on 'the tour'. We were shown where all the hammocks were stowed, where and how to put them up and stow them away every day. We were shown the kitchen, which is one of the few modern touches (thank goodness) and then the out-of-bounds officers quarters, which contained the only proper beds. We were shown the bathrooms, which are one of the other modern touches, although failing to flush the lav properly can flood the lower deck with its contents and result in levels of hygiene closely resembling those in Cook's time.

We were taken on a trial run up the rigging (a thick open mesh made of chunky rope, used to climb up to the crow's nest), and out along the wide beams, which hold the sails and were twenty metres up from the wooden jetty. What a view! I couldn't wait to climb up out at sea when the boat would be rolling and the waves crashing underneath.

An hour after we left our mooring at Geelong harbour we sailed out through the heads of Port Phillip Bay, and my stomach gave an uncomfortable lurch. We were now in the wide expanse of Bass Strait, a perilous tract of water where many yachties have come to abrupt and disastrous ends to their voyages. And already people were turning green.

During the month that followed I encountered the sea in all her moods; amazingly, I managed to keep my stomach contents safely inside, and fell for her big-time. My life became so simple – the timeless existence of sailing, directed by the cycle of the sun and the moon over the endless expanse of ocean. All that was relevant to my life was inside this little vessel that bobbed along the surface – weather, wind and four-hour watches keeping track of lights on the horizon; breakfast, lunch and dinner; the groaning timbers of the wooden hull; climbing the rigging to adjust the heavy canvas sails; cleaning, scrubbing, sanding, painting; my hammock swaying in unison with the other fifty as the boat rocked around our exhausted bodies; and my neighbour's elbow waking me each night to stop me from snoring. My worldly concerns had totally disappeared.

I was in the Mizzenmast Group. During the days when I was on bow watch, I loved to crawl along the long mast that stuck out in front of the boat, particularly when the horizontal sails were rolled and tied, because they were unnecessary in a strong breeze. This was my favourite spot, with the cool blue water rushing past only a few metres below me and the dolphins riding the waves alongside. Just me, the blue ocean and little else in between.

At night often a group of dolphins would play in the dark bow wave, silhouetted with phosphorescence as they frolicked and jumped from the water with blissful momentum.

Far too soon the *Endeavour*, her crew, the other paying passengers and I arrived in Hobart. I didn't want to go back to the land, which had quite strangely started to sway uncontrollably since I had last been on it. I had just enough in the bank to pay for the trip back across Bass Strait and up to Melbourne.

This return journey ended up being a turning point in my life, because I met Vanessa. What Ness lacks in height she well and truly makes up for with hair. *Red* hair. In fact she is flat out pushing five foot three and that is from the top of her hair because I haven't the faintest idea where her head actually starts under her piles of crimson ringlets. But there is no fear of Ness getting lost under the curls because there is a mass of raw British energy bubbling away below them. Ness, very fittingly, is a journalist. (I pity the poor sods on the other end of an investigative interview.) But, aside from her busy schedule commuting from Scotland to London for TV presenting/journo work, she is also a documentary maker and a writer. These are her passions.

This was the first time I had ever met a real documentary maker in the flesh. My dream job was actually a reality: people could do this. And they weren't just mysterious beings who had somehow stumbled into the best jobs in the world, they were normal people who worked bloody hard for their passion for very little financial gain. Ness had flown all the way from Scotland to join the *Endeavour* for a month. She was doing research for a book on Captain James Cook. Being on the *Endeavour* with Ness certainly added a new dimension to the total experience.

Life was good and, when we finally arrived in Melbourne, I was again reluctant to leave this beautiful lifestyle behind. But the reality was that I had run out of money. I approached the second-in-command to see if there was a crewing position available. Nothing at this point in time, but maybe soon. I left him my number. Ness was heading back to Scotland; I was heading back to Brisbane. What was I going to do now?

Life has funny twists in it. One of the standard twists in mine is that usually, when I leave something behind, I am glad in the long run that I did. If I *really* wanted to do it, then I wouldn't just walk away without a hell of a fight. So, when I do turn away from something, then it is generally for the best.

When I arrived back on the Sunshine Coast I was glad that I had made the break back to solid ground (which had thankfully stopped swaying under my feet after a few days off the boat). I had been lost in the freedom and beauty of the ocean, and I still missed the creaking of the hull and the simplicity of the life, but that hadn't been enough on its own. It turned out to be easy to walk away and look back at the voyage as a short-term and fun experience, a sure sign that it wasn't in my blood enough to fight to stay on board.

What *had* stirred my imagination was Vanessa. It really was possible for people to earn an income doing creative things that they loved. So why shouldn't I? It was just a matter of finding my direction.

I looked at my bank balance. Fifteen dollars overdrawn. Thank goodness for the Rancho Parento, offering free coastal board, lodgings, and car usage for indefinite periods while I tried to figure out life.

While 'working things out' on the wonderful Queensland coast, I set out to achieve one of my long-term ambitions, to overcome my fear of big waves – I wanted to learn to surf better than just to get up and then face plant. But, despite improving a little and discovering a lasting love for this frustrating but rewarding sport, in the time floating around between waves I didn't get any closer to the perfect career. Documentary making seemed like the dream, and saving the world's environment the ambition – but how did you even start when you had no camera, no skills, and negative money in the bank?

Then I received a letter in the mail from the *Endeavour*. They were looking for a crew member, and would I like to join them? It was effectively a free ticket on board this beautiful boat for as long as I liked.

As I sat with the typed letter in my hands, I thought back over the bliss of life at sea – the freedom and beauty, the dolphins, the 360-degree sunsets, the fun and the adventure. I thought of my life heading in that direction for the next – well, however long I wished. Roaming the seas with a group of friends. But, although with these imaginings came happiness and excitement, something was missing – I couldn't feel the passion. I refused the offer.

There is some indefinable moment when I know that I have trespassed on my parents' hospitality too long, and I start feeling like a loafer. That time came. Still no brilliant ideas and still negative money in the bank. So I called up my locum agency in England. If I was going to have to work as a physio to restock the coffers, at least I was going to do it earning pounds. But I had one other criterion. It had to be somewhere that I could continue to learn to surf.

Of course there were lots of jobs, but only one anywhere near a surf beach. A position was vacant in Cornwall at a geriatric care unit (*groan*!) but with one day a week spent flying out to the Isles of Scilly in a helicopter to attend the hospital outpatients' clinic (*cool*!). And Cornwall, despite being further from the Equator than icy-cold Tasmania, was reputedly the surf capital of England.

Mum and Dad lent me the money for my ticket (anything to get me out of there and into gainful employment) and so in March 2001 I was off to an English winter and my 'career' as a physiotherapist once again.

If youth and travel are about experiencing the harshest and seediest of everything, so that the rest of life seems comparatively comfortable, then living and surfing in England is about getting so frozen that you will never complain of the cold again.

A week after leaving Australia I headed with my new Cornish housemates down the sand dunes towards the roaring ocean, a borrowed board under my arm and a borrowed summer wetsuit chafing under my armpits. My first surf in England, at the end of winter when the water was at its chilliest. Surely it couldn't be that much colder than in Australia.

An icy offshore wind whistled past my bare feet and hands, making the three-foot swell stand up tall and trail a thick mist behind each wave. We reached the edge of the water. Toes went in. SHITE! I wrenched them back out. Surely water shouldn't come this cold without being frozen.

My companions were off without hesitation, running through the froth towards the grey horizon and then onto their boards to paddle out the back before they missed the break in the swell, leaving me shivering at the edge.

Baptism by fire – or maybe ice – was the only way. I stamped my foot decisively into the clutches of the ocean and started to run.

OOOOUUCH! Pain shot through my feet – like running on broken glass. And then the pain started in my hands as I lay on the board and started paddling. The others were all out the back, safely behind the set of waves that were heading towards me. Oh well, no worries, I would just have to duck-dive under these waves. Breathe in, in position, hold breath, and under ...

AAAEEEEEYYYYYYAAAAAA! Trying to stand, I held my hands around my head. As if that was going to make any difference to the searing pain tearing my skull apart. My brain was being frozen. Oh no – another wave. Hold breath ...

YOOOOOOUUUUUUUCHHHH! I was almost crying with the unexpected pain. My leg jolted and flew out from under me as my escapee surfboard pulled on the leg-rope.

Goooot to geeeeet ouuuut of heeeere before my braiiin freeeeeezes!

I struggled back onto my board. Another wave. A roll-under and back on the board again. The ice-cream headache was ripping all other thoughts from my head as I paddled frantically to get out the back before the next wave engulfed me.

I finally made it behind the breaking waves to where my head could stay above the water. As I pulled alongside my friends, the last throbs of pain faded from my skull. At least now my hands and feet didn't hurt – they were completely numb. As I looked around, I saw the bleak horizon, the tangle of waves sweeping in to the shore and the happy faces of the people I had only just met and who would be my housemates while I worked in Cornwall. They bobbed around with blue lips, chatting and laughing on their boards. Andy, Susan, Jo and Steve. Wow! I was really going to enjoy this place.

I had been to Cornwall on climbing trips before, although never for longer than a hectic weekend on the spectacular sea cliffs. But I knew I really loved the place. It has a timeless seaside charm that is preserved by its being a seven-hour drive in Friday night traffic from London. There is one long main road down the centre of the narrow prominence, and from this road branches a web of country lanes, weaving through the flower-covered hedgerows to emerge onto the rugged coastline.

The coast is absolutely beautiful. Stone-housed villages with cobbled lanes are nestled in bays behind sweeping white beaches. Rocky headlands rise above the roaring waves as the swell tumbles in from the Atlantic Ocean.

I hoped that the location would be enough to make up for being involved in geriatric care, but instead the job turned out to be a rather pleasant surprise. Although four days a week were spent trying to convince headstrong old Cornish folk that they really did want to go for a walk, one day a week was spent flying in a helicopter out to the white sands and sailing-boat-lined shores of the Isles of Scilly.

This tranquil group of flower-covered islands off the south-western tip of England has managed to stay oblivious to the frenzy of modern-day existence and its pace of life has stayed sleepy and calm. I had one patient who would actually row his little wooden dinghy from his island of residence into his physiotherapy sessions.

On this one blissful day a week I would head out to another world. As I manipulated and stretched and gossiped, I would gaze longingly out of the treatment room window, to where little sailing boats bobbed around in the harbour. After a busy morning of treating all the locals who had injured themselves sunbaking, drinking beer and gossiping, I would run down to the beach and jump into the warm Gulf Stream waters of St Mary's.

The biggest drama to hit the Isles while I was there was the importation of a double-decker bus onto St Mary's Island from 'te mainland'. The local folk were in uproar as some of the tree branches lining the small road around the island were being cut to make room for this high tourist vehicle that had been brought over by *an immigrant* from England. There was no way an outsider was going to go defacing their island!

Cornwall hooked me. The Cornish like to consider themselves a separate country to England (they have their own flag) and indeed, once you are there, this makes perfect sense. There is really no need ever to leave. In fact most of the older folk where I was working had never been as far afield as the town I was living in, only a forty-minute drive away.

My first Cornish residence was a great house that had more surf-boards than people, but also boasted the messiest kitchen I have ever seen – and that is really saying something. The permanent residents were Andy and Jo, and then me, but there never seemed to be less than a crowd in the house. Visitors would bring not only their own clean cup but their friends around to check out the mess. Cleaning it was kind of like pruning – it all just came back, but twice as thick.

The state of uncleanliness was quite ironic, given that we were all health professionals, but domestic issues were just plain irrelevant to the philosophy of the household. All that mattered was that you could do a wave check from the living room window, and could get to the ocean on foot in less than five minutes. Life, although a little unhygienic, was great.

One evening, after a particularly frustrating day with the oldies, I came home to find my housemate, 'King of Mess' Andy, dripping and glowing in the backyard. Andy was also a physiotherapist, although he didn't fit the mould that I had come to know. He was tall and skinny, without any traces of sensible health professional to be seen. He had little-boy charm oozing out of every pore, despite the fact he was in his mid-thirties. His dancing hazel eyes and ruffled brown hair had all the girls – other than me and Jo – falling helplessly at his feet. Despite his lack of concern for hygiene, he was just a fantastic person to be around, with a complete obsession and enthusiasm for surfing that was wonderfully infectious.

His eyes were radiant as he stood, clearly exhausted, next to his Malibu surfboard. 'It's absolutely beau'iful mate. You've just go'a go in. Take my board. You'll 'ave to jump off the back of the headland mate, 'cause there's no way you'll paddle out through those waves.'

I didn't like to mention that as yet I hadn't surfed in waves much bigger than three feet, and was still having some trouble standing up on those. The typical expectation is that all Australians regularly surf on a ten-foot swell. But that didn't matter. One look at Andy's glowing face told me that I needed to get out there straight away.

I clambered down the steep steps carved into the rocky headland – the shortcut for the brave – and stopped just above the level of the thundering ocean, my heart pounding. The usual expanse of sand was covered by the high tide. I had never been this close to waves this big. They were huge. They were beyond the size where they look nice, and instead they were thundering mountains of water growing and growing to a tremendous width and height before standing tall and peeling away from the headland. But they were perfect – tremendous walls of water, unravelling from a glassy surface. In the distance groups of surfers bobbed on their boards, waiting for their turn to ride these crushers.

I waited for a gap between sets of waves. Then I threw my board in, dived in after it, and paddled with everything I had to get away from the headland before a wave hit and smashed me back into it.

Shit, a wave! Then the nightmare began – a battle for air and a fight to stay away from the rocks as wave after wave pushed me under and dragged me towards the towering cliff. I prayed that my leg-rope wouldn't snap as my board was ripped from my hands again and again. Without my board I was toast. It occurred to me, in a moment of spluttering clarity, that perhaps my number was up; but then I was forced under again and all thought dissolved in blind panic.

After what seemed like an eternity, the set of waves passed and, completely exhausted, I jumped back on my board. Adrenalin somehow fed me the energy to paddle so far out to sea that a wave wouldn't break on me again.

Now, between me and the shore, the nightmare waited. I struggled for strength as I paddled across to the nearest group of surfers. At least there was some comfort that someone might notice if I was drowned trying to get in to the shore.

Swell after swell lifted and then lowered me as I spent an hour paddling in the opposite direction to everyone else, trying to get away from the breaking waves. But there was no denying it – the only way I was going to get out of this was to catch one to the shore.

I was snookered, trapped in a terrible catch-22. The smaller waves, of course, were breaking closer to the shore but, if I waited on the inside to catch one of these, then I would be crushed under the white water of the bigger ones that were breaking further out. Yet if I waited right out the back, where I was safe from the thundering white water, then I would have to catch one of the biggest ones, which were well over six foot (which means the face is more than twelve foot, double my standing height).

Finally I lined myself up. I was in position. It was huge, growing and growing as it came towards me. This was my wave, the one that would take me back to safety ... or finish me off. Twelve feet of towering water was rising up behind me. I turned to the shore and started to paddle. I had to get up enough speed to get onto it. It was on me, picking me up and up and up, the dark water in front of me dropping away far below. I surely couldn't go up any further. I felt the tug as my surfboard joined the wave's forward momentum, becoming a part of its energy. It had me. Now, turn left and stand up quick before I face plant.

I swept onto my feet in one smooth move. A miracle. And, almost without realising how it had happened, I was standing up. I was riding across this enormous wave! Behind me the white water thundered as the wave curled into oblivion; in front of me was just a huge but gently sloping wall of smooth blue water. Adrenalin-charged, I glided up and down, up and down as the wave swept forward, raw powerful energy unwinding in a graceful flow, and me sweeping along with it. Pure ecstasy.

We came to rest together at the shore. The wave was sedated, I was electrified. For an instant I turned to paddle back out for another one, but then the roaring ocean told me all I needed to know. That had been a one-off – maybe even for a lifetime, I don't know. But what a wave!

When the landlord finally kicked us out of the house (I take no responsibility as I had only been there a month), I found myself a residence that dreams are made of. I convinced a family that lived five minutes' walk from the Perranporth headland to let me convert the little old garden shed in their backyard into living quarters. I lined the inside walls with scraps of colourful old material, and bought a futon out of the *Trade-It* paper.

Equipped with a kettle, climbing gear, guitar and CDs inside, and my mountain bike and a borrowed surfboard leaning up against the outside, I created a little piece of heaven for the meagre sum of thirty pounds a week all-inclusive. Even dinner every night was thrown in so I wouldn't be in the way in the kitchen. (Maybe they had heard about the other house.) From my little home, in which I could only barely stand up straight in the very centre without bumping my head, I would wander down to check the surf conditions from the top of the headland with a Baileys coffee in hand. Bliss.

It was while living in the garden shed in Cornwall that I bought my baby.

She was even taller than me, a strong eight foot, with wide shoulders and sexy curves. I designed her myself: buoyant enough to glide gracefully, but small enough to get easily under the bigger waves. She was a bit of a show-off, a real crowd-pleaser, drawing comments from passers-by wherever we went together.

'Gee, nice colours.'

'Wow, she's beaut-i-ful.'

The day that my red and yellow flowery mini-malibu was finished we went out for our first surf together, and I knew I had found a soul mate. It was the middle of summer. We stood together at the top of the headland in the crisp late afternoon, looking out over the sweeping kilometre of beach, a huge expanse of white sand shimmering as the ocean recoiled far from the dunes.

Even from this distance I could see there was none of the usual frenzy of foam and surfers that I had become accustomed to, just a still flat blue with tiny waves lapping at the edges. Maybe too small to ride? There were no other surfers out there. A bad sign. We'd just go for a paddle then.

Bare feet numb from the cold and wetsuit gripping uncomfortably at the back of my knees, I descended the steep rocky steps of the headland, carrying my baby. I would be grateful for my tight second skin soon. A long walk out across wet sand, my footprints the only marks in the perfect white, and we were there. The ocean meets 'Flower Power', a meeting of yin and yang.

My heart was pounding. The icy water was smooth as glass, but through this crystal perfection tiny yet perfect waves peeled across before me.

We were alone.

We paddled out towards the line between sea and sky. The horizon was blurring with a vibrant red, there was a bright yellow ball sinking into its centre, but the ocean and sky below and above it were still a flawless blue. Red, yellow, and blue – the colours of my board!

Again and again my baby and I rode in to the shore together. We ducked and weaved across the faces of smooth and perfect undulations as they uncurled towards the shore. My body rushed through the air in a cutting downwards sweep, leaving my stomach behind and then whoosh, back up again to the crest before the freefall down again, a flying ride all the way in. Paddling easily back out again we would wait for the next surge from the belly of the sleepy ocean.

When the sea lay calm, we floated on her milky surface and I gazed at the darkening sky, the first stars of our first night together arching high overhead. The moon spread its fingers across the dark bottomless eternity, a fringe of blue glow on white foam. The water was cold, icy cold, but I was warm with happiness.

This was the life.

With my beautiful board and my ex flat-mates as constant play companions, I found myself living and working in Cornwall through the whole of the summer of 2001, stacking away the pounds I was earning as my life was costing laughingly little – my total living expenses, including the cost of a bit of extra food and petrol, were under one hundred a week, even if I lived it up.

But, apart from the money and the wonderful lifestyle, I reckon that if there is such a thing as destiny, it had a hand in my staying on for as long as I did. A very significant person was about to enter my life.

One day, feeling about as motivated as my elderly patients and guiltily sitting in my office drinking tea, I received a phone call from some guy who knew someone, who knew someone else, who knew that there was an Australian physiotherapist named Claire who climbed and surfed and was working in Cornwall. He had asked around and found out where I was hiding and we arranged to meet.

Little did I know that in the future I would be thanking this Australian stranger for much that has happened in my life. Clyde shared with me a passion for anything outdoorsy, and was just great fun to be around. A lasting friendship was born and it was through Clyde, about six months after leaving Cornwall, that I first heard about Hot Rock, the expedition that was to change my life in more ways than I could imagine.

Given my line of work at this time (mostly helping little old ladies recover from broken hips), it only seemed right to go home when my very little 89-year-old Nanna broke first one, and then the other of her hips in quick succession. Despite Mum's protests that I needn't stop my own life to return to Australia, I booked my ticket to Victoria. I knew too well that the statistical probability of Nanna surviving even one such break was slim at her age, and I wasn't going to let another grandma slip away without a chance to give her a hug.

Thank goodness. If it wasn't for my grandmother, I may well have been permanently claimed by the Cornish void, all memory of the world beyond this narrow peninsula of land wiped from memory. My true dreams may never have been fulfilled. This trip home was to have a devastating effect on my bank balance, but profound repercussions on my life and direction.

Nanna, being the invincible old bird that she is, defied the odds and returned to her own home in Geelong, and Mum and I planned a weekend trip up home to the Sunshine Coast. Dad had a surprise waiting for us. He had booked us a unit at the beautiful seaside town of Sunshine Beach. During the weekend we got looking at real estate and I realised with surprise that, thanks to my stint of cheap living in Cornwall, my bank balance was healthy enough to put a deposit on a unit by the beach. (Property prices didn't go crazy until about a month later.)

By the end of that weekend we had found a little place, my offer had been accepted, the contract had been drawn up and signed, and I, an officially unemployed physiotherapist, had to find myself a bank loan. Despite the fact that I had only worked for about half the time since graduation, my average annual wage, again thanks to earning pounds, was just enough to convince the bank that I was a freelance physiotherapist, and that I was a safe bet. The unit was mine – or, more accurately, I was the bank's.

And somehow, while spending that much money, it seemed like the right time to fork out a few extra bucks for a video camera. Because, although life had been plodding along very nicely, there were still two things that I wanted more than anything, and just following my heart didn't seem to be getting me any closer to either.

I daydreamed of finding my Mr Right, and I still dreamed of making documentaries.

Having pretty much given up on the former as a lost cause, I had settled on getting the ball rolling on my documentary-making career. Now that I was a real grown-up (I had acquired an enormous rug in Turkey, *and* now I had a unit to put it in) it was time to get serious.

While searching for the perfect bank loan, I researched the perfect video camera. And, never being one to start at the bottom, I ended up settling on a hand-held 3CCD broadcast-quality digital video camera with optical stabilisation, huge megapixels, a Leica lens and a multitude of other features that sounded really impressive. (Just in case anyone wanted to broadcast my early footage. Well, you never know!)

In debt up to my eyeballs, signed, sealed and delivered, I organised a physiotherapy job back in England. (This time I was heading for Thetford, a town four hours' drive north-east of London.) Bring on the pounds!

Unfortunately, one of the surprises that was waiting for me on my return was Dave, the handsome builder from Mt Isa. If only I had stayed in Australia just a little bit longer. But, as it happened, I arrived in England just in time to catch up with him before he left for Canada. I saw him for just long enough to remember how gorgeous he was, and for his sweet-talk to melt my hopeful heart, and not quite long enough to remember what a toad he was.

The next three months were spent working in Thetford and pining for an imaginary romance (based entirely on some cleverly chosen words from him), corresponding by email and the occasional phone call, writing extended prose about my devotion, boring my workmates to tears with my 'blossoming romance', and paying for my extremely expensive ticket to Canada. My plans to make a significant dent in my bank loan took a back seat. Maybe this was it – True Love.

It was only weeks until we were to meet again. I had spent so many hours of so many months daydreaming of falling into his strong arms, and in less than three weeks my dreams would at last be a reality.

I emailed my flight confirmation. I imagined him opening my email, his excited anticipation, and his surprising me by waiting for me at the airport in Vancouver. After all, I was the woman of his dreams. He had said so himself.

I checked my emails twice a day. Nothing. He mustn't have received my message. I emailed again.

Nothing. I was becoming frantic. What had happened? A terrible accident, maybe?

Then *a group email* in my letterbox! The bastard was still alive and well, *and* had been into his email account. And he had decided not to write back.

I tried to look on the bright side, but my expectant heart was breaking. Thank goodness for my 'Voice of Wisdom' to help me see things for what they were. As I headed for Vancouver, I emailed my mum:

Dear Mum,

Dave still hasn't called or written. I am really not even going to try to second-guess his reasons for being such a slack correspondent … I will just wait and it will all become apparent in the not too distant future and hey, plenty more fish in the sea. Knowing me, even if he was still keen on me I would probably get bored after a few months anyway!!!

Maybe I am just not meant to have a boyfriend that I really like EVER. How can someone who has so much luck in every other area of life be so dismally unlucky in love … anyway that's my self-pity session over.

Everything else is going really well …

Back came my mother's almost immediate reply:

Darling daughter,

I haven't really got time to write this now but as you

say 'what the heck'! Other things will wait. I feel I need to comment on this 'unlucky in love' misconception you have. What you're really saying is that you haven't made that one instant connection and that it's all been happily ever after from then on ... YET. But surely that's the stuff of romance novels. The chances are you will meet a guy one day who you'll know is someone you want to live your life with but if you don't, well, them's the breaks. At least these days women can lead a fantastic life without a man, thank goodness. Maybe you just have to wait, to be more patient, and to go out with men without the complication of thinking 'maybe this is the one'. And maybe the 'unlucky in love' perception just means you've got the sense to know when it's not right, as you did with Kel ...

I spent the next three weeks in the beautiful snow-covered Rocky Mountains, as far away from Whistler (where I knew Dave was) as I could get in the short time available. I spent my time ice-climbing, caving, and having a brief attempt at learning to snowboard on nearly solid ice, thus injuring both shoulders and my pelvis, and instilling a fear of snow which I still hold today.

I deleted Dave's address from anywhere in my life and caught my plane back to England, pride restored and feeling liberated. Maybe True Love (whatever that was) wasn't meant for tall girls. I would just have to focus on my other dreams; like, becoming a doc-umentary maker.

Unfortunately my expectations of instant genius in this area had also been sadly crushed. My shaky footage of seagulls, family, and travelling didn't quite compare to the crisply focused stories I watched on television. Disheartened, I was shying away from my camera, not sure what to do next.

Luckily, by this time Michelle and I had healed our Middle Eastern rift, so I moped around Michelle's house in London for a few days. My trip to Canada had wrecked not only my dreams but my bank balance as well. I was broke – again. There was nothing else for it but to contact my locum agency in England – again. Their return email wasn't very encouraging. *'Not many jobs around. One going in 'Out-Patients' in East Grinstead ...'*

I looked on the internet (for once in my life I was going to research my destination; I definitely didn't want any more disappointment): *Small community ... One hour train to London ... Sandstone climbing abounds ... Local crags riding distance from town ... Surrounded by Ashdown Forest, the home of Winnie-the-Pooh.* Hmmm, sounded okay. It would do for the short term anyway, until something better came up, hopefully in Scotland near my friend Ness (from my *Endeavour* days), who could teach me something about documentary making.

Piling my belongings into the rental car that went with the job, I headed south to East Grinstead and its Queen Victoria Hospital, where I would be living and working. This time I wasn't going to get caught up in some fanciful dream. I was going to put my head down and work and save so much that I wouldn't ever have to worry about money again.

As it turned out, East Grinstead, of all places, was the closest I have ever come to finding a home away from home. Other places, such as Cornwall, had been fabulous locations, but in the end what makes a home is friends and family, and in old East Grinny I found myself a part of something bigger than adventure and fun. I found a home full of great women and I became part of a wonderful group of people loosely known as The South Downs Climbing Club. We met up at the sandstone crags or the indoor climbing wall every Tuesday and Thursday night.

These evenings would be capped off with pints of local brew, pickled eggs and chatting in our favourite little pubs. Most weekends were spent driving for ridiculous numbers of hours to get to awesome wilderness areas around the UK, to camp and climb.

I had found a bunch of wonderful, supportive people: if I had a dinner party, they would come; if I had a problem, they would listen; if I wanted to go out for a coffee, I could give them a call. It's funny how you don't realise how much something is missing until you find it.

Once committed to the comfort and security of East Grinny, I was overcome with the intense desire to be creative. I bought myself a full supply of painting equipment and stayed up for long nights in my room painting the canvases or experimenting on paper.

All those colours and patterns were practically fighting to get out of my head, where they had been cooped up since I had left university and started my life on the move. It was like welcoming back an old friend into my life. But still my super-technical video camera sat inside its case, gathering dust in my room, looking at me dejectedly as I shied away from using it. Finally I decided that something had to be done about making my dreams a reality. I got out the phone book and looked up *Videographer*.

The following evening I pulled up outside No. 11 Witchcroft Street. This was the address that the lady named Claire had given me over the phone. She was a videographer and editor and, although she had sounded a bit confused by my vague request just to come and chat so I could learn something, she had said I could come and look at her set-up.

I knocked on the door. A rustle came from inside. And then – towering over me, her breasts in line with my eyes and her strong face looking down on the top of my head – was the tallest woman I had ever seen.

I stammered ... I stared ... I didn't know what to say. I felt the question fighting its way up my throat towards my mouth – the very question I had spent my whole life loathing. I managed to stop myself from blurting it out just in time, but in my mind it was screaming to be answered: *How tall are you?!*

Her voice boomed down to me. 'I'm six foot eight, just in case you were wanting to know. You must be Claire. You're not so short yourself.'

'Yeah, six foot two … you must be Claire.'

'Great. Well, do you want to come in?'

We both stooped to get in through the low doorway.

In the evening that followed I didn't learn much about videography but I did learn that there is such a thing as a Tall Persons Club, and, being a woman over six foot tall, I qualified for entry. I was duly invited to one of their monthly get-togethers, where twenty or more enormously tall people go out to dinner at a restaurant together. I decided to give that one a miss.

It wasn't long after arriving in East Grinstead that my 'financial plan' started coming undone. Clyde, my friend from Cornwall, was now working in South Wales and the parents of an English friend, Rachel, owned a cabin in a town nearby. So we all arranged to meet for a weekend of climbing, rendezvousing in a tiny seaside village.

After a few hours of roaming the beach, exploring a cave and climbing on the ancient stone walls of the nearby castle, we made our way to the quaint, run-down cottage. We struck up a warm fire in the dark lounge and sat as close to it as we could without singeing our eyebrows, with some cups of freshly mulled wine warming our palms.

Clyde pulled out of his pocket a thick brochure, his face easing into a warm smile. 'Claire, I've got something that you will love.'

I flipped through the pages as he told me about Hot Rock, the three-year around-the-world rock climbing and mountaineering expedition that had already departed England. A big truck with thirty seats was travelling the length of every continent on the globe, taking climbers on board, and seeking out the best climbing areas along the way. He told me of his plans to join the Hot Rock expedition. He was off to South America with his girlfriend in September 2002 to travel with them for six months.

The seed was planted and, as I settled into life in East Grinstead, it slowly grew in the back of my mind.

Living in East Grinstead confirmed my love and appreciation of English people. I really don't know how they have managed to get a worldwide reputation as being a bunch of whingeing Poms. As far as I can tell, they are the most optimistic and enthusiastic people on the planet. They have to be. Otherwise they would never leave their homes. I'd love to see a bunch of Aussies living in a similar climate!

Weekends away with the South Downs Climbers became a regular and exhausting routine, no matter what the weather forecast. On Friday nights, after a long week's work, I would clamber exhausted into someone's car and we would hit the M1 in Friday night traffic. We would sit in a diabolical bumper-to-bumper nightmare for anything from six to eight hours, depending on which direction we were heading (e.g. to the Peak District, North Wales, the Lake District, or sometimes Cornwall). We wouldn't stop until we got to our destination.

We would put up our tents in the early hours of the morning and I would collapse into a coma, hoping for rain so I could have a sleep in. Gradually through the darkness carloads of climbing friends would arrive and pitch their tents.

Just after sunrise someone would be up and jumping about: 'Wake up everyone – it's morning. Let's go!'

'But it's raining.'

'There's a little blue patch over there. We don't want to miss it.'

After that, there would be no stopping. Full-on action all day – a morning surf, a long day of hiking and climbing, and then an evening surf to cap it off. Or, if we were not near a beach, then just hiking and climbing from dawn to dusk, stopping for a brief picnic at lunchtime.

Early on I gave up trying to talk anyone into having a nice rest in the middle of the day. If there was dry rock, then it had to be climbed. I did manage once to convince Martyn, a lovely and lanky Pommie uni student and regular climbing partner, to lie on the beach between our morning surf and our day of climbing. I instantaneously melted into the sand, loving the rare feeling of sun on my skin and ready to be absorbed by relaxation for a good couple of hours. Martyn lay next to me, his body out straight and rigid with resignation as he looked at the sky, wondering how long he was going to have to wait for this lazy Aussie chick. After about two minutes he started to fidget, and after five I heard the rustle of sand as he looked over at me impatiently.

'Are you finished yet, Claire?'

It sure took the pleasure out of sunbathing.

When we were all too exhausted to continue for the day, or we ran out of sunlight, or it started to rain too hard to offer any reasonable hope of it stopping, then we would retire to the cosiness of one of the wonderful pubs that are scattered throughout the English countryside. We would huddle around a table with tall pints of ale and warm home-cooked meals of English stews and roasts prepared lovingly by the publican, and compare exciting climbing stories from our days on the rock. Epics would be embellished, spectacular achievements would be shared and falls would be chuckled about. Late in the evening we would retire to the camping ground and I would collapse exhausted into my tent, ready to start again early the next morning but again hoping it would rain so I could have a sleep in.

I would be dropped back at the nursing quarters in the early hours of Monday morning, wondering how the hell I was going to make it through the week. I almost looked forward to the weekends at home, where I could take it easy and just go for a ride and get some sleep. But they didn't happen very often. Going away was way too much fun. Camping in the rain became a way of life.

As the end of my visa drew close, my yearning to go home and find some stability was being overwhelmed by a conviction that this Hot Rock truck was something that I just had to be a part of. A group of rock climbers travelling around the world in a big red truck was too good to be true. Apart from anything else, this was a trip on which I could take my camera and maybe get some really good footage. But then again, I had promised myself I was going to save all my money and pay off my Sunshine Beach unit.

In the middle of September 2002 I waved Clyde off at Gatwick Airport, wondering if they would actually let him on board his flight to South America wearing half of his luggage (a strategy used by climbers the world over to avoid paying excess baggage when travelling with about forty kilos of climbing equipment).

That night I picked up the phone and booked a position on the truck. I was going to join up with Hot Rock in La Paz, Bolivia, on 10 January 2003 and from there I would head north with them for three months, up along the Andes until we reached the northern tip of South America. And from there, well, who knows.

But it wasn't until after I had paid up my money and booked my flights home and then to South America that I found out the really big piece of news. I was chatting to the organiser of the trip on the telephone and we got to talking about the people who were already on the truck.

'Oh, and there's another Aussie girl, about your age, named Mel,' he told me. 'She's just great. Oh, and she's filming the whole trip to make it into a documentary.'

'What! Are you serious?'

'Yeah ... why?'

I didn't want to say too much – like, this was a dream come true! 'It's just that I have a video camera.'

'Well, make sure you take it, Claire, because I think she would like all the help she can get. She's very talented, but she's doing all the filming and editing alone and it's a huge job. I think you guys will get along.'

I couldn't believe it. I was on my way to join a documentary maker. Life sure has a funny way of working itself out.

When the time finally came to leave East Grinstead, after eight months of living and working there, I felt somehow whole for the first time in my life, like a child who has become an adult, or like random brushstrokes that have come together to form a picture. Somehow a mist had cleared and I could see who I was in entirety. I wasn't complete – maybe no-one ever is – but I did feel whole and happy and ready for whatever was to come next.

You'd think that, after twenty-five years of wondering who He would be, if or when He would come into my life, and how well He could climb, I'd know Him when I saw him. But I didn't. *He* did ... *I* didn't.

And you'd think that, after twenty-five years of fantastic things coming from repeatedly being in the right place at the right time with the right people, I would sense serendipity when she was about to play her best game with me ever. But I didn't.

I just stormed on ahead through the twenty-third of December, 2002, completely unaware that my life had taken one of its most dramatic turns yet. In my defence, I was busy. I had places to go and rocks to climb!

This was the day I had been looking forward to for a very long time. I was heading to Brisbane to go shopping for outdoor gear that actually worked. I'd waited a long while to get properly equipped; the trouble was that I am a born bargain-hunter, and over the years I had stubbornly stuck by my principles that anything more expensive than op-shop clothing was a rip-off.

Unfortunately, you don't find Gore-Tex, ProLite and Therm-a-Rests in op-shops, so I had paid the price in tears. I had spent days at a time being wet under my old raincoat. I had returned from climbing, riding and walking in England with completely white toes and fingers, and had screamed with pain while defrosting them in the bath. I had spent countless nights cursing in my breezy tent as I shivered in my sleeping bag on a hard foam mat. My feet had gone so wrinkly in my waterlogged boots that the skin had started to break down.

I had lugged heavy and ineffective gear around the great outdoors of Australia and the world. But not this time. No way. Something big was going to come out of this trip, I could feel it.

So I walked into an outdoor equipment shop I had salivated over for years. Inside was what my dreams were made of – all the accessories and equipment I could ever want, and more.

Scott introduced himself to me and I unfolded my A4 shopping list. He glanced at the sheet and a happy smile lit his face. As he worked through my list and my pile steadily increased, we chatted. He was a climber too, and very well travelled. He was kind of short (well, relative to me anyway) and had the alive sparkle of someone who was passionate about things.

Then an amazing coincidence. Pia, one of the girls who worked in the shop, was also a climber, and was joining the Hot Rock expedition in La Paz on the same day as me. Incredible. Hot Rock was an international expedition but, out of all the shops in all the world, she worked in this one. It was meant to be.

By the time Scott and I headed for the shoe section, I had been there for over an hour. As we talked, his enthusiasm had been steadily growing and now he was literally bouncing with excitement. Gee, this guy was *really* into outdoor gear, almost to the point of weirdness.

He handed me a pair of technical sandals: 'Claire, I've just got to duck downstairs for a moment while you're trying them on. I'll be back.' And he was off.

What I didn't know then, but do know now, is that, while I was trying on the sandals and wandering around the shop, pondering their relative comfort and practicality, Scott had run full-pelt downstairs and into his manager's office. 'Ad!' he blurted. 'Guess what! I've just met the woman of your dreams! Your perfect match. You've got to come up and meet her.'

Adam looked questioningly out from under heavy lashes at his flatmate and friend, who was jumping around eagerly in the doorway. They had been friends and colleagues for many years, but Scott had never said anything like this before.

'What! Who ...?'

'Her name's Claire. She's perfect for you.'

'What? How? Is she still here?'

'Yep. I'm serving her as we speak. You've got to come up!'

And with that Scott dashed back up the stairs, two at a time.

Meantime, blissfully unaware, I was gazing critically at my reflection in a mirror, wondering whether the sandals made my feet look big.

Later, as Scott was describing the benefits of a particular water purifier, something caught my attention out of the corner of my eye. A young dark-haired man with a goatee was walking past and he was looking my way. His big brown eyes nervously met mine. Did I know him? He paused his long-limbed strides and turned resolutely towards me. He cleared his throat: 'Hi.'

Crap. Maybe he was a past patient whom I had forgotten (I hated it when that happened). Who was he? I gave the beaming smile that I always have reserved for when I have no idea who a person is. I said, 'G'day', hoping for some clue to help me out, but he just smiled awkwardly and then kept on walking, disappearing back down the long staircase.

Three hours later I left the shop fully laden, broke, exhausted, and over the moon. What a life! Young, single and ready to take on the world in comfort at last. South American rock, here I come.

Apparently, Adam sat in his office for a long time, kicking himself.

A COUPLE OF QUESTIONS TO ASK A THIRD WORLD TOUR OPERATOR BEFORE PARTICIPATING IN AN OBVIOUSLY DANGEROUS ACTIVITY

1. Is this more or less dangerous than it looks?

2. At what point will it be too late to change my mind?

3. So, what's that stretcher for on the roof of the minibus?

4. How many injuries did the company have last year?

5. Were any of them fatal?

6. Do you mind if I look at your rescue procedures?

7. So, who underwrites your insurance policy?

As a final test piece pick the toughest looking member of your group and get them to storm up to the person in charge and scream out, 'My brother took a tour with you twelve months ago', and closely watch the expression on their face.

Surprise = Might not be too dangerous

Fear = Probably dangerous

Tour guide abandons office and runs = Go back to your hostel and play cards

EIGHT

Downhill Madness

As I stepped off Transportes Aereos Centro-Americanos (TACA) flight TA35 and into the La Paz terminal, I just couldn't see what everyone had been making such a big deal about. Apart from my obvious elation at having survived a flight in a plane owned by a Third World country, nothing else felt out of the ordinary. So much for the Lonely Planet guidebook saying that you can get altitude sickness from landing at this airport (which stands at an altitude of 4100 metres above sea level). I felt totally normal. A little tired maybe, but definitely not affected by the low oxygen levels.

My biggest concern was that it was now 10.30 at night and rather stupidly I hadn't bothered to organise transport down into town (which sits at 3660 metres) – or anywhere to stay, for that matter. Oh well, I was sure something would work out.

I stood dreamily in the queue behind the empty desk in the tiny airport, waiting for whoever was going to stamp our passports to appear. Two tall Caucasian men in front of me were looking curiously in my direction. Maybe they spoke some English. I may as well try.

'G'day.'

The biggest one answered. 'Hi. Where have you come from?'

He sure was a tall man, maybe in his mid-thirties; with his broad shoulders draped in a beautifully tailored business suit, he had an air of utter superiority. His handsome and similarly suited companion looked inconsequential by comparison. I looked down at my dirty hiking boots, practical trousers and travelling shirt. Classy.

'Oh, I'm from Australia. Why, where are you from?'

'We both live in La Paz.'

'Cool! You might be able to help me then. What's the best way to get into town from here?'

I looked out of the windows into the void of darkness, broken only by the colourful lights of the strange city far below. What was out there in the darkness of this Third World city? I had no idea. And I really was feeling very sleepy all of a sudden ... almost dizzy ...

'Why, where are you going?'

'Oh ... um ... I don't actually know yet ... a hostel or something like that.'

They looked at each other curiously. The taller man answered again, his deep voice thundering down on me from a wide, strong mouth.

'You don't know? You haven't booked in anywhere?'

'Ahhhh ... nope.'

I looked sheepishly back at their disbelieving faces, trying my best to look in control but helpless enough to need their assistance. I didn't fancy going out there alone at all.

An immigration official arrived at the desk and the line of people shuffled forwards. I watched vaguely and despondently as the two men went through before me. But, instead of heading straight for the door, they waited on the other side of the desk.

The taller man was looking me disbelievingly up and down. 'Hey look, my name's Michael. Would you like a lift into town?'

I handed over my passport. I was really tired now. Kind of all relaxed and airy. How good that I didn't have to sort out my own transport. What nice people. I looked over at these two lovely guys who were going to give me a ride. They were looking expectantly back at me. Why were they looking at me like that? ... Oh yeah ... I hadn't answered ... Oops.

'Oh ... ah ... that would be great. Oh, and my name's Claire.'

STAMP.

I drifted after them, out of the airport and into the open air. I felt so light on my feet, almost like I was floating ... what a beautiful evening it was. So relaxing and calm and ...

Michael turned to me as we walked through the doors into the cold night air; I registered vaguely that he was talking to me again. 'Don't you have any bags?'

What was he talking about? ... Bags? ... What bags?

'OH, SHIT!'

I ran back inside to where all the precious climbing, camping and mountaineering equipment that I would be needing for the next three months was sitting alone on the luggage table. I had been about to leave the airport without it.

I was ushered into the front seat of a shiny black Land Cruiser. I sank deep into the cosiness of the sheepskin seat cover as the surround-sound and air-conditioning drifted around me. The huge and magnificent Michael filled the driver's seat beside me. His colleague lounged silently in the back.

Michael's attention drifted from the road to me: 'Claire, I think you should stay at my house for the night. You can find accommodation tomorrow. There are plenty of spare rooms. You don't have to worry. I'm married with a child.'

His wedding ring shone on his left hand on the steering wheel. I didn't have to think very hard about whether I should accept the invitation. I would find myself other accommodation tomorrow. *Yawn!* I was far too sleepy to be lugging my stuff around a Third-World city in the middle of the night trying to find a bed. Much better to do that in the light of day. How floaty and nice I was feeling ... and what a lovely chap he was.

A low chuckle rumbled through my driftings. 'Claire, I think you might be suffering a little from the altitude.'

I turned around to see who he was talking to. How funny – someone was affected by the lack of oxygen ... Hee, hee, hee ... Oh, he was looking at me.

'Who, me? Noooo way. I'm fiiiiiiine. Just a little sleeeeepy, that's all.'

'Don't worry. You'll feel better as we go down.'

I gazed dreamily at the pretty colours on the digital altimetre as we drove down and down and down, past 3600 metres of altitude, where the big dirty city was still hectic with people honking and selling and shouting. We dropped his friend off at 3500 metres and kept on driving down further, until at 3400 metres we reached a lovely tree-lined suburb. What fuuuuun this was! What lovely colours were blurring in front of me. Through the trees we went and then we started heading back up again. But not for long.

The security guard smiled and waved from his little shelter as we pulled in through an imposing gate. We crunched to a stop outside an enormous house and two men ran to the car. Our bags disappeared into the house and, as I floated out of the car after them, I realised that we were on a small knoll and around us was a panoramic 360-degree view of city lights twinkling all the way up the valley sides.

I followed Michael's suited shoulders up the long flight of marble steps, past another security guard sitting at the front entrance, and into the large foyer.

Michael was waving at me. Oooh! He was saying goodnight. How weird. 'Goodnight,' I said.

'The maid will show you to your room. See you in the morning.'

And with that he disappeared into the depths of the house, and in his place stood a short, round woman in an apron. I was taken to my room where a king-size bed, ensuite bathroom, a tray of bottled water, cookies and my bags waited for me.

Alone in the room, I locked the door. I wandered around the expanse of bed and out onto my own personal balcony that looked out to the city above. If this was Third World living, then I was all for it!

But as for altitude. Pfft. No worries at all, mate. I felt just fine. Absolutely great, in fact.

I searched through my luggage. No purse! I must have left it on the plane.

The following day, after being chauffeur-driven into the city, I sat in Michael's intimidating office. He gazed importantly across the enormous expanse of his mahogany desk. Behind him a wall of glass revealed the hectic Bolivian city, but in here time stood still. I was trying not to look like a complete slob as the deep leather chair threatened to engulf me.

I looked despairingly at the cup of green coca tea I held in my hand – a mixture of coca leaves and sugar in boiling water. Despite the classy presentation of this traditional drink, it was disgusting.

'You should drink it. It will help with the altitude,' Michael advised. Obediently I took another sip, and stifled a gag. 'Once you find somewhere to stay, let me know and my driver will take you and your bags there. Oh, and I'll get someone to sort out your purse. You can pick it up from here later ... One of my staff will be back soon with a map of the city for you so you can find your way around.'

He stretched his impressive bulk back in his enormous chair, and with his hands behind his head he looked at me with a mixture of amusement and curiosity. 'I used to climb as well, you know.'

'Really?' That seemed unlikely.

'Yep. I was quite an adventurer when I was young. I lived in Canada, and used to go into the mountains for weeks at a time climbing and exploring and hunting. But then I got a real job and got married and had kids. Climbing's a thing of the past for me now.'

'But you live in the Andes! Don't you miss it?'

'Sure, but that's life. Look, if you want to go out to dinner tonight then we will take you to the best restaurant in town.'

'Oh – sure, great!'

As I left his luxurious office the rest of the bank staff waved at me with courteous but questioning smiles. I was going to be the talk of the tearoom. Catching the lift down to the ground floor, I wondered at this turn of events. The fact that my head was still spinning from lack of oxygen wasn't helping me to process my situation. It was certainly bizarre – I had woken up on my first day in Bolivia in serene luxury, had been chauffeur-driven into town, seemed to have the manager of an enormous American bank looking after me, and now I had been invited out to what I assumed would be an extremely posh restaurant for dinner. What on earth was going to happen next?

I left the polished marble floors of the bank and stepped outside onto the dirty and cracked concrete paths of La Paz, and nearly got bowled over by a colourfully dressed woman in a bowler hat pushing a barrow full of assorted sugar-coated nuts. A young child with a dirt-smeared face pulled on my jacket and said something in Spanish. I had ten days to fill in here before the Hot Rock truck arrived.

La Paz, the highest capital city in the world, is situated in the bottom of a huge dusty valley. The main road runs along the flat bottom and all of the buildings creep their way up the steep brown sides. But, unlike Australia, in La Paz real estate doesn't improve with the view. The higher you go, the poorer it gets. A house high up above the city means thinner air and one hell of a long walk to get into town and back home again, and this is a walk that many La Paz residents do every day, carrying huge bundles of merchandise and food to sell in the markets.

I personally was having doubts about whether I was even going to make it up the small elevation to check into the Hostel Continental, where I would be meeting with Hot Rock in ten days. Any remaining doubts about my reaction to the altitude were shattered by a spinning head and a fight for air after my first five steps uphill.

Unfortunately the Hostel Continental turned out to be rather pricey, so I continued my exhausting search, puffing up and down side streets until I found the Hotel de Cactus, the cheapest hostel in town. It was located on Witch Street, where you could get all you ever needed if you were looking for dehydrated llama foetuses, magic herbs and spices, or witch doctors. Near the hostel's door sat a bedraggled old man reading the future for anyone who paid. Inside there was an air of desperation as penny-pinching travellers through necessity settled for rooms with stained sheets and sagging springs. I booked myself in.

I spent that first morning gawking, delighted by the strange sights of this vibrant city. The marketplaces were full of women sitting in the hot sun for the whole day behind their piles of produce, their puffy rainbow-coloured skirts billowing around their folded legs and their bowler hats tilted to the side over thick black plaits. These same women would be carrying all the unsold produce back up to their homes later that night. I felt exhausted and defeated on their behalf just thinking about it.

But, strangely enough, there were more smiles and laughter around than in any supermarket in Brisbane. I felt ashamed of flaunting my wealth by being a tourist, only to be awed and somewhat embarrassed that in front of me were people tackling poverty and adversity with happiness and humour. And all they could do was smile at me.

As I stood looking down at some yellowed rounds of cheese that had been sitting in the sun all day, I felt a gentle tapping on my shoulder.

'Hello there. Can I walk with you?'

A small sinewy old man with a thick woollen jumper, a green beret and a pointed and straggly grey beard was standing by my side. His bright green eyes sparkled up at me and a mystical aura seemed to surround him. He looked totally unlike any other person I had ever seen.

'Uh, sure.'

'My name is Marellio.'

'Hi – I'm Claire.'

I started to walk again and he pattered along by my side. He linked his arm through mine. 'Clairrre, you come with me. I want to show you La Paz.'

So began my tour of this exotic city. I spent the rest of the day being shown all of the hidden corners of La Paz. Small indoor markets were tucked away behind inconspicuous doorways. We squeezed into narrow tearooms with low ceilings, where locals sat with cheese and bread and coca tea. We talked about destiny and the environmental movement.

'Claire, we were destined to meet, just as you are destined to do many things. Each day of life, and each moment of each day, is just as important as those before and after. Everything happens because it is destined. We will meet again tomorrow.'

'Oh? Ah ... where?'

'Somewhere.'

With that he disappeared into the marketplace.

And so it was that I spent my days in a bizarre whirlwind of being shown around the colourful and poverty-stricken streets of La Paz by a bearded Syrian, punctuated by being wined and dined for dinner and lunch in the grandest restaurants of my experience, capped off with a multitude of unexplained nighttime noises and cold, dirty showers in my seedy, smelly accommodation on Witch Street. I was living in three different worlds at the same time.

By the time Pia arrived from Brisbane on my fourth day in La Paz, I had acclimatised a little to the altitude and regained my breath enough to walk up and down through the markets without stopping to rest every ten paces. And I was ready to take the ride of my life.

'Downhill Madness' it was called, and I had seen it advertised in a window as I had puffed my way through the tourist area of La Paz. It involved riding a mountain bike down what was reputedly the most dangerous road in the world, all the way from a 4700 metre pass down to a town called Coroico in the Amazon basin, at 1200 metres. Downhill on a bike for over three and a half thousand vertical metres. You don't get that sort of opportunity every day.

Pia – who had had no time to get used to the thin air, was suffering from the flu and confessed to being a little scared of bike riding, even on flat ground back in Australia – decided to come along too. I had to admit I was a little surprised.

Pia is roughly five foot of delicate prettiness with sandy ringlets, a tiny fragile-looking physique, wide blue eyes and a bubbling giggle. She blushes when conversations turn to anything distasteful and she chides friends when they swear. It wasn't until later that I found out that Pia's nickname in her job at the outdoor shop in Brisbane was 'Pia, Princess of Power' and I have never heard a more apt description of anyone.

Hidden behind her sweet, gentle exterior is a force to be reckoned with. Pia hates being thought of as a fragile little woman, because nothing could be further from the truth. She is a feisty bundle of energy, ready to take on cliffs, mountains and any other challenge that is put in front of her, even if she does take them on in a rather delightful and ladylike manner.

Because we would be sharing, I could now afford an upgrade and so we took a room in the Hostel Continental and I had my first hot shower. Well, lukewarm and clean, which was a big improvement. The next day we would be riding down the most dangerous road in the world.

Next morning, equipped with overnight bags to stay in Coroico, we headed through the early-morning hubbub to the office of 'Downhill Madness' tours, with Pia puffing and coughing by my side. Fifteen nervous western tourists stood around watching and waiting as two Bolivian men loaded the rather old-looking bikes onto the top of an even older-looking minibus. Pia stood firm. She had decided to do this and she wasn't going to be scared. I, on the other hand, was feeling more than a little nervous.

Two hours later we were standing in an entirely different location, wrapping ourselves in as many layers of clothing as we could find in our bags. Thank God I'd brought my waterproof jacket, because the icy wind cut through all other material. The change in scenery and climate was incredible.

Since we had left La Paz the minibus had groaned its way steadily up the western side of the Andes. The dense population of La Paz had thinned out to become an occasional farmhouse and some dirty goats, and then to no inhabitants at all. Eventually we had reached the top of the pass, the high point of the road at an altitude of 4700 metres, where it snuck through a gap between the high Andean peaks before plummeting down east to the Amazon Basin. We would be going the rest of the way on two wheels.

Around us the mountains rose in wind-blown barrenness; the dark brown rock was exposed and scattered patches of snow littered the ground. Before us the road carved a scar along the side of a barren valley between the mountains as it headed downwards into another world. The tour guides unloaded the ramshackle bikes, got out repair kits, and started fixing them and pumping up the deflated tyres. We tourists stood around shivering, only partly from the cold. Apparently more people died in car accidents on this road than any other road in the world, and more than one had died while riding down it on a mountain bike.

Pia stood beside her small and rusty bike looking less than impressed.

'Claire – um, how do you change gears?'

We rode around in circles for five minutes to find the gears and the brakes, then one of the tour guides shouted above the wind: 'I go in the front. No-one go ahead. Carlos will ride at the back. You go when you are ready. After a while we stop and wait.'

And with that he was off. We all nervously pedalled towards where the road headed down, uneasy with the anticipation of what lay ahead. At least it was sealed with bitumen.

Whoopeee! It was like flying. Once I had tested my brakes and was sure they were actually going to work, I let them go. The bitumen road made sweeping great bends as it curved down and down along the side of the valley. It was wide and smooth and there was only the occasional car. Very soon the air started to warm and I felt hot in my longs and windproof jacket.

When the guide stopped, I pulled up obediently behind him and waited for the others to catch up, peeling off my outer layers. What a glorious day. Pia caught up, looking flushed and elated. The slowest riders trickled in.

We were off again, zooming forever downwards, letting momentum take effortless control and leaning into the wide curves, the whirr of the tyres lost in the wind in my ears. The rugged barren mountaintops were left behind and there were now grassy valleys, where streams carved winding rocky trails through their centre. The air warmed further still and became richer with oxygen. I couldn't work out how this could possibly be the most dangerous road in the world – Bolivian drivers must be very reckless.

After an incredible few hours we came to an intersection where the bitumen ended. I pulled up beside the guide and we waited as the rest of the group trickled in.

'How's it going, Pia?'

'I'm knackered.'

Her face was looking strained. Even going downhill for this long at altitude without having acclimatised was a big ask, and the few short uphill stretches had been the final insult.

'Don't worry, Pia. It will get easier the further down we go.'

The last stragglers pulled in and our guide informed us: 'Now we start the real ride. From here the ride becomes harder. It is dirt the rest of the way and big holes. If you see a truck or a bus, pull over. We stop again soon.'

And he was off at top speed, leaving a trail of dust in his wake. I pulled out behind him, trying to keep up with the pace. A couple and a bloke were ahead of me – the four of us were keeping up with the guide.

This was definitely a different ball game to riding on the bitumen. The dirt road wound its way through some sparse and dusty bushland. It was full of potholes, and the tyres didn't grip as well on the gravel. I started paying a lot more attention to what was ahead of me. Still, as long as we were careful, I couldn't see how this was particularly dangerous. Well, not any more than your average dirt road, anyway.

Half an hour later we stopped again. My jaw dropped. Our tour guide was smiling as he waited to see the expression on each of our faces turn from fatigue to shock as we pulled in beside him. 'This, my friends, is where the fun starts. From here the road gets really dangerous. See down there? A bus went off the edge just last week, and a bit further down a cyclist went over and died, and ...'

I didn't need to hear any more – I could see quite clearly how this road could claim casualties with alarming regularity. (About one hundred a year to be specific.)

The dirt road had emerged from the bush and we were at the top of a deep plunging valley. The sides of the valley were treacherously steep, almost vertical in fact, and rose thousands of metres from the valley floor. It was almost unbelievable, but cut precariously into the right hand wall was a narrow dirt road, the continuation of the one that we were on. And it perched about a kilometre above the base of the valley. The narrow brown scar curved in and out around the folding contours of the wall as it worked its way downwards for many kilometres into the distance.

He had to be kidding. We were going to ride down that? One thing was obvious – the road was barely wide enough for one bus. But, despite this seemingly apparent fact, dotted the whole way along were vehicles of all shapes and sizes leaving a trail of dust in both directions. Huge buses, big trucks, minibuses, 4WDS, normal cars. They looked like tiny little matchbox cars teetering on the edge of oblivion.

And, as we watched in disbelief, we realised how it was that quite regularly these vehicles full of passengers end up plummeting down to a very messy end. Further down the valley we watched two large buses approaching each other, one heading down and one heading up. But they couldn't have been able to see each other, because they were on opposite sides of a bulge in the valley wall. They drew closer and closer, neither slowing down. They met abruptly at the corner, and only just stopped in time. But, of course, there was no room to pass. The bus heading uphill went into reverse. We all held our breath.

Thank God I wasn't on that bus. It continued to reverse until it came to a slight widening in the road. Surely they weren't going to try to pass each other there? Oh … My … God! The bus heading downhill squeezed slowly around the outside, its wheels barely staying on the road, below which the ground fell away for at least 500 metres. Miraculously, it passed successfully and they both continued on their way.

It turns out that this is the main road between La Paz and the other side of the Andes and so, unbelievably, it carries continuous traffic day *and night*! And, as if the challenge of driving in such conditions isn't enough, the final clincher is that the road rules on this particular road are reversed and drivers swap sides to drive on the left side of the road, rather than the right. I guess this is so the vehicle doing the hair-raising passing on the outside is the one going downhill with the assistance of gravity, and with the close up view of the edge from the driver's seat (on the left of the vehicle.)

I was starting to feel a bit guilty for having suggested this outing to Pia. 'Hey Pia, you can always get in the minibus if you don't want to ride.'

A slightly irritated look crossed her usually calm face. 'No. I'm fine.'

Besides, the bus wasn't really a better option anyway. I for one was definitely glad to be on something that was only as wide as a bike.

We pulled away from our rest stop and the side of the road dropped away below us. The guide and two of the faster blokes zoomed off ahead.

Something got into me – a kind of reckless abandon that displaced any commonsense. I knew I was good at controlling a mountain bike – I had spent enough time roaring around little bush tracks and dirt roads and I was also pretty fit on a bike, at least as fit as anyone else on this tour. If I could just let go and trust in myself, this could be the downhill ride of my life.

The scenery was amazing. Clinging to the steep mountainside above and below the road was lush vegetation flourishing in the heavy, damp air. We were still at 3000 metres altitude, but the climate on this side of the Andes was certainly different to La Paz on the dry and dusty coastal side.

I raced to keep up with the guide. He raced faster, a little disconcerted that he had a woman on his tail. Ha! I was surprising him with my recklessness. I'd show him what a woman could do. We hurtled down the hill with a trail of dust behind us, swerving to miss the frequent potholes. We stuck to the outside half of the road, to keep a constant lookout for trucks and buses ahead. I was glad he was in front. At least I had a little more time to stop and pull out to the side when we came upon traffic grinding its way slowly uphill. At these stops I would look down off the edge of the road and do a double-take. Cripes.

But then we would be off again and I would barely touch my brakes, instead pedalling in low gear when the gradient eased. When we stopped for lunch, I was covered in dust. The guide looked at me with mild amusement. 'You ride fast for a girl.'

'Thanks.'

Pia arrived. She was looking shattered.

'How's it going?'

'My hands are killing me.'

I have a top tip for anyone partaking in Downhill Madness: forget that you have brakes and think like a bird, because riding slowly is a form of slow and painful torture. The riders who were taking their time were getting nailed. Sitting on a bumpy bike and squeezing the brakes continuously was taking its toll. Their forearms were absolutely exhausted. If you just let go, the speed smooths out all the bumps and gravity does all the work. You've just got to make sure you keep an eye out for potholes, the corners, and the edge.

We settled down to a well-earned lunch. Our guides had chosen our lunch spot carefully – next to the road was a plaque for the Swedish backpacker who had recently ridden off the edge and plummeted to her death. Nice touch.

After eight hours of riding we were finding it hard to believe that we were not yet there. It had been tactfully left out of the brochure that this ride took the greater part of a very long day to complete. Quite a few of the group had either had their bikes rattle apart, had their forearms give up on them, or had just been so shattered that they had boarded the bus. The rest of us were battling through exhaustion to keep on going.

Eventually the road flattened out, but it wasn't over yet. In fact it was harder. Now we actually had to pedal. I was determined not to let the guide get ahead of me – I had stuck to him the whole way and he wasn't going to beat me now. Anyway, we had descended almost 4000 vertical metres and I felt like I was on some kind of amazing drug in the oxygen-rich air.

There was one last stretch of downhill before the road started to head up a hill. At the base of the dip was a little row of food stalls and a collection of vehicles. This was where we would stop. We raced to the finish line and pulled up together. But unlike the guide, who then started loading the bikes on the truck, I was unsure that my legs would ever work again.

We all collapsed gratefully into the chairs at the roadside stalls and drank our well-earned drinks. It turned out that we had missed the last bus to Coroico. Pia sensibly decided to head back to La Paz, but I stupidly decided to hitchhike on – I couldn't get this close to an Amazonian town and turn back.

It turned out to be surprisingly hard to get a ride up the hill. As evening approached and without any luck, I was left with little option other than to walk, assuming it couldn't be that far away. I found out soon enough that it was, in fact, a two-hour trudge up a steep, rocky road. Bugger.

But it was well worth the effort. Coroico is an absolutely lovely little township. Its cobblestone streets and brick houses are perched on the lower slopes of a mountainside and from nearly every nook and cranny you are offered views over the surrounding hills and into the basin of jungle. I checked into a very cheap hostel with a large pool and comfortable bed and 180-degree views. A fantastic end to a fantastic day.

After several days of exploring on foot the hills and countryside around Coroico, I booked onto the narrowest bus I could find to take me back to La Paz on the day that the Hot Rock team were due to arrive.

MY TOP 10 PIECES OF OUTDOOR GEAR THAT MAKE ROUGHING IT A LITTLE LESS ROUGH

1. Comfortable, waterproof, top-quality walking shoes.

2. Light-weight, self-inflating travel mattress (e.g. Therm-a-Rest).

3. Light and breathable waterproof jacket (i.e. lets the sweat out but not the rain in).

4. Comfortable and breathable underpants (my personal preference being Earth Sea Sky superfine merino boxer shorts – not very sexy but the ultimate no-wedgie technical daks.

5. Two or more sets of good-quality, stupidly expensive technical walking socks.

6. Outdoor sandals that don't get smelly – my personal preference being Chacos.

7. Lip balm with a sunscreen.

8. Light-weight travel towel.

9. Down vest (this combined with the waterproof jacket will keep you warm nearly anywhere, and doubles as a very comfortable pillow when wrapped around clothes).

10. Head torch (LED lights last much longer so you don't need to carry as many batteries).

NINE

A Contiki Tour for Climbers

The next morning Pia and I waited in the foyer of the Hostel Continental. It was the time we had been told Hot Rock would be arriving. We were about to meet thirty people we had never laid eyes on, and with whom we would be living and travelling for the next three months.

It was pretty easy to pick them out. As we sat nervously on the old sofa opposite reception, three very dirty and smelly young blokes struggled in carrying big crates. Not long after them, some equally dirty girls heaved through big tubs of cooking paraphernalia. Then came more tubs and pots and boxes and then the backpacks. More and more new people with a mixture of exhausted, happy or grumpy expressions were carrying pack after pack into the foyer. The piles grew until there was only a narrow path through to the stairs.

The bewildered young girl at reception stood with her mouth

gaping, as if she wasn't quite sure what to do about the flood of bodies and equipment that had bombarded her peaceful domain. She had the good sense to just stand and stare because there was absolutely nothing she could do against this mighty force. She, Pia and I were in the process of being Hot Rocked.

We sat and waited, unsure of what to do next, until amidst the chaos we were hailed by a robust blonde woman in her mid-thirties. This was Fiona.

It takes a special kind of person to decide to spend three years leading a Big Red Truck filled with a fluctuating group of climbers, seeking out climbing areas around the world. Our two expedition leaders, Fiona and Dave, had been with the truck since it had left England eighteen months before, and had very distinct roles.

Fi was sturdy, tanned and strong, in jeans and a T-shirt and with her long blonde hair pulled back in a messy bunch. She was the designated driver of the twenty-tonne truck, and the group's 'mother with attitude'. Her features were feminine, but she had a bulldog charm about her that said, 'Be good and I'll play; be bad and I'll bite'. At our first meeting she gave us a rundown of truck life and our place in it, and she left little doubt as to who was captain of this ship.

She dealt out our on-board duties with a boisterous smile. I was to be on tent locker duty with Mike, which involved stashing all the camping gear into the high external locker when we packed up camp. Pia was on water collection duty with Annie and Leanne, which meant ensuring the water containers were never empty, and putting the right amount of chemicals in them to ensure the water was safe to drink.

We were put into cooking teams of two people who would be responsible for the whole group's breakfasts and dinners for two days and two nights at a time. This meant all the shopping, preparation and washing up, and the daily cleaning of the truck. We were told of the complications of different personalities living so close together, and that we were to come to her before things became a problem. We were told that, if we were not there when the truck had planned to leave a place, we would get left behind. We were informed that we should wash our hands after toileting and before eating or we would get upset tummies. (I took particular notice of this last instruction.)

Then we were warned about 'truck days', and I felt my first serious flicker of apprehension. We had to be in Colombia to meet with the next influx of new Hot Rockers by a certain date, so we wouldn't be wasting time in transit. Sometimes it would be two or three days of driving between areas of interest, and these days would be spent just driving and camping. We would be on the road – and hence trapped inside the truck – from dawn until dusk before we got out to set up camp. But we were told not to worry – there were plenty of ways to stay entertained, and we would get used to truck days in time. I had a premonition of the torture that lay ahead but little did I guess that, rather than getting easier, over the next months truck days were to become the bane of my life.

Dave, the other expedition leader, was otherwise known as Gaffer and I'm sure he was somehow descended from a line of Greek gods. Not only was he tall, tanned and muscular with blond locks and a wide, white-toothed smile, but he had the quiet nobility of a being who was above your average mere mortal. He was a born leader and what Dave said went, without any question or doubt. His bare feet were calloused and blackened from a year and a half of seldom wearing shoes and considering showering a very low priority, and his jeans and shirt were equally stained and full of holes. But his glowing dignity and supremacy were untainted.

Unlike Fi, whose primary concern was the truck and its passengers, and who wouldn't herself climb unless her life depended on it, Dave was a climber and adventurer to the core. As such, he was in charge of knowing where the best climbing areas were and finding out about all the secret local spots, and then organising us all to get there.

Fi and Dave were a mighty team. I left our initial briefing with some of my concerns about fitting into this ramshackle group fading. These two masters of group organisation had already slotted us into the well-oiled machine, and there was no turning back now.

Dinner that first night was followed by a rowdy presentation of awards by Johnny 9.5, an English guy with a peroxide blond mohawk, who had earned his nickname by chopping off half a finger while on wood-collecting duty. In-jokes were laughed at and awards of wine were handed out sincerely. Tearful goodbyes were said to those leaving the truck in La Paz, and a welcome was extended to us newcomers.

Then I spotted Clyde. I had almost forgotten that I had a friend on board the truck. He and his girlfriend were hectic on cooking duty but, despite not being able to talk to them, I relaxed. At least I knew that, besides Pia, there were two people I would get along with.

Suddenly the rest of the crowd felt less intimidating and, as I watched them with interest rather than concern, I amused myself with trying to piece together the different characters that I would be living and travelling with from now on. The most obvious was a tall, blonde and beautiful woman who was walking around the room with a glitter pot smearing sparkles on everybody's cheeks. My instant distrust of someone who looked like she should be lounging by a pool in a *Cosmopolitan* magazine was soon replaced with disappointment. This stunning young woman was Mel, the film-maker. She was far from the robust, somewhat butch and hard-edged woman whom I had for some reason been expecting and looking forward to working with. I kept quiet about my camera.

My initial expectation of throwing all my bags into the Hot Rock truck and then heading straight off for three months of extremely hard-core climbing with a bunch of people obsessed with solid rock died an early death. When a truck is enormous and old, and has already travelled from England through Europe, the Middle East, from the tip to the tail of Africa, and then been shipped across the Atlantic, before travelling half the length of South America, often into wild mountainous settings, it is guaranteed to have the odd problem here and there. Most of them could be tackled by Fi and her tool kit while on the road, but sometimes a part died completely and a new bit had to be ordered in. We weren't going anywhere for a while because the truck was to be stuck in La Paz for a week while it waited for some repairs.

So, while some Hot Rockers went in search of La Paz's finest beers, the rest of us set out to find some local climbing areas. When we did find them, they were awful. Rather than rock, I would say they consisted of boulders held together with dried mud. This kind of rock works like a sieve – it separates out the obsessed from the merely enthusiastic. Quite a few Hot Rockers, having heard the reports, didn't even bother to go and look.

Enter Dave, aka expedition leader, Greek god look-alike, king of climbing and organiser of Hot Rock adventures. He hired a run-down old bus and we set out for five days of trekking, camping and climbing in the Cordillera Blanca, where some spectacular cliffs were sure to be waiting.

But instead of good rock, we were about to discover the civil war in Bolivia. After two hours of travel out of central La Paz, up through the very high and poor region of the Alto Plano into the desolate countryside, our bus stopped. In front of us stretched a kilometre or so of stationary vehicles and before them the road was blocked by hundreds of seated Bolivians. It was a protest. We were stuck in a roadblock.

Because none of us came from countries where protests ended

in deaths, we climbed out of the bus, grateful to stretch our legs, and strolled casually through the crowds, taking the odd photograph and finding the little food stall that had of course been set up. We sat by the road eating our fried-egg rolls and drinking. We didn't see any of the guns, and didn't quite notice the anger in the eyes of some of the protesters.

Five hours and countless egg sandwiches later, our bus did a twenty-point turn to get out of the now enormous queue of vehicles and headed back to La Paz. The next day we heard that shortly after we left the protest three people had been shot, two of them young men who had died from their wounds.

A few days after our failed bus trip, things were coming to a head in the city. The main road through its centre was blocked entirely with people in colourful clothing and bowler hats protesting loudly against the police. The streets were filled with shouting civilians, cars were honking continuously trying to fight their way through the traffic, and there was a feeling of increasing tension in the air.

I braved the turmoil to go to an automatic teller machine to withdraw some money. In Bolivia, unlike anywhere else I can recall, these machines give you your money before your card, making it insanely easy to grab the cash and forget the plastic. Of course, after thinking very carefully that I mustn't leave my credit card in the machine, I left my credit card in the machine.

Twenty seconds later I realised my dire mistake, but my lung-exploding sprint back to the teller was to no avail. In less than a minute the card had gone. I was devastated – not only by the loss of my only credit card, but by the fact that someone had probably been watching over my shoulder and had just gone and taken it for themselves.

Holding back tears, I started a desperate hunt for an internet café that had international telephones so I could call and cancel my card. I ran down the hill to the main street, which was surging with angry protesters. The air resonated with irate Spanish shouting, blaring loudspeakers and the honking of furious drivers. The crowd marched in one direction and I headed down the footpath in the other. Then a new energy hit the protesters. The crowd was no longer walking but running up the street and the rhythmic chanting had become chaotic screaming. Shop owners were slamming shut their doors and windows, and I was standing in stunned immobility. What the hell was going on?

I turned in the confusion to move in the same direction as everyone else, but I was too late. A cloud swept up the street and enveloped me and those around me, and suddenly I could no longer see. It felt as my face had been enveloped by fire. My nose and mouth were screaming, as if I was inhaling hot flames, and tears were streaming down my face obliterating my vision as my eyes felt like they were being scratched with scalding sand. I covered my face with my shirt and ran up a side street, finally pushing through a swinging glass door and into the clean air inside.

It wasn't until late in the evening that my eyes stopped smarting and I could breathe through my nose and mouth without feeling a deep burning sensation. I had just had my first, and hopefully my last, experience of being pepper-bombed. In the middle of the ensuing chaos, I managed to call my mum and she cancelled my card.

Two days later the truck was ready and we left La Paz. And two days after that, civil war broke out in the streets of this crazy city, resulting in the destruction of the front of Michael's bank, hundreds of deaths and complete chaos. It appears that we made it out just in time.

If I had known anything about the history of Bolivia I would have realised that the chances of getting stuck in a civil war in La Paz were actually pretty high. Since Bolivia gained independence from Spain in 1825 it has had a rather tumultuous existence, with almost 200 governments in 180 years, many being overthrown with violent uprisings. This latest coup was the result of a proposed tax increase. The population (of which sixty per cent live in poverty) was not impressed and the protests forced the current president to flee the presidential palace and eventually caused him to resign and go into exile.

Yet another chapter of Bolivian politics was beginning as we happily escaped to calmer places. At last the Big Red Truck, the two team leaders, its twenty-two paying passengers and more camping and climbing gear than you could ever imagine were on the road, heading towards – well, I wasn't exactly sure. I knew we were heading north along the Andes but, apart from that, I would just have to see what travelling South America in a big red truck full of climbers had in store for me. Hopefully a lot of high rock faces.

It became rapidly apparent that travelling with Hot Rock was to be unlike anything I had ever experienced. There certainly were perks to being on a 'guided tour'. I didn't have to think about where I would be sleeping for the night, where I would be getting my next meal, or whether I could afford either of the above. I didn't have to think about where or when I wanted to go, and there was no chance of getting lonely. Things that I might never have thought of doing, if travelling on my own, were suddenly already organised for me and I just had to follow the crowd. It sure took the stress out of travel.

I recently heard Hot Rock described by an outsider as a 'Contiki Tour for climbers' but, although this is probably halfway to an accurate description, it is not quite right. Most Hot Rockers are on the truck primarily because they are passionate about out-door adventures, not for the social scene. However, it soon became obvious that Hot Rock was not only about climbing.

In fact, for the first month and a half it wasn't much about climbing at all. It couldn't be. Firstly, because the good climbing is widely spaced in this vast continent and we were trying to go in more or less a straight line towards the top to meet our schedule.

And secondly, it turned out that, with a typical lack of attention to detail, I had organised to go on a climbing expedition in the Andes in the wet season.

After crossing from Bolivia into Peru we pulled up in Copacabana on the shores of Lake Titicaca, unpacked the tent locker, pitched our tents to create a miniature city in the sunset and waited for the cook team to make our dinner. Dave had organised a boat to pick us up in the morning and take us out to the Isla Del Sol, one of the biggest islands in this incredibly huge inland sea. We would camp on the island's shores for the night and then go out in the two kayaks he had hired. The day after, hopefully, we'd be picked up. It was all just so easy.

Looking out across the lake at the sunset sky, it was hard to imagine that we were still high in the mountains. It looked for all the world like the ocean stretched out before us. But I knew this was not the case. To the south was ancient Tiahuanaco, 'the city at the gate of the sun'; to the east were the Cordillera Blanca mountains thrusting skywards from the earth; to the north-west were the mountains in which hid the famous ruins of the Inca city of Machu Picchu and the Inca Trail. Wild, famous and ancient places lay in every direction. What a country this was, and it was all out there ready for us to discover. And, with Dave and Fi in charge, how could anything possibly go wrong?

But then again, easy isn't always easy.

The next morning we all woke up together, ate breakfast together, then packed up camp together. We hit the markets together, boarded the rickety old boat in the rain together and played card games for the three-hour boat ride together. We all turned green together, and then cheered together before landing on the Isla Del Sol together. We set up camp together ...

Just as everyone was cracking open their first beer together, I headed into the hills. There is only so much constant companionship a girl can take! It was doing my head in.

And I was not the only one. Mike, a tall and lanky English bloke, with enormous laughing brown eyes, heavy, thick lashes and the unscrubbed look of a mountain man, headed off in the other direction alone. It was good to know I wasn't the only antisocial one.

I made my way through some ancient Inca ruins, out to a headland, and climbed across a narrow slice of rock to a prominence of red grassy earth. Here I sat and watched the world in peace. Below me were the shouts and laughter from some Hot Rockers in the kayaks but, rather than wave, I hid myself from view.

The next morning I snuck away from the silent tents for a long walk on my own and, for the first time since joining Hot Rock, I nervously took out my video camera. It began to pour with rain. I put the camera away. So much for my debut into documentary making.

Hours of wind and rain later, I ran down a rocky scramble to a little village on the other side of the island, and to my delight found a colourful sign. Soggy and dripping, I followed its red arrow through the low door and into the back room of someone's mud-brick home. This was the 'café' and if the sign was to be believed they offered coffee, hot chips and egg sandwiches. Lo and behold – filling the snug interior from wall to wall were a crowd of Hot Rockers! We chatted and laughed as water dripped onto us through the thatched roof. Warmed and full, we found our boat moored just near the café and got a ride back to camp.

It wasn't until a month into the trip, when we were two days into the Inca Trail and on our way towards Machu Picchu, that I finally had the gall to get my camera out in front of the others and use it. How could I resist? In front of me was a shot out of a David Attenborough documentary – a hummingbird with its beak in a red flower. I was exposed.

Getting out my camera was in fact a moment of revelation. After I broke the seal, I couldn't stop filming – everything!

Everywhere I looked there were colours and shapes and scenes just begging to be captured.

Walking at a steady pace became a thing of the past; instead, running ahead or lagging behind became the norm. After five days of gruelling walking, we struggled into the ancient ruins of Machu Picchu, which, I have to say, no amount of photographs can ever prepare you for. I had taken about four hours of footage and was on my road to film-making – well, in my head, anyway.

Over the next two months we journeyed north through the Andes. Dave discovered all the fabulous out-of-the-way climbing areas, while Fi navigated the Big Red Truck through a range of suss situations, including very dodgy bridges and horrendous bogs. And miraculously, whenever we finally got there, we always found flat areas big enough to set up camp.

But, although we found some fabulous rock, staying active and climbing in the often icy cold wind and thin oxygen-deficient air was not as much fun as you'd imagine. Some of us were more motivated than others and quite a few of the expedition members gave the truck bar a bigger workout than any rock face we encountered. Contributing to a lack of motivation was a range of stomach bugs that made their way around the truck. Toilet paper became a prized possession when in remote camping areas.

Despite my ongoing struggle to adjust to the altitude, a persistent chest infection and several bouts of the runs, I preferred to get away from the truck and those who almost continuously inhabited it at every opportunity. I had filming to do and Mel was inspirational.

Mel had lived a truly adventurous life of travel and filming action sports around the world before she heard about Hot Rock. She learnt that there was a man filming the full three years of the expedition to make a doco and had asked if she could join him. He had agreed but, just before the truck left England, he had pulled out. Mel, being the kind of person who doesn't shy away from a challenge, decided to do it on her own. She left Australia with no money and her three video cameras, and committed herself to three years of travelling around the world, filming. She figured that, if nothing else, at least she would have a bloody good time.

Unfortunately, a good time doesn't pay for much food or film (the latter being the priority), and she had so far been unable to secure a producer or a budget for her project. So she spent a great deal of time in front of her laptop editing the footage into short videos, which she sold to the Hot Rockers when they left the truck. This was her only income and, when I met her, she was getting worn down. She just couldn't finish the whole of the Hot Rock expedition without some money coming in from somewhere.

She was more than happy to have someone helping with her project, even if I didn't have any experience or ability. It was just good for her not to be doing it all alone. With this in my mind I filmed with all my heart.

However, despite the opportunity that seemed to be opening up before me in the shape of my dream career, in other respects things with Hot Rock were starting to wear a bit thin.

By far my worst problem with being a Hot Rocker was the Truck Days. For someone who can't bear to sit still for prolonged periods of time and who revels in peace and tranquillity, these were a form of unrelenting torture: days at a time of noisy captivity. They would start at the crack of dawn when, after being fed, we would bundle our belongings into the tent locker. Then we would all climb aboard, the hatch would be shut and the truck would rumble onto the road, filling the cabin with diesel fumes.

We would then be stuck inside for the rest of the day, and inside the truck was far from luxurious. There were two tables with seats facing them but, apart from these, the rest of the truck was set up with old bus seats. Every so often, the truck would stop for a wee break, during which girls would squat on one side and boys stand on the other, but we would soon be shouted back on board. A lack of showering added to the pungent atmosphere.

I watched on as Pia and some of the others chatted and laughed and played cards throughout the never-ending days. How did they do it? My attempts at joining in ended quickly with motion sickness, and anyway I couldn't rid myself of my feeling of being a caged animal. I would dream of getting off the truck all day but, by the time it finally pulled over for the night, I would feel so disgusting that I couldn't be bothered moving anyway and, after a quick and exhausting dinner, I would curl up in my tent, thinking about starting it all again the next day.

After less than eight weeks with Hot Rock, when we reached Huaraz, a little town in Peru, I was more than ready for a change. And a change was about to find me.

The whole of Hot Rock made an executive decision to stay in Huaraz for a few days. It was going to take more than one day of hot showers to remove the ingrained dirt and body odours that had developed after months of camping. Besides, just out of town were some fantastic boulders to climb on and in town were comfortable beds, restaurants, bars and luxuries that only months in a tent can make you fully appreciate.

It's interesting how, after travelling in an exotic place for a while, if you find something that is familiar and almost like home you are uncontrollably drawn to it. In Huaraz we found the Extreme Bar, a far trendier bar than you would expect in a small, remote town in Peru. It ended up being the place that most of the Hot Rockers inhabited in the evenings. From the ceilings hung paper lanterns, deep couches shrugged in dark corners and 'American Pie' blasted from the surround-sound. It was not unusual to find one of our crew behind the bar serving someone else from our crew.

We were back again on our third night in Huaraz, for yet another evening of pool-playing, and over a glass of Benquelo's infamous and potent Pisco Sour, Gary and Danny were sitting looking devious and excited. Something in their manner drew my attention away from the shouted conversation I was having with Mel.

Trying to tune into their words over Led Zeppelin, I managed to hear mutterings of a 'big route' (no, not what you're thinking; in climbing lingo, that means a big climb, usually several hundred metres), of breaking away from Hot Rock, and talk of a spectacular glacier-filled valley somewhere near town. My ears pricked up.

As the night wore on and Benquelo, the owner of the now-familiar bar, kept the Pisco Sours coming, the plan was revealed. Gary, a scruffy 35-year-old South African who had paid to stay with Hot Rock for the full three years, had come up with an idea to create a big route in the mountains above Huaraz. He felt that, given that we had spent the last month climbing on Peruvian climbs, it was time we gave something back.

He planned to (with the help of whoever would join him) find a stunning line up the rock walls of the valley, preferably a couple of hundred metres high, and turn it into a bolted rock climb (a 'sports route'). The team would have to clean off any loose rock and dirt, then drill bolts into the rock about two to three metres apart, the whole way up. After we had finished our task, Peru would be able to boast what we hoped would be a fantastic multi-pitch, fully bolted climb. This was a big thing for the Peruvian climbing community because mostly they lack the finances to invest in a rack of 'natural protection', and hence rely on the pre-placement of bolts to climb cliffs. Gary had already been liaising with the Peruvian mountain guides at their headquarters in Huaraz and they had told him about a wonderful glaciated valley full of potential rock-climbing faces that were over a hundred metres high, where they owned a cabin that we could stay in for free. In fact, one of the Peruvian mountain guides, Michael, was keen to join the expedition despite the obvious foolhardiness of the plan.

There were a number of very good reasons why this was quite a silly idea. Firstly, Huaraz sits at an altitude of 3090 metres and we would be going up from there, so we would be battling against the thin air and cold weather. Secondly, being the wet season meant there was a high probability of rain or snow, which would make climbing very difficult and dangerous, if not impossible. And thirdly, we were in a Third World country with limited time, which would make the logistics of organising such an expedition from scratch difficult, to say the least.

But for climbers like Gary logic doesn't come into play when a good plan is being devised. And Danny is a Chilean with a passion for climbing which rises above and beyond all other considerations. As far as they were concerned, it was a damn fine idea. And I too had to admit it sounded pretty exciting. By the end of the evening I was in. I was going to be the expedition's cinematographer. I would be filming my first ever 'documentary'.

By the end of the next day we had a team of eight – Gary, Danny, Mike (the Englishman), Johnny 9.5, Colin (another Pommie), Sandro (a nineteen-year-old Swiss chap), Michael (our Peruvian mountain guide) and myself. Seven blokes and me. Hot Rock would be leaving Huaraz without us, and we would be meeting them again in two and a half weeks, a world away in Quito, Ecuador. No more truck days for a whole three weeks!

I had to be crazy. I mean, why did I get myself into these situations? What the hell was I doing stuck on a mountainside with three blokes at 4750 metres – freezing, hungry, shattered with exhaustion, struggling for breath in the thin air and now stopped in our tracks with a 400-metre cliff dropping away between us and our destination? Sunset was rapidly approaching. No food, no water, very little warm clothing, and not enough rope. And the hail that was battering our shaking bodies wasn't helping morale much either. Suddenly the mad cow waiting back at the hut looked like an appealing prospect.

The day before, we had arrived in the Llaca Valley, which had been a miracle in itself after several serious bogging situations in our clapped-out old minibus carrying about 500 kg of gear and us. But, as I looked around me after we arrived at our destination, I knew that the three days of preparation in Huaraz and the 'interesting' bus ride that followed had all been worth it. Without a doubt we were in one of the most incredibly stunning places I had ever seen.

The Llaca Valley is a deep U-shaped valley scraped from the rocky mountainside by a glacier of unimaginable size, which had since receded to the mountains, leaving the valley floor to grow wildflowers and grasses. Sparkling waterfalls decorated the steep rock walls, draining melted snow from the mountains above and feeding rocky streams at our feet.

Above the valley magnificent snowy mountains rose to the blue sky, with huge seracs – pinnacle-like masses of ice – overhanging and crevasses slashing their sides. The low rumble of avalanches echoed through the valley walls to us. From their midst a younger but still enormous glacier plunged towards us through the centre of the wide valley, carving a smaller moraine inside the larger expanse. Our new home, the *refugio* (hut), was positioned beside a gurgling stream at the base of this moraine.

We stood and stared. What a spot.

The first sign that this place wasn't going to let us have an easy run came soon after we arrived. When you embark on a mountain climbing expedition at high altitude in the Andes, one of the dangers that you are not prepared for is that of animals, especially not of the farmyard variety.

As we had unloaded bag after bag of gear, I noticed out of the corner of my eye that we were being watched. I hadn't been too worried. It was a pretty little thing with black and white spots, big brown eyes and tiny horns. And, as far as I was concerned, cows were just rather cute creatures that hung about chomping on grass and batting their big brown eyelashes with sedentary curiosity.

But how sadly mistaken I had been. This cow had issues.

After we had waved goodbye to the minibus, we left the hut behind to search the valley for a suitably enormous and spectacular cliff to drill in our bolts. We had to get started on creating our multi-pitch bolted climb as soon as possible if we were going to get it finished in time.

The cow had followed, and my initial thoughts that it was just being friendly had quickly faded. 'Hey, guys, do cows ever put their heads down and scrape their hoofs as a sign of affection?'

Despite our unhappy chaperone, which at this stage was too timid to forcibly charge us, we continued up the valley, walking along the wall of the younger glacier with eyes peeled for a possible site. After several hours we found the perfect climbing route. It looked to be about 200 metres high and it headed up a near-vertical rock face of the valley wall alongside some huge overhanging roofs. It topped out right near the snow line. The views from it would be incredible, looking down onto the glacier and across to the over-hangs.

Having chosen the climb, we headed back to the hut for a feed and a good night's sleep. The next day, our first full day in the Llaca Valley, would be spent hiking with all our climbing gear and the heavy bolt driller around to the top of the cliff, abseiling off, attaching fixed ropes the whole way down so then we could climb up and down these ropes as we cleaned the rock and drilled in the rest of the bolts over the following week. The environmentalist in me cried at defacing the pristine rock, but otherwise the plan sounded foolproof.

In the crisp Andean morning air we set out. At the hut we had left behind Johnny 9.5, Sandro, Danny and the mad cow, which had aborted its charge soon after we had sprinted across the creek. We headed off up the stunning Llaca Valley towards the high mountains, confident that we would only be gone for three or four hours. 'Back for lunch' were our parting words.

We carried little other than our climbing equipment, as this alone was weighty enough. That's the last time I trust the advice of a Peruvian mountain guide, no matter how smiley and lovely he is.

Three hours? *Yeah, right!* Maybe for an acclimatised and extremely fit person with no pack in dry season conditions! We were all carrying over twenty kilos, which was increased after an hour when Colin turned back, unable to continue with the first hints of altitude sickness sapping his strength. We shared out the crucial contents of his pack and he headed back down to the hut.

Since that moment we had struggled onwards and upwards until, after two hours of walking, we came to a high and steep rocky embankment. Unfortunately, what would have been just a difficult scramble without ropes in the dry season, was actually a slimy, wet deathtrap. So we set up the ropes and, with frozen fingers and 25kg packs pulling back on our shoulders, we skidded and slipped our way up towards the snow line. Four hours after leaving the hut, we were still heading higher and higher, trying to find a safe line to traverse across to the top of the climb.

We hit an altitude of 5000 metres, the highest I had ever been, before we were able to traverse. So much for having to gradually acclimatise to high altitudes. My lungs were gasping for air and my fingers were icy cold. None off us had eaten since breakfast. We were still a long way from home.

As we started traversing the mountainside towards where we hoped the top of the climb was, the clouds came in. Not just thin clouds, but a thick, soupy, white mass which obscured all except what was directly in front of us.

Then it started to hail. Small hail at first, but it steadily became bigger and heavier.

By this stage our 'three-hour' mission had already turned into six hours and we were seriously regretting not packing any food. I was getting the shakes and feeling dizzy. Mike was cheerful as usual and making jokes. Michael was looking a little concerned and mimicking bird songs in the wind as he shivered in his thin T-shirt. But Gary was looking depressed. He was suffering from the altitude as much as I, but he had bigger things on his mind. His last six months had been a series of expedition failures.

Gary didn't much like not reaching his goals. Mountains had shunned him from their tops; climbs had thrown him off. He just wasn't having a good run. And now this trip, rather than being his redemption, was looking like adding another cross to his score-board. If we couldn't get to the top of the climb today, then his plans were stuffed.

But the strangest thing was that, through all of this, I continued to film. I just couldn't really care too much about whether or not we succeeded in creating our multi-pitch climb. I had discovered an obsession. Despite my screaming lungs and empty stomach, I was running ahead with the camera to get footage from in front. Then I was lagging behind to film pretty flowers and rocks. It was impossible not to be excited and inspired by the incredible scenery, even though its power and severity were somewhat intimidating when searching for the elusive top of the climb in the cloud and hail.

I have to thank Gary and Michael for the fact that I wasn't wandering around in the mountains well into the night because, without them, I most certainly wouldn't ever have found the top of the climb. Somehow they managed to work out just where we should start walking back down the mountainside to place us right at the top of the cliff that we had been looking up at that morning and the afternoon before. That seemed like a lifetime ago.

So there we sat – cold, starving, breathless and exhausted, but at last in the place we had been aiming for all day. Cloud blotted out the distant mountains and filled the void before us, and hail clinked on our helmets and the rock around us.

But, just when we thought the end was near, the worst news was yet to come. The whole reason for our being in this position was suddenly in doubt. Our plan to fix ropes from the top to the bottom had been a good one if the climb had been 200 metres, because we had lugged with us 260 metres of rope. But Gary's face now dropped and his hopes took their biggest assault yet – his GPS was now telling us that the climb was actually 400 metres. We hadn't carried enough ropes. Our whole plan to bolt a multi-pitch climb rested on our fixing those ropes the whole length of the cliff.

The cloud around us was turning pink with the glow of evening. Damn it. Oh, to be back with the cow. The truth was that I still didn't care about the possible destruction of our plans. By this stage all I cared about was getting to some food and warmth again because my windproof jacket and thin fleece were doing little to stop my body from shivering, and I *hate* being cold! Oh, and I don't deal with being hungry very well either – I am definitely not a good person to get shipwrecked with.

Mike, Michael and I huddled shivering against each other, chuckling at the ridiculous nature of our situation, until the cold eventually wiped the smiles off our faces. I gave Michael my bright orange waterproof pack-liner, which looks something like a huge garbage bag for toxic waste, and he huddled inside it in his T-shirt. We watched through the hail as Gary drilled two bolts into the top of the cliff. His lips were blue, his nose red and his beard full of small hailstones as he pushed the drill into the rock. We watched very closely as he attached the longest of our ropes to the bolts and then threw it off the edge. He would abseil to the end of this rope and then decide if his GPS calculation had been accurate, and would make a plan of action from there.

We were to follow him over the edge of the cliff in half an hour, giving him time to sort out the rest of our abseil down. It sounded like a fair plan. At least, at the end of this 100-metre rope, we would be closer to our hot chocolate.

We watched and waved as he slipped the rope through his belay device and vanished over the edge and out of sight. Then a miraculous thing happened. As Gary disappeared, so did the clouds. Not slowly and quietly, but instantly. It was like one minute we were in a hailstorm and the next minute the skies were open and blue and the sun was shining on our shoulders, warming our bodies and instantly lifting our spirits.

After half an hour Mike abseiled over the edge, trusting his whole body weight to the two bolts that Gary had drilled earlier. Then when his weight left the rope, leaving it slack, I fed it through my belay device and stepped out over the edge of the cliff myself, with no idea of what epic situation awaited me below. Instantly my world went from horizontal to vertical and the ground was suddenly hundreds of metres away. I smiled goodbye to Michael, who hunched, still shivering, inside my orange pack-liner.

Looking down at the stretch of perpendicular rock and the dangling rope below, I was overcome with relief. There was no way this was 400 metres. This wasn't as bad as we'd thought.

After two hours of abseiling down the five fixed ropes, my feet hit the ground and the last stains of sunset were washed from the sky by the night. The moon shone overhead and stars sparkled bright through the thin, clear atmosphere. The cliff had only been 200 metres after all. Thank God for that, because there wasn't much left in me. Twelve hours of extreme physical activity with heavy packs at the highest altitude of my life – with a chest infection, in the hail and with no food – had taken its toll on my body. But I sure had captured some great footage.

Danny was waiting for us at the base of the cliff and he carried my pack back to the hut.

As I ran the last few paces over the threshold into the *refugio*,

I was even filled with love for the cow, despite my buttocks just escaping her lowered horns.

During the next six days in the Llaca Valley we hauled ourselves up and down the fixed ropes, cleaning the climbing route of loose rock and vegetation, and drilling in the bolts. It was a bigger job than I could ever have imagined, but Gary was determined to finish it. The climb was spectacular and, if we could bolt the whole thing before we left, then it would be accessible to any Peruvian climber with minimal gear.

On the seventh day I took a break from the climb and from the by-now-very-smelly blokes, and went for an exploration up the opposite side of the glacier. My progress was slow, even without the weight of climbing gear on my back. Rather than getting used to the high altitude I seemed to be getting worse, with even the smallest tasks requiring a huge amount of effort. I had been waking at regular intervals every night gasping for air, feeling like I was suffocating. I felt physically wrecked.

However, it was a perfect day and I slowly plodded along the trickling streams, my feet sinking into the soft grass that was dotted with bright blue and yellow daisies. On my left a high cliff rose up into the skies; the rock was scarred from the glacier carving it aeons ago, leaving telltale streaks sweeping across it in dramatic lines. Along its length sparkling waterfalls drained melting snow from the mountains above.

Then I beheld a sight that brought all my energy flooding back. One of the waterfalls was caught in a moment of brilliance and I was there to see it. The gentle breeze had been swept up into a whirl and was lifting the fifty-metre high mist of water in a spiral dance in the sunlight, with rainbows trickling through the eddying droplets.

I couldn't just stand back and watch. I threw off my clothes and ran towards it, forgetting that this water had only moments ago been ice. But even the piles of still-frozen snow around my feet couldn't deny me my ecstasy. My filthy body was being cleaned by the most beautiful and pristine of showers.

Feeling transformed, I lay out stark naked in the sun to dry. The blue sky showed no trace of clouds and the hot high-altitude rays warmed the back of my body. I didn't think to apply any sunscreen as I drifted into a contented sleep. Oh, how I needed a good sleep.

On the eighth day, our time was running out. We still hadn't finished bolting the highest pitch of the climb and in two days the *collectivo* (minibus) was due to come and pick us up. It looked like we were going to run out of time to climb it from bottom to top ourselves.

But my interest in the climb was being dulled by a new and overpowering sensation. My blissful sleep by the waterfall had lasted for several hours and my short moment of joy when I awoke, feeling refreshed and invigorated, turned to horror when I looked at those areas where the sun doesn't usually shine, which had taken on a new and frightening hue. By the end of the day I couldn't sit down, and felt like I was hauling around a raging furnace.

There was a full moon. We built a large fire in front of the *refugio* and, as I stood still to avoid the searing pain of moving my butt cheeks, the boys danced around its flames. The cow, obviously able to recognise madness when it saw it, for once ran away. The snowy mountains glowed down at us from above.

As the evening wore on, the moon started to work its magic on Gary and Danny. They were hatching plans again. There was no way they were going to run out of time to finish their task, not when we were this close to success. At midnight they packed their bags and headed away from camp. Despite protests from the rest of us, they were adamant. They were going to finish off bolting the highest section of our climb in the moonlight.

Crazy as it sounds, that's exactly what they did. Thanks to the collective madness of a Chilean and a South African, we woke on our last day in the Llaca Valley with our climb finished and the fixed ropes removed so we were able to climb our creation from bottom to top. It was perfect. Through the 200-metre vertical journey were many of the rock features that make a route exciting and interesting to climb: chimneys, roofs, slabs, arêtes, cracks and corners. There were hard sections and easy sections, exposed sections and protected sections. The views from every pitch of climbing were spectacular, with snowy mountains around us and the valley dropping away before us. We had created a truly fabulous climb.

In honour of Gary, Danny, the moon and the cow, we called our climb 'Mission Lunatica'. Our *collectivo* returned on the arranged day and we left the Llaca with some sadness at turning our backs on such a beautiful place, but with pride in our accomplishment and great relief to be heading back down to a world where there was plenty of oxygen. I personally wasn't sure how the hell I was going to be able to sit down in buses for the thirty or so hours it would take us to get across the border to Quito to meet up with Hot Rock. The lobster-red skin on my buttocks had started to come up in huge blisters.

Shortly after our return to civilisation, Gary found out something rather interesting about Mission Lunatica. It turned out that, completely by accident, we had broken a world record. It's one of those obscure records – sort of like being the person who has eaten the most metal in the world. However, it is kind of cool because, to the average person who doesn't understand climbing lingo, it makes me sound pretty hard-core. Mission Lunatica is, as yet, the undisputed 'Highest Altitude Multipitch Sports Route' in the world, topping out at an awesome 4740 metres above sea level.

To put that into perspective, it is not even close to being the longest or the hardest or the highest climb in the world. All it means is that, as yet, no-one has bothered to go and bolt a climb which is longer than one length of rope *and* can be climbed from bottom to top using only pre-placed bolts for protection *and* that also ascends to 4740 metres, or higher. It says nothing about our level of skill whatsoever.

Still, it sounds pretty cool. And I was now the proud owner of all the footage of a world-record-breaking adventure!

Instead of catching the rather pricey direct bus from Huaraz to Quito, we opted for the cheaper option and took four long days of epic travel involving five different buses, while still lugging about 300 kg of gear. My poor bum.

When we finally made it to the hostel to meet with Hot Rock and the Big Red Truck, it felt almost like coming home to family.

Surely we were nearly there. I was feeling my usual tension at the end of a long truck day – my limbs were beginning to twitch and I was getting a mounting feeling of desperation to get out of this confined and crowded space and do something. Surely I should be getting better at coping with truck days, but instead I was getting worse, much worse. The fact that the pressure of sitting was painfully bursting the blisters on my butt wasn't helping the situation.

Once again I wondered at Pia and some of the others, who were still looking quite calm, collected and chatty. I marvelled at their ability to get their heads around these days of confinement and boredom. I shifted uncomfortably in my seat. We must get there soon.

Then, at last, a cheer went up. There above us rose Mt Chimborazo. Freedom was ours at last – as the truck's iron steps banged to the ground, we stampeded gratefully from our prison. Here beside the road was to be our campsite for the next eight days.

We huddled against the howling wind. I looked up from the road at the towering mass of mountain. At 6310 metres, Mt Chimborazo is the highest mountain in Ecuador, and in fact its snow-caked peak is further from the centre of the earth than Mt Everest's, as it sits almost on the equator at the earth's widest point. But no, this doesn't mean that the air is thinner at the top.

Strange how, after hours of dreaming of movement, my body now decided that it was vehemently opposed to even the slightest effort. As the icy wind whistled around my ears, one by one I bent all my tent-pegs trying to drive them into the rocky ground next to the truck. I was puffing and panting as the wind cut through my clothes and tore the corner of my tent from my icy fingers. Around me the others were bent over their flapping tents, absorbed in the same miserable struggle against the wind and concrete-like surface. Finally, I managed to get my tent up in a fashion and crawled in, to hide from the cold and the wind.

Over the following days the wind just didn't let up, and even the most passionate climbers were having trouble finding enthusiasm to make the one-hour trek to the cliffs and back. For me, the days seemed mostly filled with the whistling of the wind, the duties of camp life and regular trips to the toilet.

My body had given up on trying to cope with the minimal oxygen; my chest infection was ripping all my energy away with rasping coughs *and* my belly was retaliating against almost three months of Third World food. It didn't make me feel a whole lot better when Colin turned to me and said with a smirk: 'I 'ad a friend about your age who 'ad a cough like that, and she died a year later of lung cancer.'

Great!

More and more I was wondering if I really wanted to continue with this trip and head into Colombia to face the cost and uncertainty of getting home from there. I had paid for food, transport and accommodation to go as far as Colombia – where there was awesome climbing in a warm, dry and sea-level location – but what was the point?

My climbing motivation had hit an all-time low. I was cold,

I was sick and, despite having met some great people, I just wanted to get away from that truck. A strange kind of stagnation seemed to have hit Hot Rock.

Mel was also showing the signs of strain. The producers were failing to contact her and her budget was wearing very thin. Her project was on the edge, but she didn't want to give up. Her belief in, and commitment to, the project was infectious.

Crunch time came on day five. The wind dropped off a little and the sky cleared. I had spent the morning climbing half-heartedly, trying to convince myself that this was good fun. But, after struggling back to the truck coughing and spluttering, I knew that I needed to get away from the group and make some serious decisions. I put my walking boots back on and as many layers of clothes as I could find and, without telling anybody, headed away from the camp. I walked through the fields and down to the stream and followed its snaking path down the valley.

I followed the icy water as it gurgled and trickled along, eventually entering a high-walled curving canyon. I felt more alive than I had for a long time. I knew I didn't want to say goodbye to this adventure for good, but nonetheless a plan was forming.

I would head straight from here to Quito, and get a flight back to Australia. Once home, I would try to get sponsorship for Mel and me to continue filming the Hot Rock adventure, with a view to making a documentary series. I would aim to join up with Hot Rock in LA again in July of 2003, fully funded by some generous Australian millionaire I would unearth, or with a producer and a budget to continue for the following year and a half.

This plan would not only suit me, but would be helping Mel. It was perfect. What could possibly go wrong?

I got back to the truck, packed my bags, said my goodbyes, and started my journey home.

While I was in Quito organising my flights home I met two Americans who had organised sponsors to finance their trip through South America. They were filming with hand-held digital cameras and they proudly showed me some of their footage. There were some monkey shots, where the monkey very inconsiderately kept ducking out of frame ... despite hurried attempts to follow it. There was some rather shaky footage of roads filmed through the dirty windscreen. And, of course, there were drunken bar scenes (need I say more).

Quite frankly, my confidence started to build. If someone was willing to give these jokers money, then my quest for funding was going to be a breeze!

ADAM'S ALL TIME BEST EVER PANCAKE RECIPE

To be pre-mixed and taken on any camping trip with lemon and honey, for a gourmet breakfast. Hearty and healthy!

^{2}/3 cup oat bran

^{3}/4 cup plain flour

2 tbsp LSA (linseed, soy and almond mix)

1 tbsp sugar

^{1}/2 tsp baking powder

^{1}/4 tsp bicarb soda

^{1}/2 tsp cinnamon

^{1}/2 tsp ground ginger

pinch of salt

1 egg, lightly beaten (for camping substitute powdered egg, or cradle egg in top of pack and don't use pack as a seat)

1^1/4 cups buttermilk (for camping substitute powdered milk with 1 tsp lemon juice)

1 tbsp cooking oil

Combine dry ingredients. Beat egg, buttermilk and oil until just combined, then add to dry ingredients. Stir until just combined. Spoon batter into hot, greased pan and cook over medium heat until golden.

TEN

Back in the Lucky Country

March 2003, and I was home again. I had set myself three months in which to find myself A\$30 000 to finance a year and a half of filming Hot Rock, before I headed over to the US to meet the truck in LA.

As a first step, I headed for QPIX, the Queensland organisation set up to support upcoming film-makers. I hoped to score my big break. Surely they would recognise a great idea when they heard it.

I spent half an hour selling the wonderful idea of 'Hot Rock' to the patient-looking office attendant there. She gave encouraging nods and mmms in all the right places and finally, as it became obvious I just wasn't going to go away empty-handed, she gave me the phone number of a local documentary producer of some standing.

Mark Chapman was very friendly on the phone, despite being quite surprised that I had his number, but he was unable to see me immediately as he was 'very busy'. We organised to meet in three weeks' time.

Maybe I was just going to have to find myself a private sponsor, I figured. The way I saw it, the Sunshine Coast was literally teeming with people with way too much money. More than they could ever need. At least one of them must want to put some of it towards an enthusiastic young Australian with a dream. A mere $30 000 would be a drop in the ocean to them.

It was just a matter of letting them know I was there. So I set about getting myself and my cause known on the coast.

I thought I'd start with the press. It's quite amazing how desperate local journalists are for stories. After calling all the local papers I lined myself up to do an article with the *Sunshine Coast Daily*. This would be a good practice run before hitting the big time. Much to my surprise and to the amusement of John, my parents' wise-cracking gardener, within a day there was a photographer around at my parents' house doing a shoot.

The very next day, there I was in a large colour photograph sitting on a rock in the backyard (set up to look like the top of a climb, but the pawpaw tree behind me may have given the game away slightly). I cringed. The headline read: *Claire Prepares to Scale New Heights*.

As I pulled into our drive later that day, John approached the car with a smirk: 'G'day, Claire. Nice shot of you on the rock under the pawpaw tree. Very convincing!' Chortle, chortle.

I did an equally cringe-making radio interview and this time it was my brother James who pulled in on his way home from work. He had a slightly horrified look on his face:

'What are you doing, Claire? The whole of my work was listening to that bloody interview!'

I continued to be haunted by my moments of fame for weeks

afterwards. How could so many people notice my efforts, recognise me, and care enough to comment? And, worse still, not a single one of those millionaires out there bothered to get in touch.

So much for the bloody media! It was time to go back to the drawing board. I was clearly going to have to start work at ground level, and try approaching individual shops. And, where better to start than the travel outfitter shop that Pia had worked in before she had left to join Hot Rock, and where I had had my gear splurge before South America? They had personal contact with the expedition through Pia, they would benefit from advertising in a documentary, and they had been so very friendly. Damn it, it was worth a try.

'What's the worst that could happen?' I heard the 'Voice of Wisdom' in my head tell me. 'They can only say no!'

I swallowed my pride, headed down to Brisbane, stood tall with my portfolio tucked under my arm and pushed open the shop's glass door, dreading the handshake, when my sweaty palms would give me away.

A young girl met me at the counter with a wide welcoming smile.

'Oh hi – uh, I'm Claire. I was wondering if I could speak to the manager. I'm looking for sponsorship for a documentary.'

'Sorry, Adam isn't in today. But if you'd like to leave your details, he can give you a call back.'

I scratched down my name and number, figuring my note would probably soon be lost in a pile of papers. She took it and her eyes drifted briefly across my handwriting, as if checking that all the information needed was there. Then she froze. Something seemed to have caught her attention, although I couldn't imagine what.

'Is that all okay?' I asked.

'Claire Brownsworth?'

'Yeah, that's right.'

A delighted smile now lit her face.

'Claire, I'll be sure to let Adam know that you dropped by.'

I left the shop disheartened. As if they were ever going to call me. But my glumness was short lived. After all, I had the interview of a lifetime to attend – and this had to be the solution to my problems because I was running out of ideas. During the next week I prepared for my forthcoming meeting with Mark Chapman. I was convinced that Mark was my man, so I put together a proposal for a 'Hot Rock' series, with VHS copies of some footage and my lovely portfolio. I even unearthed my best posh gear to wear for the occasion; before setting out, I checked all angles in the mirror, put on some lippy and practised oozing confidence and sophistication (and possibly a little too much of my mother's Chanel No.5).

But, even as I talked to him, I could see the flaws in my plans emerging. Firstly, half of the three-year Hot Rock expedition had already happened. Secondly, Mark was snowed under with projects already. Thirdly, it didn't take a rocket scientist to realise I had no experience whatsoever, and it wasn't really my project anyway. And fourthly, and most importantly, neither Mel nor I wanted to produce a Hot Rock soap opera, filming everyone's intimate moments and personal crises, and this apparently was what sold.

I left Mark's office with lots of useful tips, but without a shred of hope that he was going to take us on board. I was beginning to run out of ideas as I sat despondently at home trying to figure out my next step.

'Claire!' It was my mother calling. 'Phone for you – it's Adam.'

Adam? I didn't know an Adam.

'Hello? This is Claire.'

'Oh, hi. This is Adam ... You left a message for me about sponsorship.'

'Oh. Yes!'

The shop, my message – of course! This was it. My breakthrough at last! I knew it!

'Well ...' I launched with more confidence and enthusiasm

than usual into my by-now-well-practised sales pitch, before he had a chance to get a word in. Once I had finished, there was a short pause.

'Gee, that's a really great idea, Claire, but – '

Another one bites the dust.

But this Adam chap sure was a friendly guy. After a while, I had forgotten the reason for the call as we chatted away about Hot Rock and Pia. I tried to recall if Pia had told me about her manager. But I couldn't be sure. She had mentioned a few of the staff, but I didn't think she'd said anything about the manager.

The conversation of course soon turned to climbing. He sounded like he was pretty into it: 'Yeah, there sure are some great climbing sites near Brisbane, but I always seem to end up bouldering *alone*. Wednesdays and Thursdays are my weekend and it can be *really* tough to find a climbing buddy in the middle of the week ... *really* tough.'

I hadn't been climbing since I'd returned home. I was hankering for some adrenaline. Would it hurt to ask?

'I'm around during the week. I mean, if you're ever desperate, you know my number ... I mean for someone to climb with [*Oh, God!*] but don't expect to do anything too hard.'

'Oh ... yeah ... um ... sure.'

That obviously wasn't going to happen either.

I had been home a month, running around crazily, and so far I had not seen even a hint of success. I was running out of ideas. I needed some serious help, and quickly.

My aunt Chris is a journalist; she's also a mother, wife, author, TV personality, and screenplay writer. I am proud to say she is the kind of woman who gets things done. I decided to book myself a flight down to Canberra to visit her for a weekend, with no idea of how her powerful life force would slingshot me into a wholly new and exciting orbit.

I arrived on the Friday and Chris patiently listened to my plans to find sponsorship to continue on Hot Rock. She asked whether I had considered doing a film course.

I told her I'd thought about it and decided not to. Hands-on experience with Hot Rock was going to get me a lot further than any stupid little film school course.

'Riiiight. But did you realise that the Australian Film and Television School in Sydney runs a two-year documentary making master's course? But it's *very* hard to get into. They only take four people a year.'

On the Saturday, while Chris was attending a business lunch, I received a long-awaited email from Mel. It had occurred to me the week before that I had been working away in Australia trying to get us funding, without really knowing whether she wanted me to be a part of her project. Originally, when I had told her of my plans, she had seemed enthusiastic but I felt sure she hadn't taken me seriously. So I had written to her asking how she felt about my being a part of her project.

When I read her reply, I had an abrupt reality check. I had only ever expected to participate as work experience, but for the first time she spelled it out to me – even though I was spending so much money and time on this project, I would have no ownership of the final product. After all, it was all her blood, sweat and tears that had started it off and kept it going for a year and a half already.

Suddenly what I was doing seemed completely daft. The clincher was that she was not at all sure she was going to stay with Hot Rock anyway. The wheels could come off at any moment. The Hot Rock idea was on very shaky ground indeed.

On the Sunday Chris sat down and watched my Mission Lunatica footage – my first-ever documentary in unedited form. I watched her face nervously as I played through some of the high-

230

lights, and waited for the telltale sign of drooping eyelids. But, much to my surprise, she was full of enthusiasm; in fact it seemed she loved it. And Chris, of all people, would surely tell me it was crap if it was. If she thought it was okay, then maybe I had something to work with. My confidence was building.

As I sat on the plane home I mulled over the new plans I had formulated over that weekend. I wasn't going to rejoin Hot Rock. I wasn't going to be heading back overseas again. Instead I was going to use my footage from the Mission Lunatica expedition to create my first-ever documentary, and maybe even sell it to a TV station.

But, most importantly, I would be using my first documentary in my application to get into the film course and then, if successful, I would be studying in Sydney for two years. Perhaps I was going to be a student again, but this time in a course that suited me.

The phone rang three days after my return from Canberra. I had been consumed by a whirlwind of enthusiasm for my new ambition, enslaved by the exceedingly tedious task of trawling through, transcribing and logging my six hours of footage.

I jumped up at the shrill ringing. Fantastic! An excuse to stop.

To my amazement it was Adam. He quietly asked how I was and then – hooray – he wanted to know whether I was free to go climbing the following Wednesday. Climbing again at last.

Wednesday came, and at twelve o'clock on the dot the front doorbell rang. I opened the door and there stood a strangely familiar young man dressed in obviously well-loved outdoor gear. Despite seeming a laid back and confident character, he shifted a little nervously as he introduced himself with a smile, clearing his throat several times. He was a fair bit shorter than me, with dark hair and lively deep brown eyes, and a little goatee on his chin.

I mumbled a few words and then sprinted for my room. I tore half my clothes out onto the floor, desperately trying to find an outfit that looked, well, like I hadn't thought about it too much. I packed up my climbing gear. Adam waited patiently on the front step.

We made our way out to the Glass House Mountains, a small range of volcanic plugs that stand proud from flat farming land about one hundred kilometres north of Brisbane. We were going to climb at Ngungun, one of the lowest of these mountains, as the cliffs have a great range of short climbing routes which are only a half-hour walk in from the road.

The afternoon was over too soon with only two climbs done before daylight ran out. So as we packed up our gear and headed back to the car, we concocted a plan for the next day – a nice long multi-pitch climb on Mt Tibrogargan, the highest of the Glass House group. This was a climb that Adam had heard of, but hadn't done before. He was not sure of the starting point, a guarantee of a long and adventurous day.

The next morning we set out early, got lost, started the climb in the wrong spot, ended up climbing on horrible, loose rock, and eventually found our way to the top of the cliff late in the afternoon. The sky was softening over the mountains. I had hardly noticed the little pack Adam had been wearing until he pulled it off his shoulders. 'Feel like some lunch?' he asked.

My stomach was growling. Then from his little pack emerged a dazzling selection – an avocado, a capsicum, a pear, a cucumber, rye bread, gourmet cheese, crackers, dates, a tomato, and some chocolate for dessert. We munched and chatted and looked out over the world.

Eventually, the sun told us that it was time to leave our perch, and we reluctantly abseiled back down the cliff. As we packed up our climbing gear at the bottom, I watched out of the corner of my eye as Adam methodically sorted out his things into his pack. There was no hurry – as soon as we got back to our cars, this awesome day would be over. Adam would be heading back to Brisbane and I would be heading home.

With a wave and a cheerful grin he got into his car. Dammit. I watched his tail-lights disappear. But what was I thinking? I topped him by about three inches.

Oh well. It didn't matter. I had places to go in life, didn't I? I sure had more than enough to keep me busy. To begin with, one thing was for sure – I couldn't start a course at the end of the year with absolutely no money in the bank. There was nothing else for it but to get a job and start saving. Even working as a physio now didn't seem too bad a prospect, with such a clear goal in sight. Work until the end of the year, and then start my dream career for real!

I settled for some locum work, found an agency and put myself on their list. I was going to be heading down to the Gold Coast to work for a private practice in two weeks' time – on the move again. My comfortable life at home would be no longer. I would just have to take the laptop and all my editing stuff with me wherever I went, until I sorted out my application for the film school.

Just three days after the Glass House adventure I was interrupted once more from my editing by a shy male voice. Climbing again next Wednesday – Adam would drive up to the coast to meet me at my place at 9 am. He was probably just desperate for climbing partners.

Then an email from my aunt Chris popped up in my inbox, asking if I'd ever considered writing a book. A book? I hadn't ever heard anything more daft in all my life. What on earth did I have to write a book about?

But then again, writing would surely make a perfect complement to documentary making. In an industry where it seemed to be hard to get started, surely if I had a book to my name it would stand for something. Anyway, maybe it would be quite fun. There was only one way to find out.

So I started writing and to my immense surprise I loved it.

The following Wednesday came at last, and at nine o'clock on the dot came the knock on the door. This guy was scarily punctual. Again he waited patiently as I ran around packing my climbing things.

The sky was a perfect blue with not a breath of wind, and Adam and I spent a long day bouldering in the winter sunshine on the

Noosa National Park headland. Here the low red sandstone cliff is separated from the ocean by a large flat rock platform. We were not using ropes that day, just traversing the rock near to the ground.

I stood in close behind Adam holding my hands almost on his shoulders, to make sure he wouldn't land on his back if he fell off the overhanging rock. He didn't. In fact he didn't even come close to coming off during the strenuous and difficult moves. I tried a few futile attempts at copying before being subtly directed to the easy section.

'Hey Claire, you should try these ones over here. They are *really* fun.'

In the middle of the day we ran straight off the rocky platform and into the cool ocean. Then, dripping and refreshed, Adam laid out the gourmet picnic he had packed. As the sun went down over the rocks, we downed a bottle of red. It seemed the perfect romantic moment, except that we sat two metres apart, and we both kept our eyes trained almost continuously on the horizon. Oh well, it was a beautiful horizon. Maybe he drank red wine and watched the sunset with all of his climbing partners. I wished for a fleeting moment that I was three inches shorter, then reprimanded myself for that ridiculous thought. If I were a 'normal' height the whole path of my life would have been different and I wouldn't have been sitting there anyway.

Somehow between writing a book proposal, attending short courses in film-making, editing 'Mission Lunatica' and doing locum physiotherapy jobs around the Gold Coast and Sunshine Coast, we managed to go bushwalking, tight-rope walking in his backyard, climbing, exploring, surfing, and to cook a never-ending supply of fabulous food. Until eventually it sank in that my slightly closer proximity to the sun didn't make the slightest bit of difference. Adam wasn't only happy about having a buddy to climb with during the week after all.

My enthusiasm for heading down to Sydney for the AFTRS

documentary course was starting to wane. But, as with all big decisions in life, the answer was there for me when I needed it.

The day came at last for me to meet with a second producer, this time in Sydney, to show him my edited version of 'Mission Lunatica'. He watched the twenty-minute promo, which had taken so many months of blood, sweat and tears, and I heard for the first, and I'm sure not the last, time the words that so many before me have heard: 'It's good, but –'

It just didn't cut it for the big time. It wasn't quite what he had been expecting. There just wasn't anything dramatic enough captured in the footage to hold an audience on television.

That was all the excuse I needed. I put my film school application on hold and resolved to hone my documentary making skills in Brisbane. It looked like I would be sticking around my hometown after all. Cool.

Adam and I had known each other for less than three months when I decided that the plunge needed to be taken. And, having made the decision, there was absolutely no way I could wait until he got around to suggesting it.

I had never even considered taking this enormous step with a boyfriend before, but now I just had to do it. As we lounged in his living room I built up the courage. What if he said no? I broke out in a cold sweat. It was now or never.

'Hey, Ad!'

He looked wide-eyed my way, sensing something big was on my mind.

'Do ... well, do you want to move in together?'

After a moment of stunned silence, his face broke into a somewhat surprised and excited smile.

'*Yes!* Of course I do!'

Phew! Thank God for that.

And without pause, we started planning our search for rentals. We wanted to be somewhere tucked away in the bush, but within commutable distance of the city. We wanted to find a high-set house under which we could build a climbing wall. And we didn't want to be able to see our neighbours. Surely that wasn't too much to ask?

On our allocated day of rental hunting we headed out of the city to some of the suburbs that fitted our criteria. But after being taken by a multitude of 'helpful' real estate agents to low-set brick veneers that were located on street corners, on bare blocks next to loud neighbours, we gave up and slumped exhausted in the car outside a suburban supermarket, traffic roaring past, pedestrians hurrying and litter on the sidewalk.

Less than an hour's drive from this bedlam was the mountain where I had grown up. There was still hope for saving this from being a wasted day – we decided to make our escape and head for the hills. I hadn't been there for years.

We started our drive up the winding mountain road. Soon suburbia was left behind and the smell of gum leaves drifted through the window. The air freshened and cooled as we drove higher and higher. I knew every bend and bump in this road.

There was a light drizzle of rain splattering on the windscreen as we approached the village. Still just two shops. We cruised past the first of these and onwards, closer to my childhood home.

The second little shop was still there but it had been revamped almost beyond recognition. No longer did it boast flaking white paint and cracked louvres and cans of produce well past their use-by date. Instead an outside area offered palms and wooden tables sheltered by large umbrellas; indoors, the warmth of a potbelly stove glowed in the corner near a lounge and a low table. We ordered a cappuccino each and sat down outside under one of the umbrellas and pulled jumpers around our shoulders.

Through the cool mountain air, the symphony of birds met no

competition. No cars, no rumble of traffic. Bliss.

A blast from my past appeared around the corner and stopped dead: 'What the ...? Don't tell me you've come back!'

'G'day, Andrew. No, not really. Just here for coffee. This is Adam, my boyfriend.'

'Hi. Hey, did you know that May Hillery is selling?'

Only been back for five minutes, and already back in the rumour mill. You've gotta love small towns. But May was selling? She must have been living on the block near Rivendel for fifty years at least. I had spent my childhood in fear of her finding me on her land, my tent had been surrounded by wild pigs in her leg of the creek, and now she was leaving.

After our coffee we drove along the winding mountain road to the national park picnic area. So many childhood memories clung to each bend in the road, each tree, each different bird song.

We pulled up in the carpark and, opening the boot which faced into the forest, kicked back on the mattress that was still there from our car camping trip the weekend before. We looked out past our feet at the trees and watched and listened as the soft curtain of rain muffled the happy songs of the birds.

'Hey, Claire, this place is fantastic!'

A week later we pulled off the main road and onto the hidden driveway of May's property. I hadn't been down this driveway for about fifteen years. Down through the thick bush it plunged, down to where it crossed a small creek and then back up again before emerging into the sunlight on the top of a knoll. On the left a giant staghorn and a tree fern overlooked the drive, and behind them the rundown old cottage that had once been a hunting shack sat in the sun amongst an enormous rambling garden full of flowers.

A slight figure knelt in the front garden plucking out weeds with a kitchen knife. May had barely changed in all those years. She bounced up with a vigour which belied her seventy-six years as we crunched to a stop.

'Hello, dear. So good to see you again after such a long time.' She remembered me!

We followed her through the wood-panelled kitchen and into the sunroom, where a writing desk sat in dappled light looking out through open windows onto the blossom-filled garden. After our brief tour of the cottage, we headed off into the bush to explore the boundaries of the eighteen-acre block.

I was confident I knew this land and the tributaries of the creek like the back of my hand. After all, I had spent my childhood exploring this very place. Of course we managed to get totally lost, and then in a frenzy of excitement when I noticed a familiar landmark, I ran at full pelt through a tangle of spiny lawyer vine, its claws ripping across the skin on my face.

We finally arrived back at May's house at sundown, rather concerned about how distressed she would be to see the blood splattered over my shirt and dripping from my face, after taking so long to return.

She greeted us with a grandmotherly smile and a tea towel-covered plate in hand. 'So did you have a nice time, dears? Here, have a rock cake.'

Just over three months into our relationship, we signed on the dotted line. May, although sad to leave, seemed happy to be passing her beloved land to someone who had some claim to it.

Adam and I were now the joint owners of a healthy mortgage, and the new caretakers of eighteen acres of rambling bush, a creek, a rainforest, a dilapidated cottage, a driveway, rusty old water tanks, power poles and a magical rambling garden alive with flowers and birds. Oh, and a hell of a big carpet snake (that we called Rastus) that lives in the roof and that would welcome us home when we returned battered, exhausted and bruised from the adventures we were already planning together. It was one of life's simple miracles. I knew without a doubt that I had found him – the guy for me.

A LITTLE DUCK
MICHAEL LEUNIG

With a bit of luck
A duck
Will come into your life.

When you are at your peak
Of your great powers,
And your achievement towers
Like a smoking chimney stack,
There'll be a quack
And right there at your feet
A little duck will stand;
She will take you by the hand
And lead you

Like a child with no defence;
She will lead you
Into wisdom, joy and innocence.
That little duck.

I wish you luck.

ELEVEN

Big Wuss?

Four months after buying the house we moved in and four weeks after moving in we left the spiders, mice and Rastus the snake behind to head off for three weeks on the South Island of New Zealand.

I left with mixed feelings of excitement and dread. My time had come to be introduced to the world of high alpine mountaineering, using crampons, ice axes, ropes and snow stakes to ascend snow-covered peaks. Out there exhaustion and potential death were never far away.

This was Adam's ultimate playground – a place he described as taking him to the limit of his skill and endurance but at the same time humbling him. Here the mountains were ultimately in control of what he could and couldn't do, and whether he would survive.

This trip was to be the greatest test yet of my bravado and ability to take myself into the extremes. One mistake, one stumble, one moment of carelessness, or indeed something completely out of my control like an avalanche, could mean death.

Adam was to be my guide, and we had planned our ascent of the steep and treacherous snowy south-west ridge of Mt Aspiring.

My one previous experience with snow – being tobogganed off a ski slope in Canada after injuring both shoulders and my back in a particularly uncoordinated snowboarding-learners moment – hadn't been a good one. But that was a minor detail. I felt ready to face my deepest fears and keep a level head to reach our goals.

Three weeks later we sat quietly sipping cappuccinos at the airport in New Zealand waiting for our flight home.

'Claire Brownsworth please report to gate 16. Your flight has boarded and is ready for departure.'

We threw down the sandwiches we'd been casually eating.

'Crap!'

I followed Adam's lanky form, daypack flapping as he sped through the crowds towards our gate. Running late again … some things hadn't changed.

But others most certainly had. There was no doubt about it but this holiday had changed things. I had found myself hunched on all fours trembling on the side of Mt Aspiring, knuckles white around the handles of both ice axes, feet planted deep into the slippery whiteness, too afraid to move or look up as Adam stood comfortably upright, as cool as a cucumber and saying, 'But Claire, it's only a thirty-degree slope'.

I had always known I was a bit of a wuss deep down, but I had up until this point kept it pretty well hidden and taken pleasure in pushing through my fears. However, balancing on that steep slippery slide of snow, with nothing stopping me from catapulting downwards into a crevasse or off the edge of the mountain except for the metal spikes on the soles of my boots, had introduced me to terror. Everywhere I looked all I could see was death and disaster waiting for me, and these thoughts had left me a quivering and useless mess.

Despite perfect weather conditions, I had been adamant that we turn back from our summit bid on Mt Aspiring. It had not been a proud moment. I didn't much like this new role of being the chicken.

Three weeks after our return the memory of my failure had not faded. Instead, it was billowing out like a huge grey cloud, throwing an ever-growing shadow over everything. Instead of New Zealand opening my world to new adventurous possibilities, those mountains had introduced me to fears that I might never overcome – and worst of all, these fears might mean that Adam and I were not suited. I mean, what was the point if the challenges Adam lived for I couldn't or wouldn't do with him, and the stuff I found challenging and exciting he found easy. I certainly wasn't cut out to be the girlfriend who shared a house and ate meals with him while sitting on the sidelines when he did all the fun stuff, only going along when he was planning an 'easy' day. YUCK.

The crunch came on a Friday three weeks after our return as I watched the tailgate of Adam's car head down our gravel driveway. Ad was heading off for an evening of work at the shop, and then going straight from there to a weekend of climbing with his mate Gareth, and I felt as though a part of me was heading off and might never come back.

He was going away climbing and camping without me, with his friend who climbed harder and better than me. Sure, I had been invited but I had declined, knowing that it was a half-hearted invitation. They wanted to do far harder climbs than I could even consider and my presence would just hold them back – like New Zealand all over again.

What had happened to my fairytale romance? Wasn't I meant to climb or surf or ride off into the sunset with my perfect man and then live happily ever after taking on the world with him by my side? It just wasn't working out how it should.

And despite racking my brain for a solution I just couldn't think of any way to fix this. My life up to this point had been one of freedom, adventure and independence. This was the path I knew. Whenever I had felt unsure and unsettled before, I had been able to cheer myself up with the thought that I could leave to move onto greener pastures so it didn't really matter. But this time I couldn't leave. I was trapped. I had always seen problems in my previous relationships as confirmation that they just weren't right. But with Adam I had lost my trusty escape valve. This had to be right because, well, it just did. But it wasn't.

This was crazy – I needed to get another perspective, and now.

I dialled the numbers. I still wasn't sure I was doing the right thing even as I waited for the woman's voice to finish her greeting at the other end of the line.

'Hi. It's Claire. Is Adam there?'

After a moment, his cheerful voice bounced down the line. 'Why, hello there!'

'Hi.'

'Hey Claire, are you all right?' Concern and confusion.

'No.'

Five minutes later I put the phone back in its cradle. He was coming straight home from work.

At five thirty the next morning I stood once again at the back door and watched as the bumper bar of Adam's car disappeared down our driveway. The bellbirds were singing his farewell and serenading my entry into a new stage of life. It had taken us both into the depths of talking endurance and fatigue but eventually I had figured it out.

I had found Adam and we had found a paradise to live in together. We had become everything for each other – climbing partners, travel buddies, a renovating team, home-owners, and best friends. Suddenly, to my own friends' amazement, I had gone from being Miss Notoriously-Messy-And-Independent, taking on the world on my own, and ready to take on new challenges and find new friends and climbing buddies wherever I went, to being the other half of Adam and oddly domesticated and settled. I had been blissfully happy.

But somewhere in this transition I had, like I'm sure many before me, tied all the threads of myself into our relationship. What I had been experiencing since New Zealand was in fact a severe identity crisis: next to Adam I didn't feel brave or adventurous at all – in fact I felt like a total wuss. Where had the old me gone? It had been swallowed up by 'us'!

It was clearly never going to work long term. I needed to get the old me back and NOW.

After our intense night of talking Adam and I had decided that he should definitely still go away on his weekend of climbing with Gareth. This weekend was going to be my first weekend of being just me for what seemed a hell of a long time. I was going to get back to having some fun and adventures of my own.

He headed off at sparrow fart on Saturday morning.

I put the kettle on.

I made a cup of coffee.

I sat down with my coffee.

Hmmmm …

The phone rang. Thank goodness.

'Hello?'

'G'day Claire. It's Nathan. What're you up to today? 'Cause I was wondering if you fancied going climbing or something?'

Phew. Saved.

'Yeah, awesome. There's a really nice little cliff in the bush up here … and it's in the shade. Oh, and there's a waterhole up here too. We can go for a swim after.'

'Great. I'll be there soon.'

We spent a long day of thrashing through the bush, getting horrendously lost, finding our way again, climbing in the stinking heat, swimming, and talking about life, the world and everything. The climbing was great. I felt strong and smooth on the rock, doing climbs that were well within my ability, and was totally in my element.

I waved goodbye to Nathan and collapsed exhausted into our red velour sofa and contemplated. It didn't matter at all that I would never do the hardest climb, and maybe never climb a treacherous snowy mountainside or do half the things that Adam and other people out there wanted to do. Exciting adventures in my life had always been about finding my own mental and physical limits and exploring them, not trying to live up to anyone else's. In fact, I was kind of lucky that I got a rush doing things that were far less likely to end in disaster.

Rastus' long heavy body scraped through the insulation overhead and a mouse skittered through the wall.

I hoped Ad was having fun nailing himself on ridiculously hard climbs in 42-degree humid heat. I sipped leisurely at my glass of iced water.

I was back, and ready for anything.

When eventually the day arrived to come face to face with the Beerwah Bolt Route I was twenty-six, I had a book to write, a home to renovate, a documentary-making career to launch, a physiotherapy career to ditch and a point to prove – I was determined to rediscover the thrill of taking on challenges beyond my comfort zone, and leave the memory of New Zealand behind me.

Our plans for this expedition had started pretty soon after Adam and I had met, when we were still looking for excuses to see each other. We had decided that we would do an overnight ascent of the overhanging cliff near Beerwah's summit. I was then still trying to impress him with my fearlessness. He was trying to find an excuse to get me to stay over – even if it was overnighting on his portable climbing ledge (portaledge).

During the months following our shy meeting we had been ready to go twice, but both times – secretly to my relief – the weather had come in and ruined our plans.

Unfortunately, the initial delays and then our terrifying trip to New Zealand had taken away my bravado and left me thinking far too much about the fact that this would be my first ever aid climb. Instead of climbing using the natural features of the rock and clipping into placed gear or bolts for protection (as with Mission Lunatica and all the other climbs I had ever done), this being a bolt aid climb meant we would be ascending without using any natural features in the rock, instead hauling up a line of old fixed bolts, by alternately clipping two webbing ladders one at a time to the bolts. With two of these ladders and a plethora of other heavy and complicated gear we would ascend the 130 metres of smooth rock with the two enormous overhangs near the summit.

This would be made all the more exciting by the fact that we would be relying one hundred per cent on another person's handi-work as our lives would be suspended on the pre-placed bolts at all times. Oh, and the portaledge would also be suspended on these bolts below one of the roofs a hundred metres above the ground.

As we progressed up Mt Beerwah towards the base of the cliff, perspiration ran into my eyes and down the side of my face and I began to feel certain that we must indeed be mad. Maybe we should turn back and do this in cooler weather (the perfect excuse). Ahead of me Adam bounced along, singing to himself, completely unflustered by the heat, or his even heavier pack. I realised the futility of my thoughts. There was going to be no stopping him now.

I stood at the bottom of the Bolt Route and looked up to see the two roofs jutting ten metres out over the steep mountainside below. Ten metres is one hell of a long way. We set up our ropes and gear and Adam explained how to follow him up once he had set up a belay.

Before I knew it, Adam was on the third bolt and moving upwards quickly.

He was leading the first pitch with ease and my nerves and excitement were building as he clipped the rope higher and higher. He got to the top of the forty-metre pitch in no time, set up at the belay and fixed his end of the rope. From here, using a second rope, he pulled up the sack with all our gear in it while I tried to make sense of his instructions on how to haul myself up the fixed rope using my two jumars – toothed cams that bite into the rope and which are used to ascend fixed ropes.

With my feet still on the ground, I looked up at Adam past my protective gloves, then I glanced down past my harness laden with gear, and past my thick, protective knee pads, to my specialised aid-climbing boots. I was a modern-day gladiator, equipped for action. Now all I had to do was get my weight off the ground. Easier said than done.

I could feel my knees bruising, even through the thick knee-pads, as I flailed up the rope. But after a couple of metres, I started to get into the swing of it. Despite the immense effort required for each movement, it was nice finding a rhythm as I worked the jumars upwards and steadily unclipped the rope from where Adam had clipped it to the bolts. My heart was thundering and my biceps burning by the time I reached Ad at the first belay.

'Good one, babe. You did that really well. Now it's your turn to lead.'

'My what?'

'Your turn to lead. You'll need the practice for when you lead over the roof pitch tomorrow.'

'When I do what tomorrow?!'

But seconding hadn't been so hard and, although leading was a completely different technique, it hadn't looked too difficult when Adam had done it. I looked up from where we dangled forty metres above the ground and saw the long line of bolts heading up to the roof.

All right, try anything once. We transferred all the gear onto my harness and Adam explained the technique again. The bolts stretched up above us in a continuous line, placed about a body length apart. I was to clip one of my 150-centimetre webbing ladders to the nearest bolt, then move my feet up its sagging rungs (spaced about thirty centimetres apart) while gripping the hand loop at its top until I was high enough to reach up and clip the second ladder to the next bolt. I would then grab the hand loop at the top of the higher ladder, put my foot into the high ladder, transfer all my weight onto it, unclip the lower ladder, and then start climbing up the high ladder to clip the first ladder to the next bolt and then repeat the process over and over again until I reached the top of the pitch.

How could I possibly go wrong?

I reached up, clipped my right hand ladder to the first bolt, and put my foot into a high rung. I stood up tentatively and reached with the other ladder, easily clipping it to the next bolt. This wasn't bad at all.

It was easy to feel confident with Adam's relaxed encouragement. Besides, he wouldn't be getting me to do this if he didn't think it was safe.

'Oh, and Claire, just be careful about how you put your weight on those bolts. They're pretty old and I reckon some of them are about ready to pop out.'

'Great!'

I started to shake.

But despite my nerves, I was going great guns. Every move was meticulously planned and every plan was evaluated – which rung of the ladder should I put my foot in, what was the risk, what could go wrong, was I safe, was Adam watching, how did my butt look from his angle (just joking ... partly). When in doubt I would do a short trial run before committing to the movement. In fact, if I'd had all day, I would have impressed anyone with my superbly cool, calm and smooth approach to my first aid-climbing lead pitch.

But it was not to be. Unfortunately I forgot to consider a most crucial factor: we hadn't left the ground until 2 pm. I was so absorbed that it was a complete surprise when I noticed the sun sitting low on the horizon. I still had five bolts to go to reach the roof and after that I had to set up the belay. And soon it was going to be dark!

This was not good. I started to rush, and with rushing comes bad decisions. And with bad decisions comes delays. The sun had disappeared, the sky was darkening, and my hands and knees were trembling when I got to the final bolt below the belay. Then my exhausted breathing stopped for a dreadful moment as my eyes landed on this small piece of metal.

The bolt was old and tiny and bent downwards – that is, extremely dodgy. If this bolt pulled out or broke or my ladder slipped off it, then I would catapult down to below the last bolt and our plans would be stuffed. There was no way I was going to be able to reach the belay if this bolt wasn't there so I would have to turn back, and down-climb in the dark. Adam hadn't told me how to down-climb an aid climb!

With my relaxed confidence now completely shattered and my heart pounding, I swore under my breath as I hooked my ladder over the bolt. It slid away from the rock on the downward-angled metal and sat balanced tentatively on the narrow bolt head. All logic told me not to trust my entire seventy-five kilos to this flimsy arrangement.

I tentatively moved a little of my weight onto the sagging rung of the ladder, fixated on where it hooked over the bolt head. My heart stopped as it moved slightly out then jammed up hard against the downward-facing head.

I gripped the ladder and committed one hundred per cent of my weight to the weakened bolt. I heaved with my right arm and pushed with my right leg, reaching as high as I could manage with my left ladder.

Goddammit! I couldn't reach. I was going to have to move up to the next step on the ladder. This was just cruel.

Shaking uncontrollably and on the verge of panic, I manoeuvred myself up the ladder, waiting for the snap and a terrifying ten-metre free-fall.

Eventually, I got my foot high enough in the ladder to reach up and clip the bolt, but by then my cool was shattered. In the dim light of my head torch I fumbled like a novice to set up a safe belay from the confusing tangle of new gear. If I had kept my head together this would have taken me five minutes, but alone and suspended almost a hundred metres above the ground in the dark, I experienced the equivalent of a mental block in an exam. I couldn't believe it – it was like Mt Aspiring all over again. But this time I had no choice – I couldn't turn back.

Half an hour later and near to tears, my quivering voice shouted down through the darkness.

'Ad, I think I've finished. Um, is it okay if I've used the ladders in the set-up?'

(Nervous pause.) 'Um … honey … no … we'll need them free to start the climb in the morning.'

Sob. 'Oh noooooo!'

Over the next half-hour Adam shouted up advice and words of encouragement until eventually, in response to my regular sobs, he gave up and said, 'Look, babe, you're in the situation now so you are just going to have to work it out. You know you can do it.'

He was right. If I could just get a grip on myself, I could do it.

I looked out at the moonlit horizon, took some deep breaths, and started again.

Finally, I was able to belay Adam up to my perch. Shivering, and feeling about as useful as the cold wind, I dangled in my harness, watching Adam in the light of the head torch as he calmly tidied up the mess of ropes, hauled up the bag of gear and then constructed the portaledge. I had a lot to learn.

Eventually, I lowered myself tentatively onto the canvas ledge and wrapped myself in the sleeping bag. The portaledge is six foot by four foot of canvas stretched on a metal frame. It comes with an optional fly but, because of our natural roof, we had left this feature behind to save weight, leaving our ledge totally open and exposed to the drop on three sides. This is a perk for the guys, as they only have to roll over onto their side to wee off the edge. Not so for girls, for whom relieving a bursting bladder involves a delicate balancing act over the edge. But for now I had other more pressing concerns on my mind.

I reached a shaky hand to the pack. If I had ever deserved a glass of red wine it was now! Plastic wineglasses came out, the gourmet sandwich selection was laid out and, wrapped in the warmth of the sleeping bag, I started to remember that this was meant to be fun. And really it was one of the most beautiful spots I have ever camped in.

The storm clouds from earlier in the day had disappeared. The sky was bright from an almost full moon and the stars glistened above us. The breeze had dropped and now the insects from the bush below vibrated the still night air. After a glass of wine and some food in my stomach I could see the funny side of the last few hours. And, as with all epic climbing experiences, the intensity of the fear started leaking from my memory and was replaced by the glory of the moment. I mean, I had just led my first-ever pitch of bolt aid climbing.

Still, I could not rid myself entirely of the nervous feeling in the pit of my stomach. That roof might be all lovely and comforting now, providing us with shelter if it rained, but tomorrow morning we had to climb out and over it, and apparently I was going to be leading. It crossed my mind that the sensible thing would be to abseil down from here and forget about the roof, but something inside me stopped me from voicing these thoughts. There was no turning back now. The challenge was waiting and, after being such a goose today, I had to redeem myself. Or at least try.

There was only so long that I could pretend to be asleep, in denial of the task ahead. I tentatively opened one eye. Overhead the roof stretched out menacingly over the drop below. I closed it again. Maybe I would just sleep a little longer …

The bag stirred beside me: 'Good morning! Check out this awesome roof – you are going to love it.'

Damn. 'I'm asleep.'

'Why do I not believe you? Seriously, babe, it is a beautiful day.'

Bugger. I heaved myself up to lean against the rock. The panoramic view was incredible. Over the lip of the portaledge my immediate world dropped away to reveal the other Glass House Mountains, wrapped in swirls of mist as they rose abruptly from the patchwork farms. The ocean in the distance met with a clear sky that was quickly brightening with the morning sun. Around us small birds brought back morsels of food to their cheeping babies hidden in holes in the rock face. They flitted around worriedly, obviously not realising how much trouble I'd had even getting this far.

Adam prepared our breakfast. I tried to ignore the rumbling and gurgling in my stomach.

'Honey, have some cereal.'

'Um, no … I think I'll pass.'

'You're not going to have any breakfast?' This was the first time Adam had known me to refuse food.

'No. I think it's best not to.' Gurgle. Rumble.

'You should eat. You'll need the energy for the roof pitch.'

'There's coconut in that cereal, right?'

'Yeah.'

'Coconut is a laxative, right?'

'Aaaahhhh. I see.'

Coconut or no coconut, the rumbling moved downwards until the very thought of holding things inside while on the ledge was quite distressing, let alone embarking on a scary and strenuous climb. I watched Adam munching away, and again started wondering about abseiling down from here and forgetting about climbing the roof altogether. My ponderings were interrupted by the rustling of plastic.

'How about a bag, honey.'

Now I reckon that I am pretty relaxed about weeing. I have been climbing, mountain biking, bushwalking, surfing and going on adventures with mixed company to areas where there are no toilet facilities for long enough to have lost most of my coyness in this area. Weeing off the portaledge had been more technically difficult than embarrassing.

However – and this is a big *however* – for me, as I'm sure for most people, the issue of going to the 'proper' toilet is a bit of a sacred cow. (See – I can't even write the word for a 'number two' without blushing!)

It's really quite weird, because we all do it. But, even though some of us like to joke about it, none of us wants to admit to any personal involvement in it. In fact, anything to do with the contents or functioning of the rear regions is just plain personal.

Needless to say, for me, there are definitely certain boundaries that I like to keep between myself and others when it comes to toileting of the solid variety. A comfortable amount of distance is ideal, but a visual barrier and a stationary receptacle I deem as essential. None of these is easy to come by on a portaledge.

Adam, on the other hand, has spent many nights camped on

portaledges on high cliffs, sometimes for up to nine days and, as a result, has no such hang-ups. In fact he has the control of his bowels down to a fine art. He equates it to the Italians in World War I, who were renowned for their rather antisocial ritual of defecating in the trenches prior to going into battle. This was said to enhance performance and therefore to increase the likelihood of survival. This, he says, is also true for climbers.

As he loves to point out, is there any greater picture of liveliness and happiness than a puppy after it has – well, you-know-ed – on the side of the path, bounding off with renewed vigour and zest for life? So after finishing both helpings of cereal, Ad happily demonstrated how to perform his art into a bag while humming away merrily.

There was no way I was going to do it. *No way*. The only way it was ever going to happen was if Adam had a blindfold on, ear plugs, a portable toilet and a peg, and that just wasn't going to happen. Crossing my legs even tighter together, I looked up at the intimidating roof and imagined myself straining with all my strength as I hauled my weight out across it. My tummy let out a curdling churn that echoed through the roofs.

'Claire, you do realise that it's either now or you will get so desperate you will have to go when you are halfway out on the roof. Take it from me – that won't be pretty for you or me.'

Oh God, no. The thought of even waiting that long was enough to make me groan.

Our relationship reached a new level as I stood, feet propped on the lip of the portaledge, bottom over the chasm below, plastic bag held in place, growling at Adam to keep his eyes closed and to stop laughing at me. The distress of watching him nonchalantly tie up the bag after I had finished was tempered only by my intense relief. Now I was as ready for battle as I would ever be.

As I headed up the two metres towards the roof, I tried to remember the futility of my nerves the night before. The only way

I was going to do this was if I stayed cool, calm and collected. My life would not be in danger, much. I knew that. There was really nothing to worry about – other than that, once committed to the roof, there would be no turning back. And that I would be dangling on my ladders above a hundred-metre drop. And that, if I fell off, I would be suspended from the last clipped bolt in mid-air. Really everything would be just fine. I reached out to the first bolt on the roof and clipped my ladder to it.

As I worked my way further out over the void, the exhilaration and exposure overwhelmed my fear. When standing on the ladders they would spiral around, making it tricky to reach to the next bolt, but giving an awesome panoramic view of rock ... then farms ... then ocean ... then rock. I made slow but steady progress out over the roof as Adam reclined, belaying me from the portaledge below.

For the first time in my life I aided over the lip of a roof and up to where the belay was. I remembered all the pointers Adam had given me the night before, and set up a perfect belay in record time. And soon Adam had packed up the ledge, and climbed up to meet me. I welcomed him with a proud and very relieved kiss. I couldn't believe it – I had done it without a single glitch.

Was I kidding myself thinking that was fun? No way! That was bloody awesome – pushing through any self doubts, then stripping back everything with a good dose of fear, and arriving at where I wanted to go – on top of the world.

We sat quietly sweating in the shade on the summit of Mt Beerwah, a distance apart but tied by an intangible bond of a challenge conquered together (well, a challenge for me, anyway). The mottled grey rock dropped away just in front of our feet, down the cliff that had loomed in my mind for months and that had been our whole world for more than twenty-four hours. Beyond that the horizon was a line of blue ocean, curving out to reach towards infinite possibilities. Another of Adam's delectable picnics was laid out on the rocks and between swigs of red wine we talked of life, the world and other places to go – the kilometre-high cliffs of Yosemite where we would spend a week or more living on vertical rock, the highlands of Papua New Guinea where glaciers were perched above jungle-covered mountains, the sea cliffs of Thailand … maybe we could even sail around the world one day. In the glow of success even Mt Aspiring seemed worth another go.

But right now life was just a combination of exhaustion, heat, sore muscles, elation, delicious food, great company and tasty wine – God I was knackered. And then into my mind popped a gem of toilet-door wisdom I had gleaned the day before in the Mt Beerwah pit toilet:

> *Life should NOT be a journey to the grave with the intention of arriving safely in an attractive and well preserved body, but rather to skid in sideways, chocolate in one hand, wine in the other, body thoroughly used up, totally worn out and screaming 'Woo-hoo what a ride!'*

At least, according to the pit toilet, I was on the right track.

GLOSSARY OF CLIMBING TERMS

Aid Something other than the rock that a climber uses to assist their ascent.

Aid climbing Climbing using means other than holding on to the natural features of the rock.

Belay (verb) Using a rope to secure a climber as they climb.

Belay (noun)/**Belay station** A set-up in which a climber has attached themselves to a number of anchors to secure themselves in their position. This can be with bolts or natural protection. From this belay station the leader can safely belay up the seconder. This is necessary at the top of a climb, and at the end of each pitch on climbs that are longer than one rope-length.

Bolt aid climbing Climbing using pre-placed bolts as 'aid'.

Bolts Artificial anchors placed in holes drilled into the rock.

Bouldering Climbing reasonably close to the ground without the use of ropes, and often with the use of a thick mat to cushion any falls.

Climbing route The specific path that a climber takes up a cliff.

Crampons Metal devices with spikes along their length, which are attached to the bottom of specialised boots for walking on steep snow. The spikes dig into the snow to prevent the foot from slipping. They have front points (spikes at the front) which, when kicked into ice, are designed to grip into the ice, and so are used for ascending steep ice.

Free climbing Climbing using the natural features of the rock. The rope and other equipment are only used as a safeguard against injury, not as a means to assist in climbing or for rests.

Ice axe A specialised axe designed for mountaineering. The axe is designed to penetrate and hold in ice, and is used in ascending steep icy slopes. There is a fine art to swinging an ice axe well. The ice axe is also used for balance on steep snow in a similar manner as a walking pole, by holding onto the axe end.

Jumars Mechanical clamps that grip onto a rope and slide up it, but not down.

Karabiner An aluminium alloy ring equipped with a spring-loaded snap gate.

Lead climbing The type of climbing where the climber starts at the bottom of the cliff with all their ropes, gear and climbing partner, and works their way up, clipping the rope through pieces of protection as they go.

Leader The person who climbs the section of rock first. The leader starts the climb from the bottom with one end of the rope tied into their harness, and clips the rope through pieces of protection (natural or bolts) as they ascend. Their climbing partner belays them.

Multi-pitch climb A climb that is longer than one pitch.

Natural protection Pieces of specialised equipment that are designed to fit into natural features of rock (e.g. cracks and horizontal breaks) and that, if placed well, should hold a fall if the climber comes off.

Pitch The length of rock between belays (no longer than one rope-length).

Portaledge A platform that hangs from the rock face, on which a climber can sleep.

Protection Anchors used to safeguard the climber (can be either bolts or natural protection).

Rack The collection of natural protection that a climber needs for free climbing without bolts.

Seconder The person who follows up the leader and unclips and takes out any natural protection as they ascend (usually the person who has been belaying the leader).

Snow stake A long metal stake that is used in mountaineering as protection (in the same way that natural protection is used in rock climbing). The stake can either be hammered into snow or buried to fix it in place.

Sports climb A climb that is bolted the whole way up (i.e. the climber does not need to place any natural protection).

Top-roping The type of climbing where the rope is threaded through a karabiner at the top of the cliff and is fed through this karabiner like a pulley. The belayer keeps the rope above the climber taut as the climber ascends.

Tying in The process of tying the rope to a climber's harness with a safe knot.